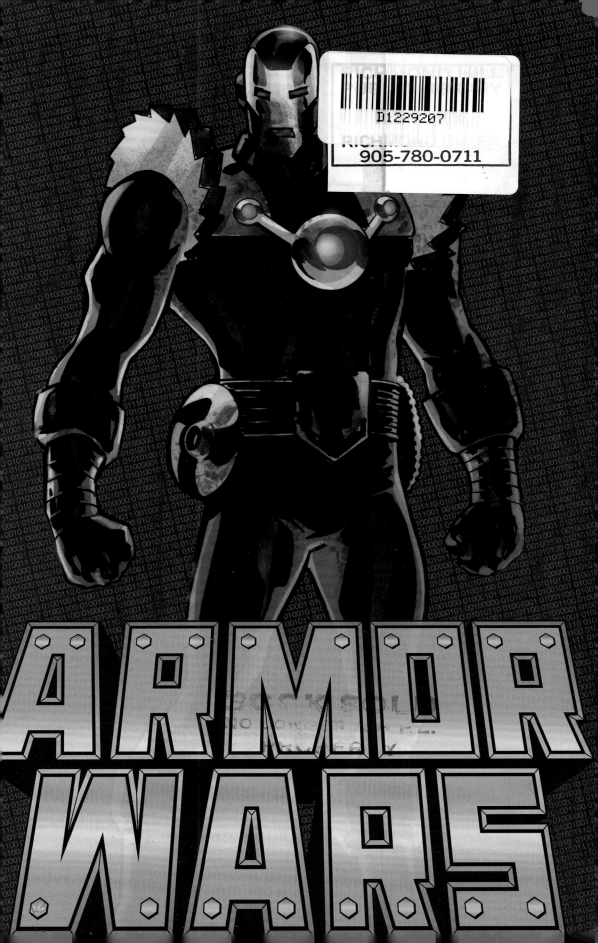

ARMOR WARS

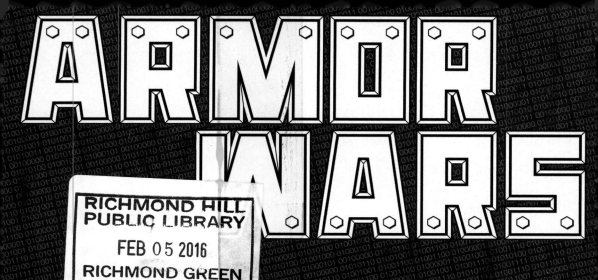

ARMOR WARS

WRITER
JAMES ROBINSON

#1/2

PENCILER
MARK BAGLEY

INKERS
ANDREW HENNESSY & SCOTT HANNA

#1-5

ARTIST
MARCIO TAKARA

COLORIST
ESTHER SANZ

LETTERER
TRAVIS LANHAM

COVER ART
PAUL RIVOCHE & ESTHER SANZ (#1/2, #1-2)
AND PAUL RIVOCHE & JORDAN BOYD (#3-5)

ASSISTANT EDITORS
CHRIS ROBINSON
& EMILY SHAW

SENIOR EDITOR
MARK PANICCIA

COLLECTION EDITOR ALEX STARBUCK
ASSISTANT EDITOR SARAH BRUNSTAD
EDITORS, SPECIAL PROJECTS JENNIFER GRÜNWALD & MARK D. BEAZLEY
SENIOR EDITOR, SPECIAL PROJECTS JEFF YOUNGQUIST
SVP PRINT, SALES & MARKETING DAVID GABRIEL
BOOK DESIGNER ADAM DEL RE

EDITOR IN CHIEF AXEL ALONSO
CHIEF CREATIVE OFFICER JOE QUESADA
PUBLISHER DAN BUCKLEY
EXECUTIVE PRODUCER ALAN FINE

ARMOR WARS: WARZONES! Contains material originally published in magazine form as ARMOR WARS #1-5 and ARMOR WARS #1/2 CUSTOM EDITION. First printing 2016. ISBN# 978-0-7851-9864-2. Published by MARVEL WORLDWIDE, INC., a subsidiary of MARVEL ENTERTAINMENT, LLC. OFFICE OF PUBLICATION: 135 West 50th Street, New York, NY 10020. Copyright © 2016 MARVEL. No similarity between any of the names, characters, persons, and/or institutions in this magazine with those of any living or dead person or institution is intended, and any such similarity which may exist is purely coincidental. Printed in Canada. ALAN FINE, President, Marvel Entertainment; DAN BUCKLEY, President, TV, Publishing and Brand Management; JOE QUESADA, Chief Creative Officer; TOM BREVOORT, SVP of Publishing; DAVID BOGART, SVP of Operations & Procurement, Publishing; C.B. CEBULSKI, VP of International Development & Brand Management; DAVID GABRIEL, SVP Print, Sales & Marketing; JIM O'KEEFE, VP of Operations & Logistics; DAN CARR, Executive Director of Publishing Technology; SUSAN CRESPI, Editorial Operations Manager; ALEX MORALES, Publishing Operations Manager; STAN LEE, Chairman Emeritus. For information regarding advertising in Marvel Comics or on Marvel.com, please contact Jonathan Rheingold, VP of Custom Solutions & Ad Sales, at jrheingold@marvel.com. For Marvel subscription inquiries, please call 800-217-9158. Manufactured between 12/4/2015 and 1/11/2016 by SOLISCO PRINTERS, SCOTT, QC, CANADA.

10 9 8 7 6 5 4 3 2 1

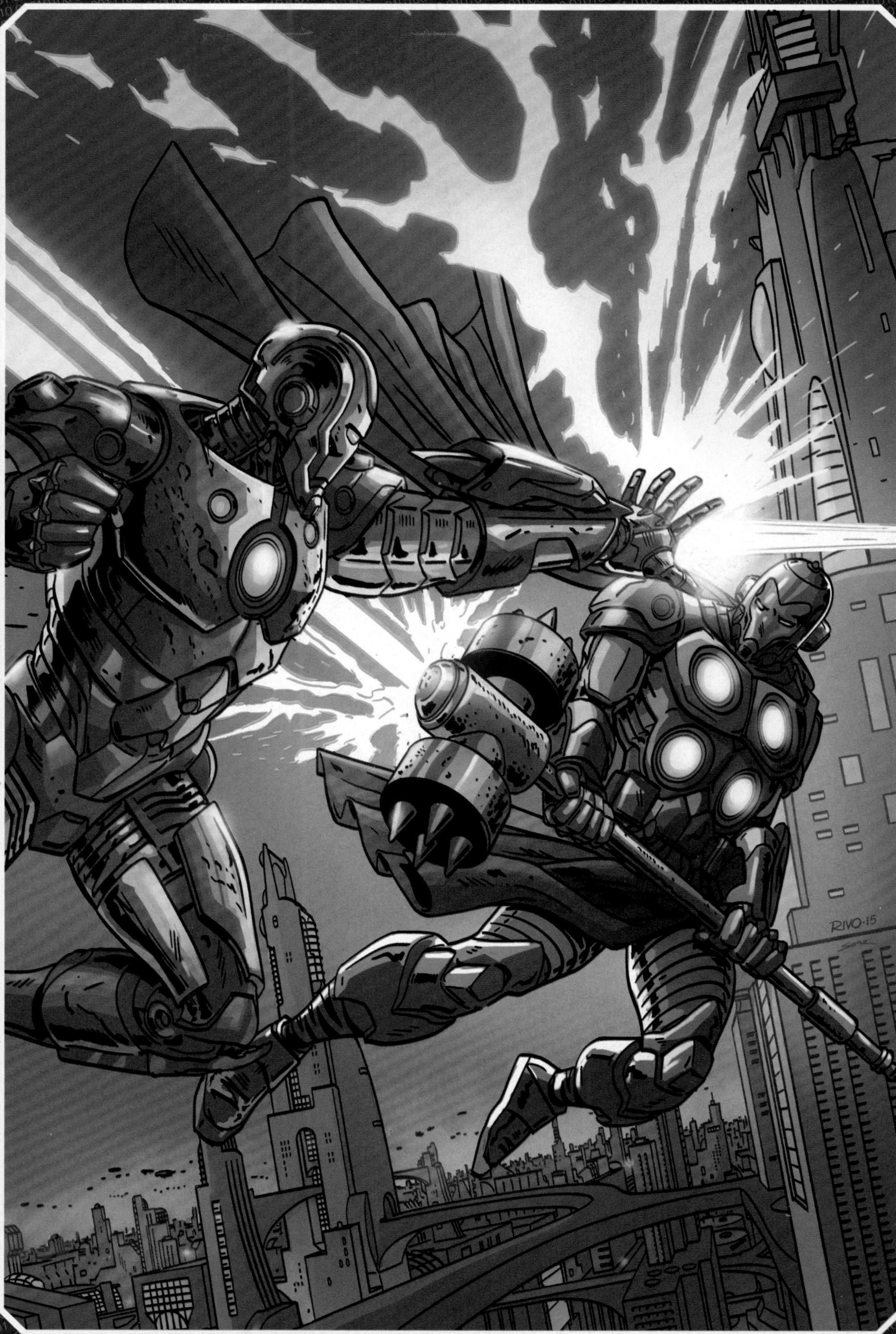
RIVO·15

1/2

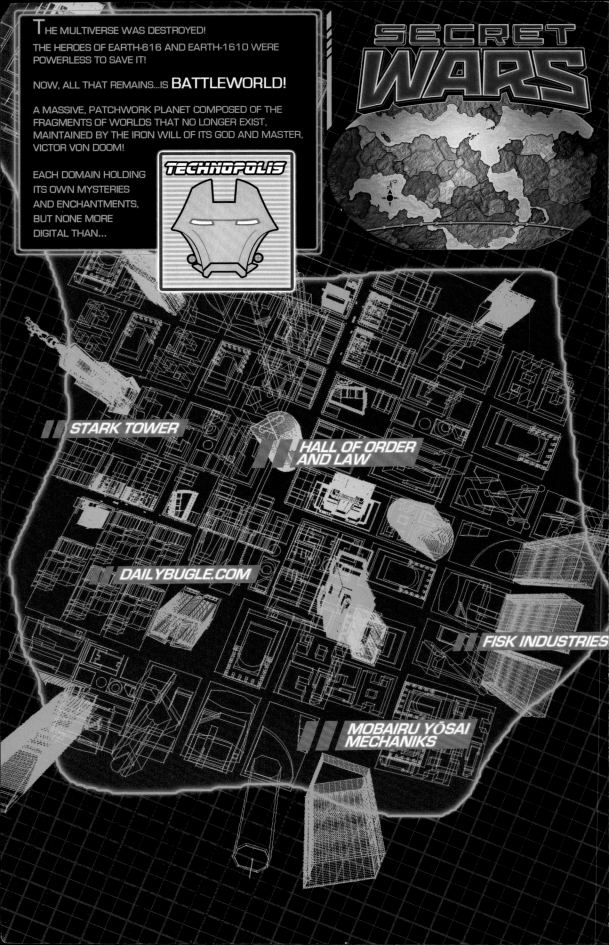

THE MULTIVERSE WAS DESTROYED!

THE HEROES OF EARTH-616 AND EARTH-1610 WERE POWERLESS TO SAVE IT!

NOW, ALL THAT REMAINS...IS **BATTLEWORLD!**

A MASSIVE, PATCHWORK PLANET COMPOSED OF THE FRAGMENTS OF WORLDS THAT NO LONGER EXIST, MAINTAINED BY THE IRON WILL OF ITS GOD AND MASTER, VICTOR VON DOOM!

EACH DOMAIN HOLDING ITS OWN MYSTERIES AND ENCHANTMENTS, BUT NONE MORE DIGITAL THAN...

TECHNOPOLIS

SECRET WARS

STARK TOWER

HALL OF ORDER AND LAW

DAILYBUGLE.COM

FISK INDUSTRIES

MOBAIRU YŌSAI MECHANIKS

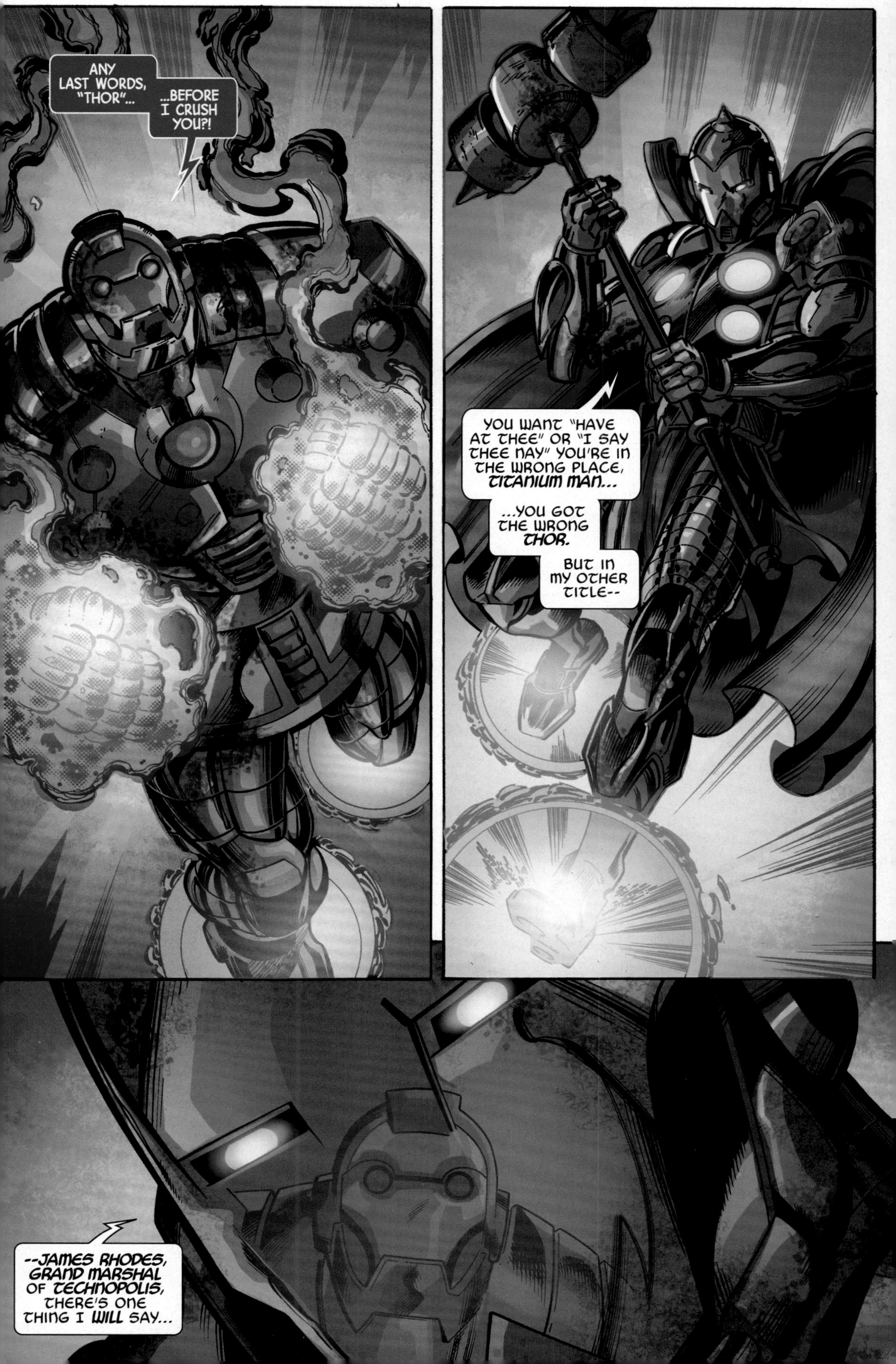

ANY LAST WORDS, "THOR"...
...BEFORE I CRUSH YOU?!
YOU WANT "HAVE AT THEE" OR "I SAY THEE NAY" YOU'RE IN THE WRONG PLACE, **TITANIUM MAN...**
...YOU GOT THE WRONG **THOR.**
BUT IN MY OTHER TITLE--
--JAMES RHODES, GRAND MARSHAL OF **TECHNOPOLIS,** THERE'S ONE THING I **WILL** SAY...

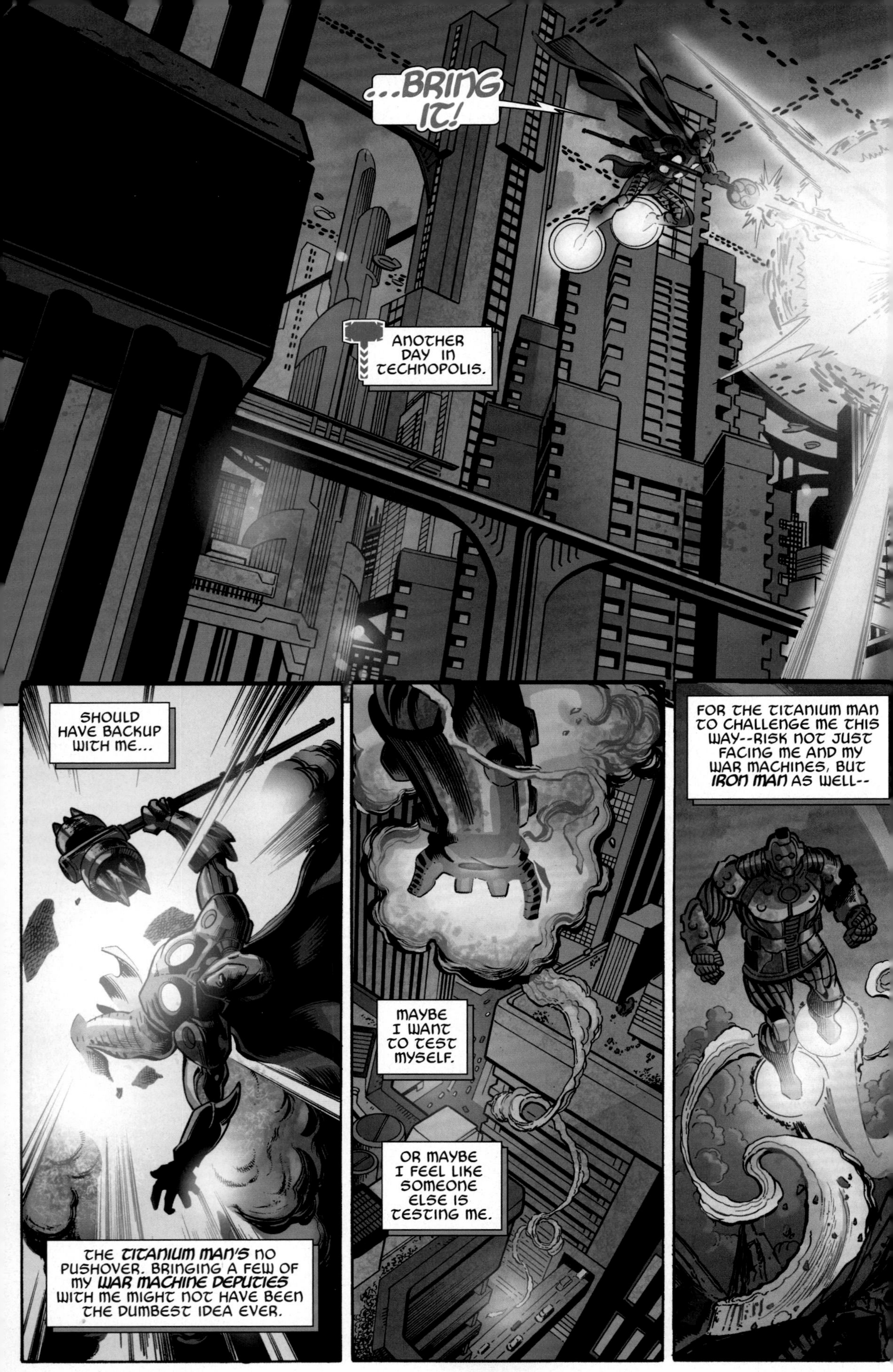
...BRING IT!
ANOTHER DAY IN TECHNOPOLIS.
SHOULD HAVE BACKUP WITH ME...
THE TITANIUM MAN'S NO PUSHOVER. BRINGING A FEW OF MY WAR MACHINE DEPUTIES WITH ME MIGHT NOT HAVE BEEN THE DUMBEST IDEA EVER.
MAYBE I WANT TO TEST MYSELF.
OR MAYBE I FEEL LIKE SOMEONE ELSE IS TESTING ME.
FOR THE TITANIUM MAN TO CHALLENGE ME THIS WAY--RISK NOT JUST FACING ME AND MY WAR MACHINES, BUT IRON MAN AS WELL--

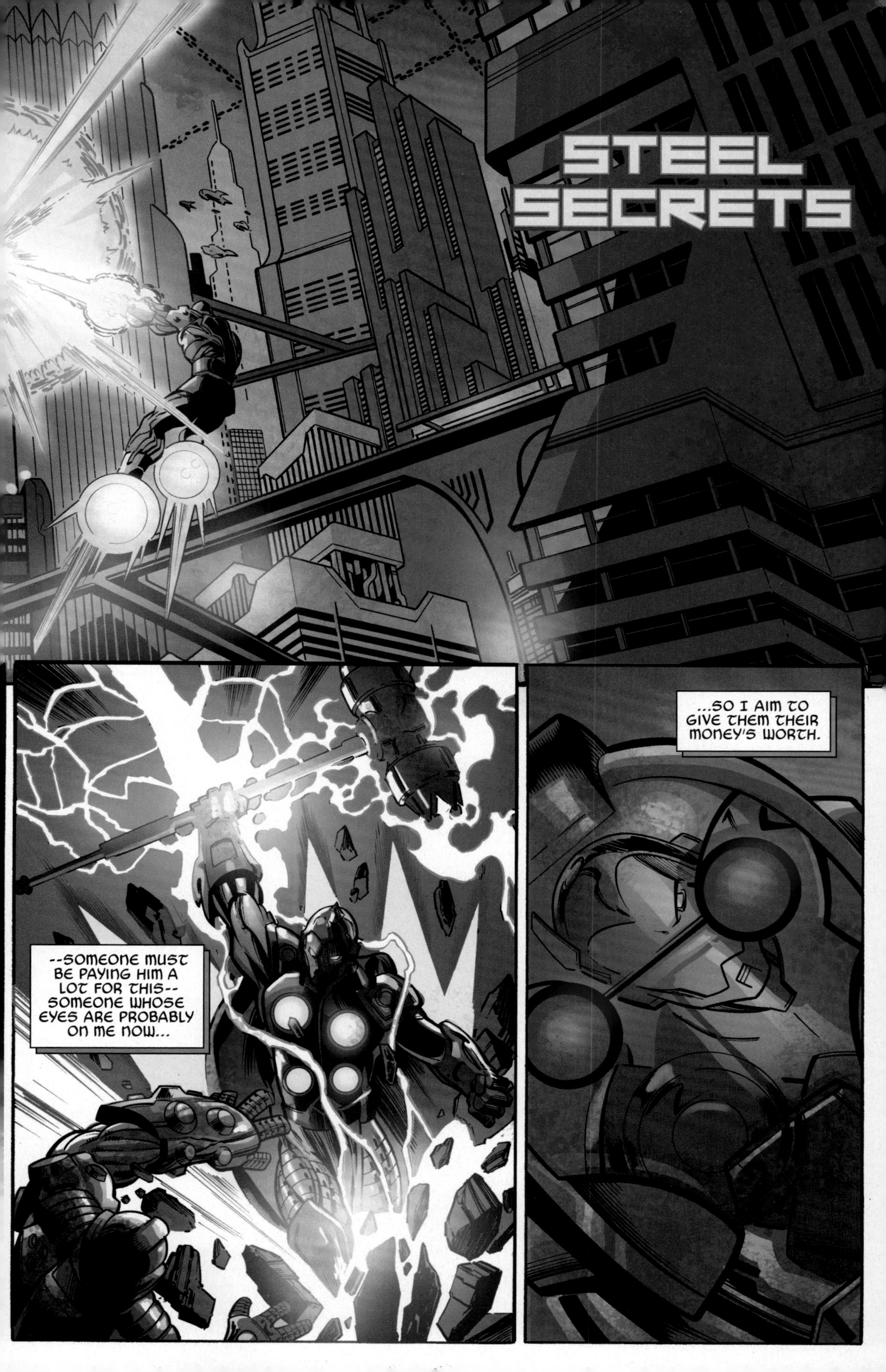
STEEL SECRETS
--SOMEONE MUST BE PAYING HIM A LOT FOR THIS--SOMEONE WHOSE EYES ARE PROBABLY ON ME NOW...
...SO I AIM TO GIVE THEM THEIR MONEY'S WORTH.

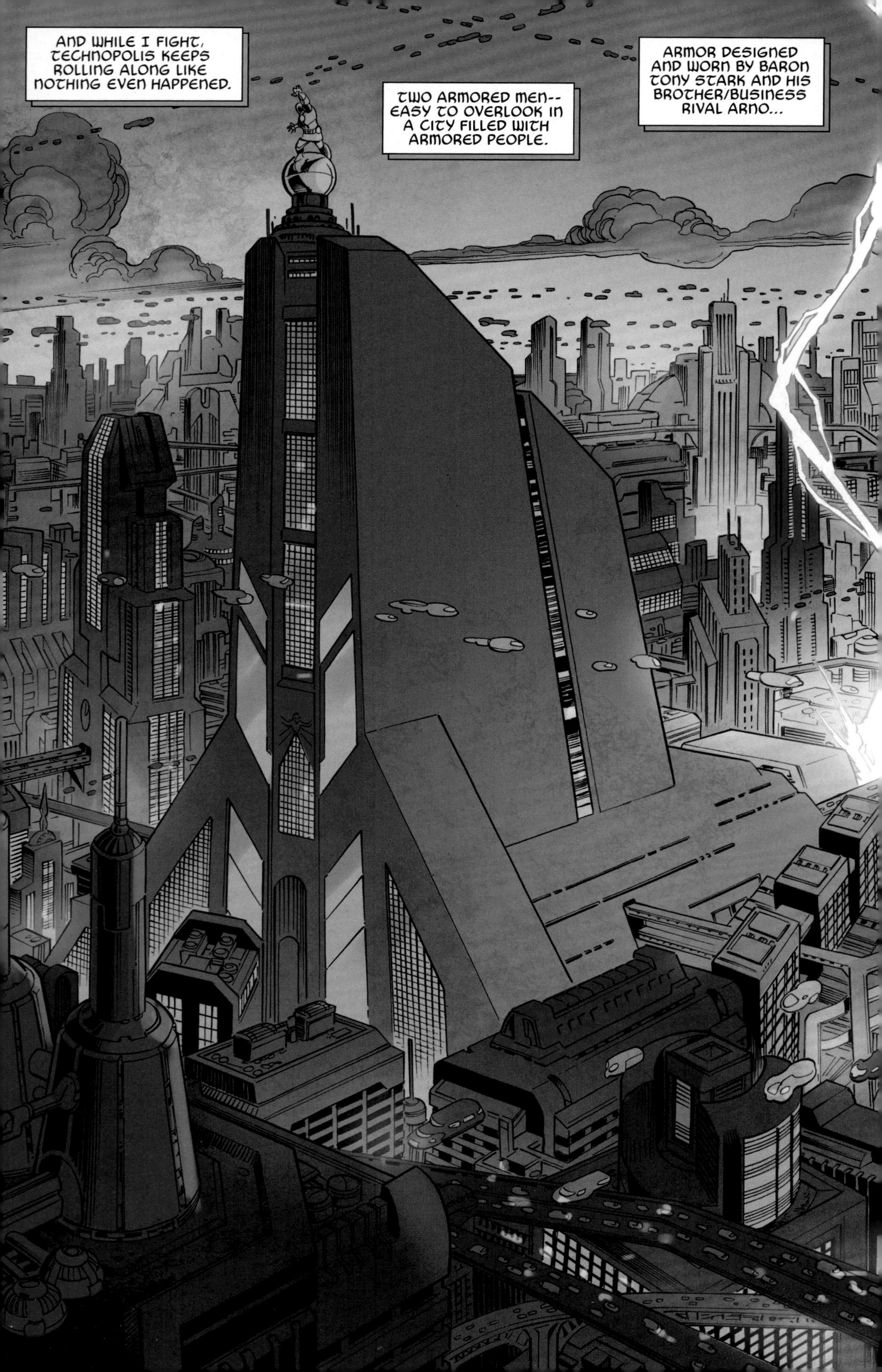
AND WHILE I FIGHT, TECHNOPOLIS KEEPS ROLLING ALONG LIKE NOTHING EVEN HAPPENED.
TWO ARMORED MEN-- EASY TO OVERLOOK IN A CITY FILLED WITH ARMORED PEOPLE.
ARMOR DESIGNED AND WORN BY BARON TONY STARK AND HIS BROTHER/BUSINESS RIVAL ARNO...

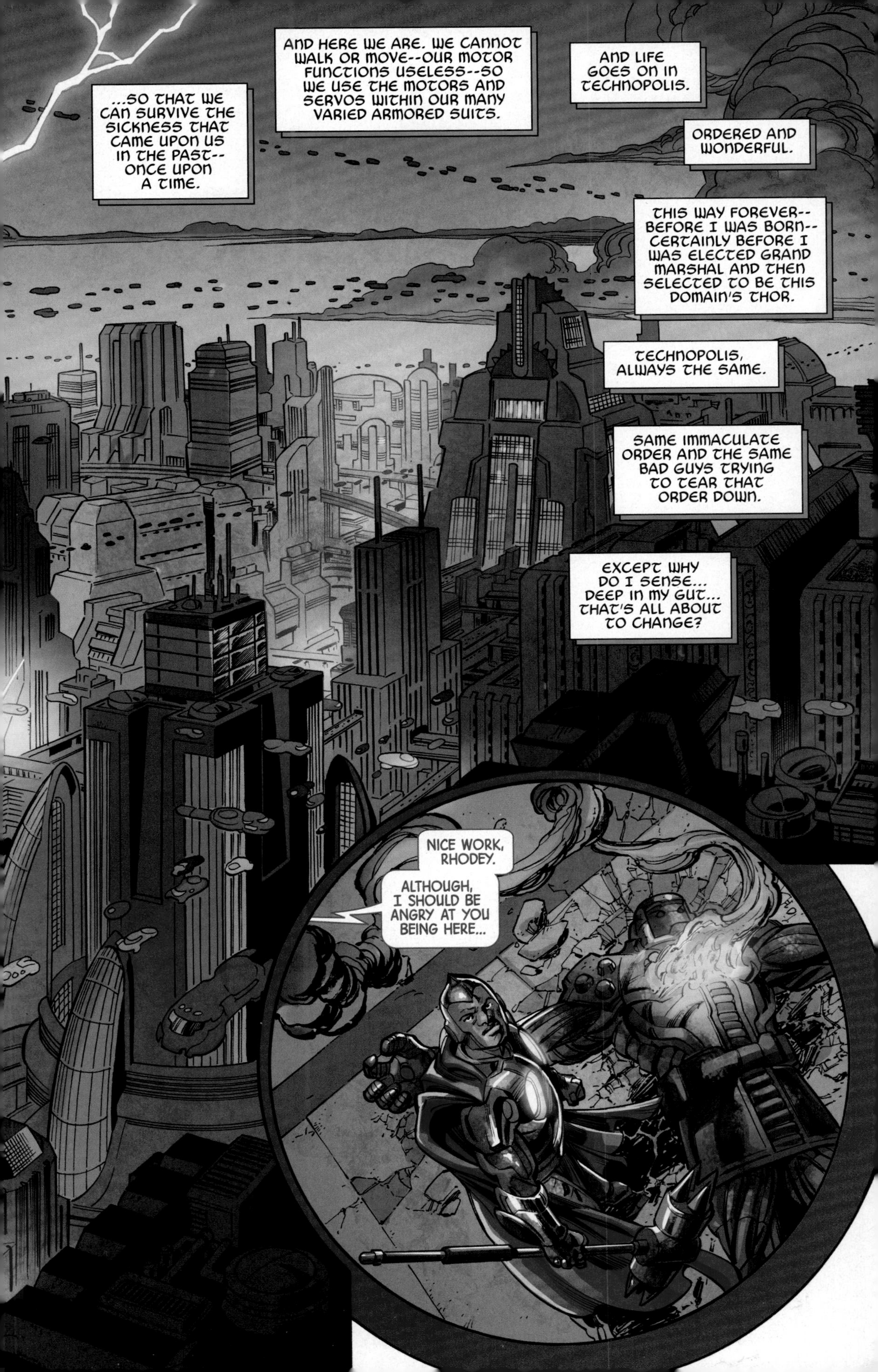
...SO THAT WE CAN SURVIVE THE SICKNESS THAT CAME UPON US IN THE PAST--ONCE UPON A TIME.
AND HERE WE ARE. WE CANNOT WALK OR MOVE--OUR MOTOR FUNCTIONS USELESS--SO WE USE THE MOTORS AND SERVOS WITHIN OUR MANY VARIED ARMORED SUITS.
AND LIFE GOES ON IN TECHNOPOLIS.
ORDERED AND WONDERFUL.
THIS WAY FOREVER--BEFORE I WAS BORN--CERTAINLY BEFORE I WAS ELECTED GRAND MARSHAL AND THEN SELECTED TO BE THIS DOMAIN'S THOR.
TECHNOPOLIS, ALWAYS THE SAME.
SAME IMMACULATE ORDER AND THE SAME BAD GUYS TRYING TO TEAR THAT ORDER DOWN.
EXCEPT WHY DO I SENSE... DEEP IN MY GUT... THAT'S ALL ABOUT TO CHANGE?
NICE WORK, RHODEY.
ALTHOUGH, I SHOULD BE ANGRY AT YOU BEING HERE...

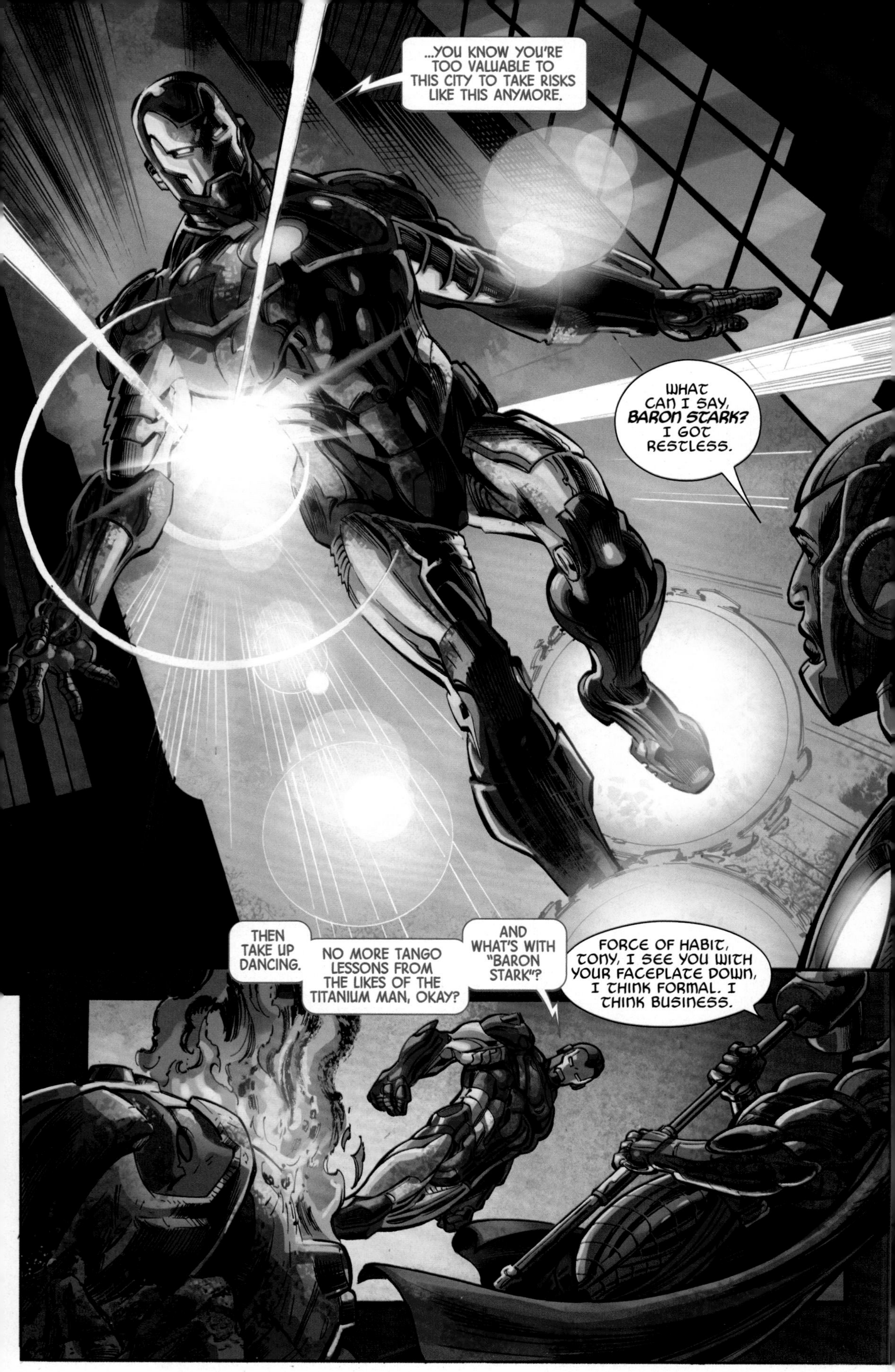
...YOU KNOW YOU'RE TOO VALUABLE TO THIS CITY TO TAKE RISKS LIKE THIS ANYMORE.
WHAT CAN I SAY, BARON STARK? I GOT RESTLESS.
THEN TAKE UP DANCING.
NO MORE TANGO LESSONS FROM THE LIKES OF THE TITANIUM MAN, OKAY?
AND WHAT'S WITH "BARON STARK"?
FORCE OF HABIT, TONY, I SEE YOU WITH YOUR FACEPLATE DOWN, I THINK FORMAL. I THINK BUSINESS.

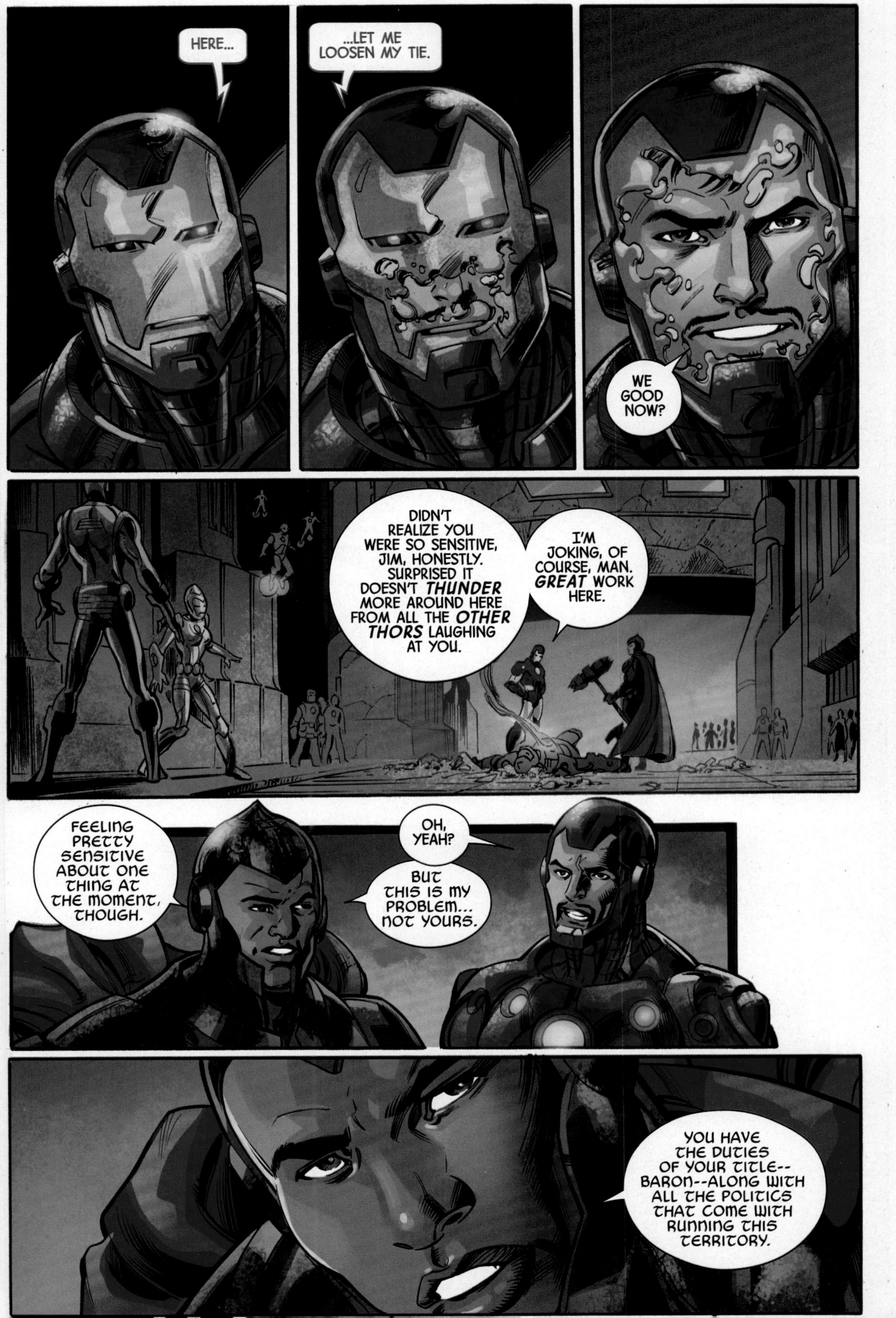
HERE...
...LET ME LOOSEN MY TIE.
WE GOOD NOW?
DIDN'T REALIZE YOU WERE SO SENSITIVE, JIM, HONESTLY. SURPRISED IT DOESN'T THUNDER MORE AROUND HERE FROM ALL THE OTHER THORS LAUGHING AT YOU.
I'M JOKING, OF COURSE, MAN. GREAT WORK HERE.
FEELING PRETTY SENSITIVE ABOUT ONE THING AT THE MOMENT, THOUGH.
OH, YEAH?
BUT THIS IS MY PROBLEM... NOT YOURS.
YOU HAVE THE DUTIES OF YOUR TITLE--BARON--ALONG WITH ALL THE POLITICS THAT COME WITH RUNNING THIS TERRITORY.

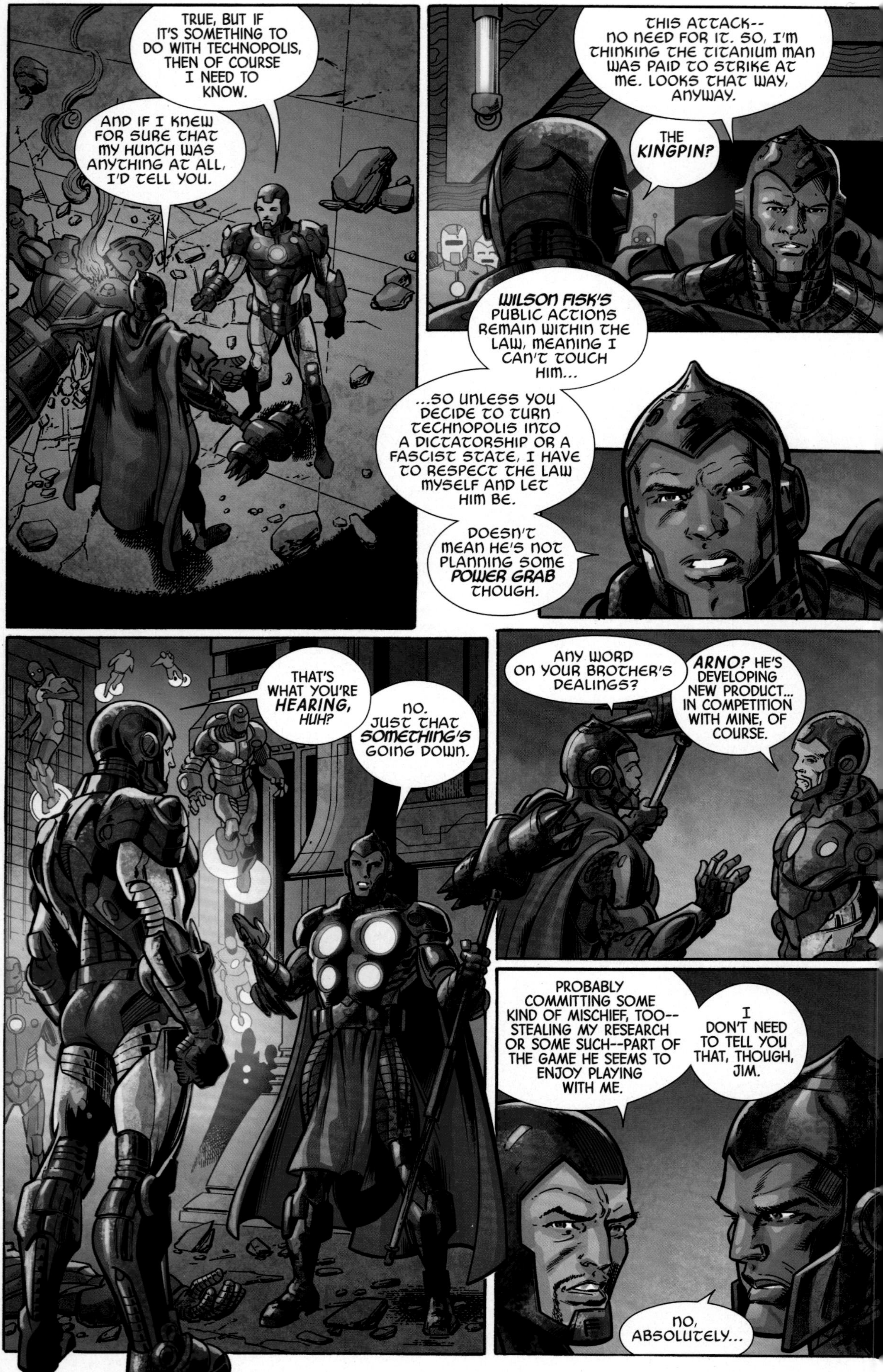
TRUE, BUT IF IT'S SOMETHING TO DO WITH TECHNOPOLIS, THEN OF COURSE I NEED TO KNOW.
AND IF I KNEW FOR SURE THAT MY HUNCH WAS ANYTHING AT ALL, I'D TELL YOU.
THIS ATTACK-- NO NEED FOR IT. SO, I'M THINKING THE TITANIUM MAN WAS PAID TO STRIKE AT ME. LOOKS THAT WAY, ANYWAY.
THE KINGPIN?
WILSON FISK'S PUBLIC ACTIONS REMAIN WITHIN THE LAW, MEANING I CAN'T TOUCH HIM...
...SO UNLESS YOU DECIDE TO TURN TECHNOPOLIS INTO A DICTATORSHIP OR A FASCIST STATE, I HAVE TO RESPECT THE LAW MYSELF AND LET HIM BE.
DOESN'T MEAN HE'S NOT PLANNING SOME POWER GRAB THOUGH.
THAT'S WHAT YOU'RE HEARING, HUH?
NO. JUST THAT SOMETHING'S GOING DOWN.
ANY WORD ON YOUR BROTHER'S DEALINGS?
ARNO? HE'S DEVELOPING NEW PRODUCT... IN COMPETITION WITH MINE, OF COURSE.
PROBABLY COMMITTING SOME KIND OF MISCHIEF, TOO-- STEALING MY RESEARCH OR SOME SUCH--PART OF THE GAME HE SEEMS TO ENJOY PLAYING WITH ME.
I DON'T NEED TO TELL YOU THAT, THOUGH, JIM.
NO, ABSOLUTELY...

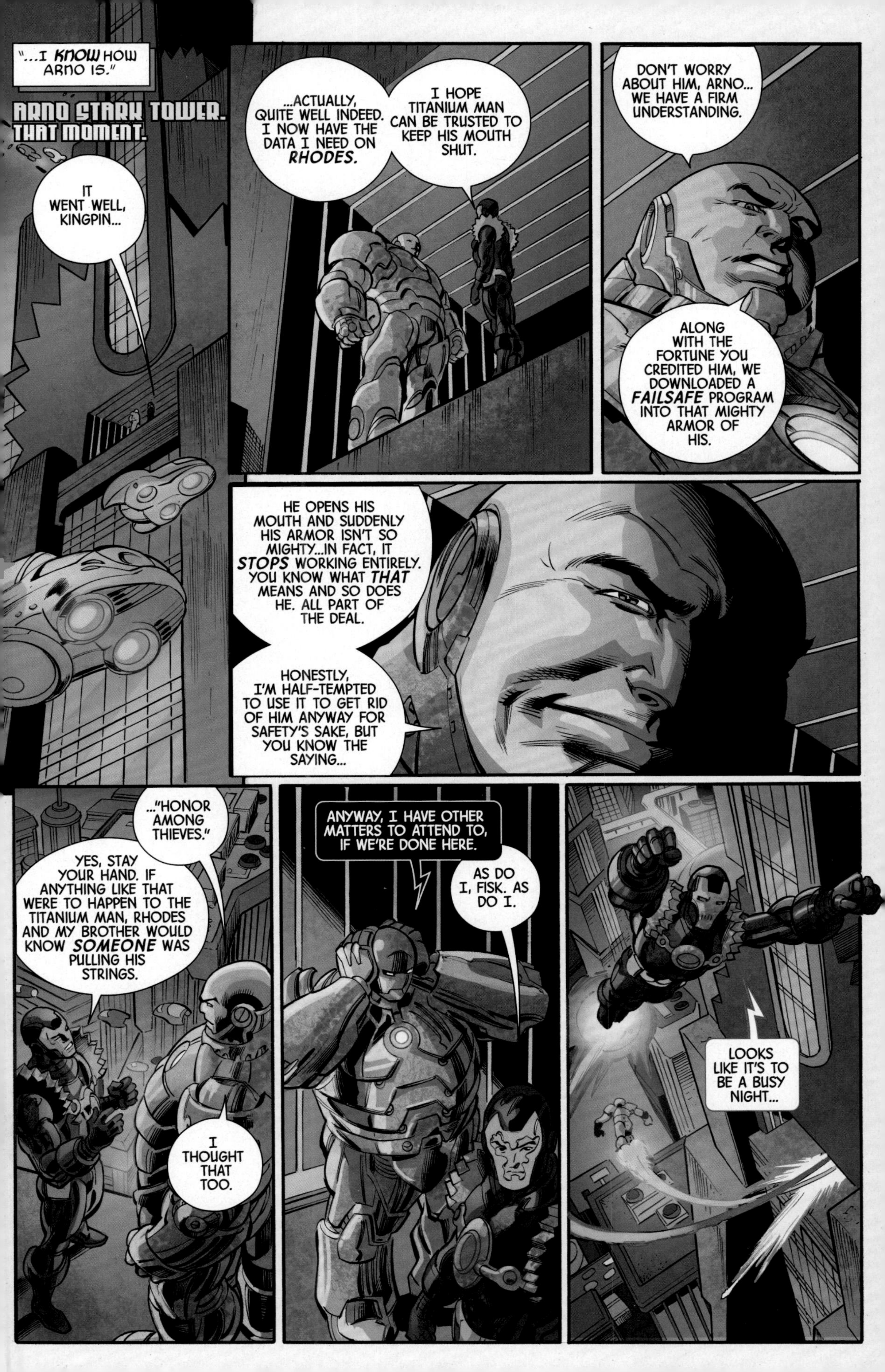

"...I KNOW HOW ARNO IS."
ARNO STARK TOWER. THAT MOMENT.
IT WENT WELL, KINGPIN...
...ACTUALLY, QUITE WELL INDEED. I NOW HAVE THE DATA I NEED ON RHODES.
I HOPE TITANIUM MAN CAN BE TRUSTED TO KEEP HIS MOUTH SHUT.
DON'T WORRY ABOUT HIM, ARNO... WE HAVE A FIRM UNDERSTANDING.
ALONG WITH THE FORTUNE YOU CREDITED HIM, WE DOWNLOADED A FAILSAFE PROGRAM INTO THAT MIGHTY ARMOR OF HIS.
HE OPENS HIS MOUTH AND SUDDENLY HIS ARMOR ISN'T SO MIGHTY...IN FACT, IT STOPS WORKING ENTIRELY. YOU KNOW WHAT THAT MEANS AND SO DOES HE. ALL PART OF THE DEAL.
HONESTLY, I'M HALF-TEMPTED TO USE IT TO GET RID OF HIM ANYWAY FOR SAFETY'S SAKE, BUT YOU KNOW THE SAYING...
..."HONOR AMONG THIEVES."
YES, STAY YOUR HAND. IF ANYTHING LIKE THAT WERE TO HAPPEN TO THE TITANIUM MAN, RHODES AND MY BROTHER WOULD KNOW SOMEONE WAS PULLING HIS STRINGS.
I THOUGHT THAT TOO.
ANYWAY, I HAVE OTHER MATTERS TO ATTEND TO, IF WE'RE DONE HERE.
AS DO I, FISK. AS DO I.
LOOKS LIKE IT'S TO BE A BUSY NIGHT...

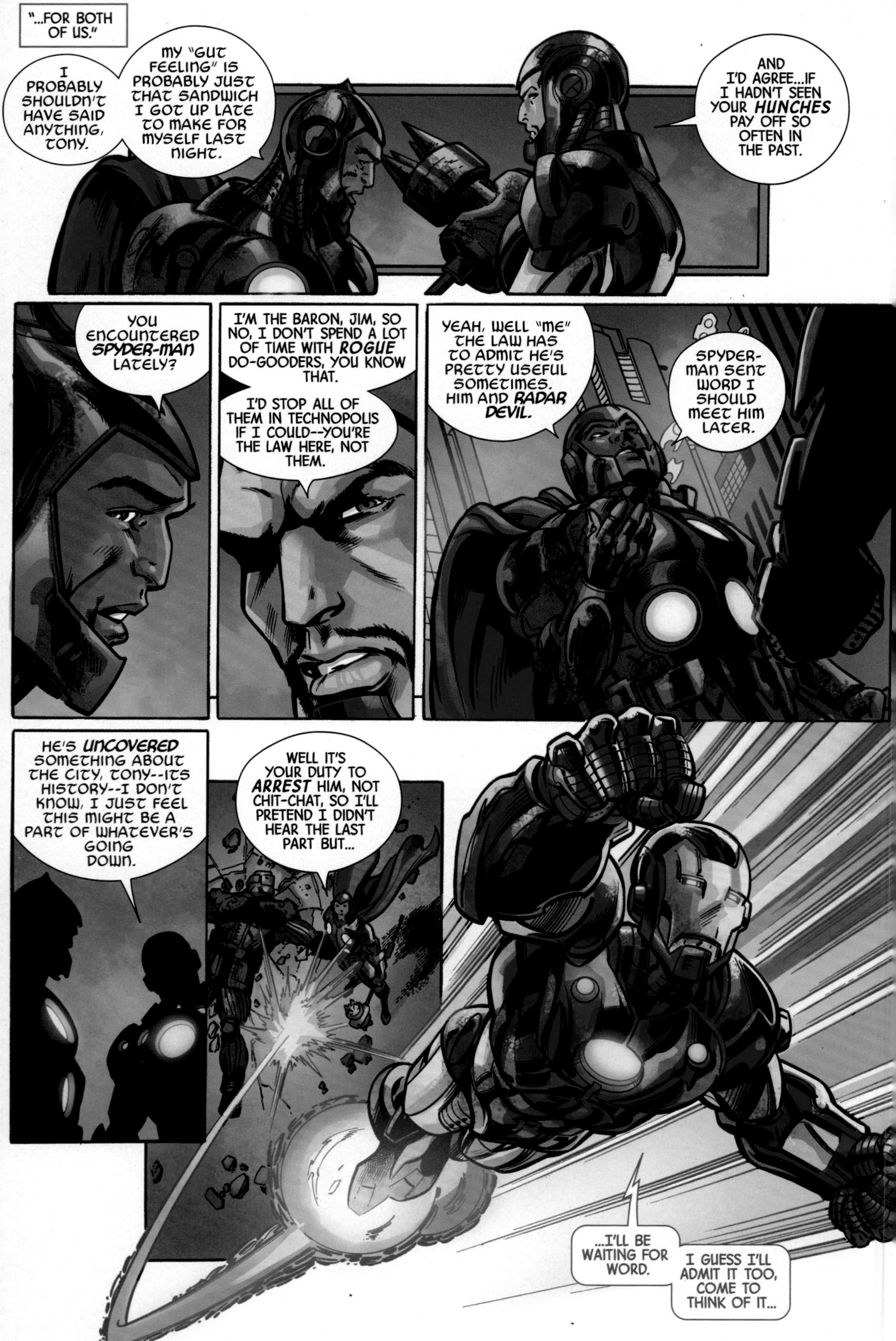

"...FOR BOTH OF US."
I PROBABLY SHOULDN'T HAVE SAID ANYTHING, TONY.
MY "GUT FEELING" IS PROBABLY JUST THAT SANDWICH I GOT UP LATE TO MAKE FOR MYSELF LAST NIGHT.
AND I'D AGREE...IF I HADN'T SEEN YOUR HUNCHES PAY OFF SO OFTEN IN THE PAST.
YOU ENCOUNTERED SPYDER-MAN LATELY?
I'M THE BARON, JIM, SO NO, I DON'T SPEND A LOT OF TIME WITH ROGUE DO-GOODERS, YOU KNOW THAT.
I'D STOP ALL OF THEM IN TECHNOPOLIS IF I COULD--YOU'RE THE LAW HERE, NOT THEM.
YEAH, WELL "ME" THE LAW HAS TO ADMIT HE'S PRETTY USEFUL SOMETIMES. HIM AND RADAR DEVIL.
SPYDER-MAN SENT WORD I SHOULD MEET HIM LATER.
HE'S UNCOVERED SOMETHING ABOUT THE CITY, TONY--ITS HISTORY--I DON'T KNOW, I JUST FEEL THIS MIGHT BE A PART OF WHATEVER'S GOING DOWN.
WELL IT'S YOUR DUTY TO ARREST HIM, NOT CHIT-CHAT, SO I'LL PRETEND I DIDN'T HEAR THE LAST PART BUT...
...I'LL BE WAITING FOR WORD.
I GUESS I'LL ADMIT IT TOO, COME TO THINK OF IT...

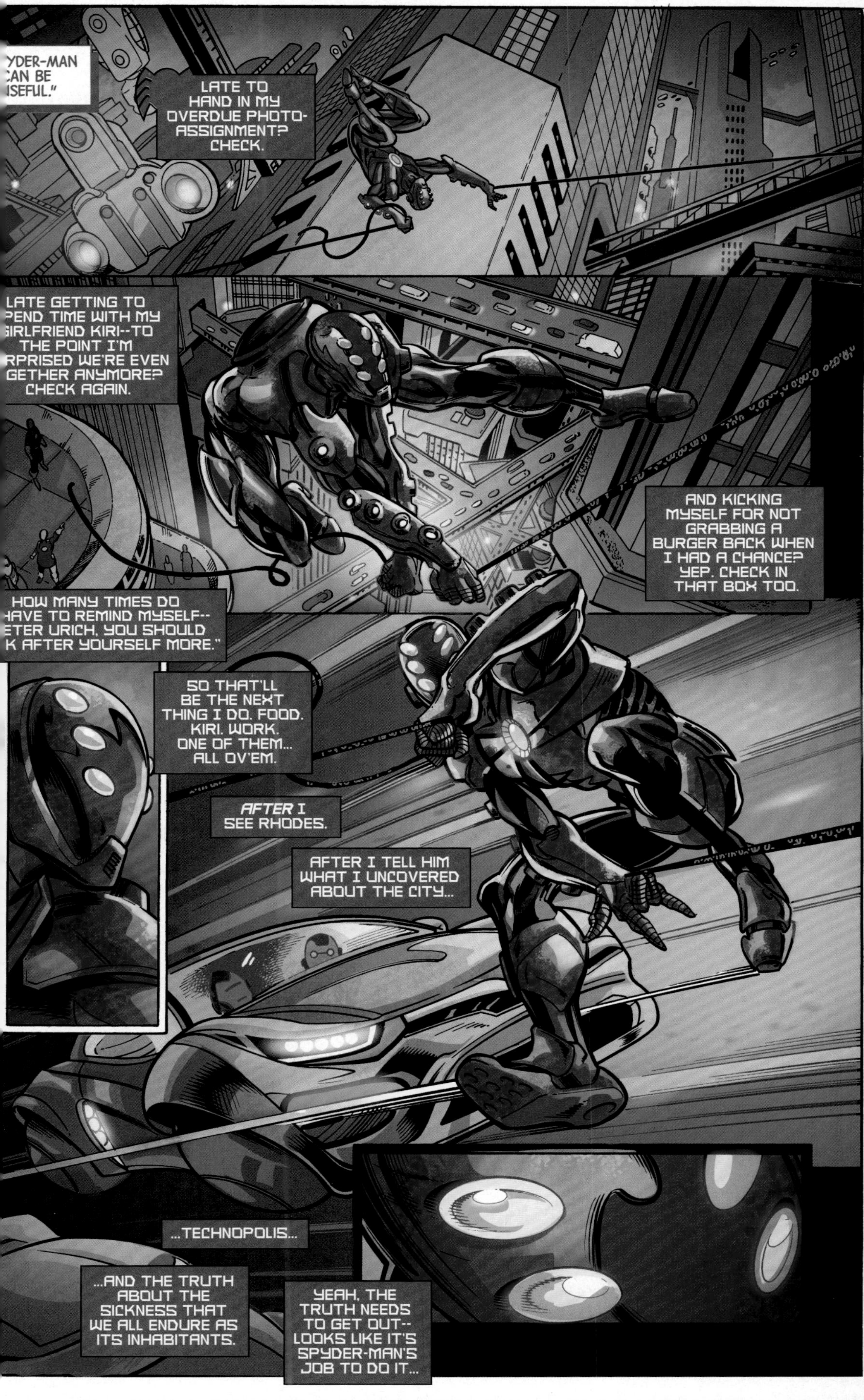

YDER-MAN
CAN BE
SEFUL."
LATE TO HAND IN MY OVERDUE PHOTO-ASSIGNMENT? CHECK.
LATE GETTING TO PEND TIME WITH MY GIRLFRIEND KIRI--TO THE POINT I'M RPRISED WE'RE EVEN GETHER ANYMORE? CHECK AGAIN.
AND KICKING MYSELF FOR NOT GRABBING A BURGER BACK WHEN I HAD A CHANCE? YEP. CHECK IN THAT BOX TOO.
HOW MANY TIMES DO HAVE TO REMIND MYSELF-- ETER URICH, YOU SHOULD K AFTER YOURSELF MORE."
SO THAT'LL BE THE NEXT THING I DO. FOOD. KIRI. WORK. ONE OF THEM... ALL OV'EM.
AFTER I SEE RHODES.
AFTER I TELL HIM WHAT I UNCOVERED ABOUT THE CITY...
...TECHNOPOLIS...
...AND THE TRUTH ABOUT THE SICKNESS THAT WE ALL ENDURE AS ITS INHABITANTS.
YEAH, THE TRUTH NEEDS TO GET OUT-- LOOKS LIKE IT'S SPYDER-MAN'S JOB TO DO IT...

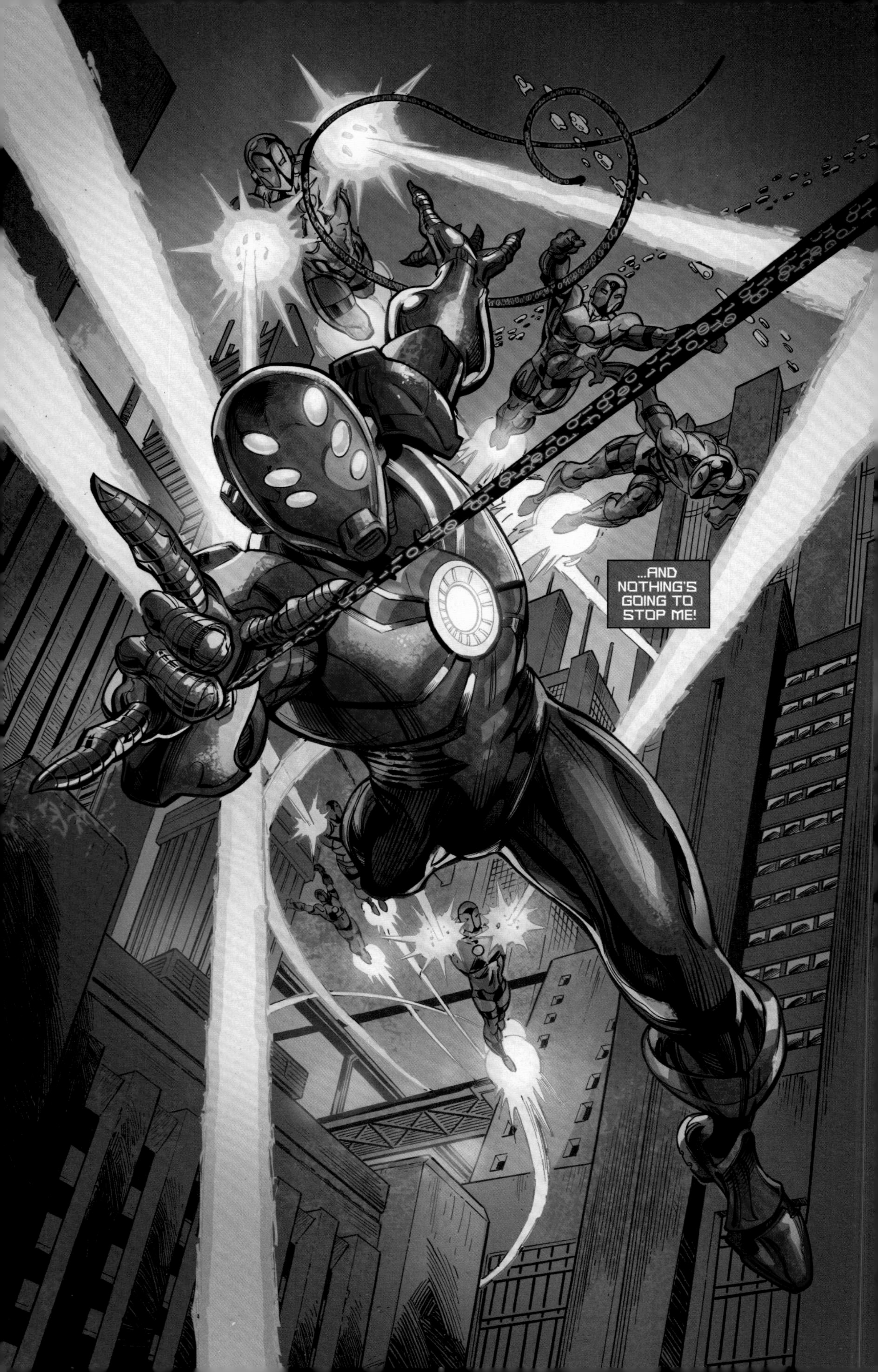
...AND NOTHING'S GOING TO STOP ME!

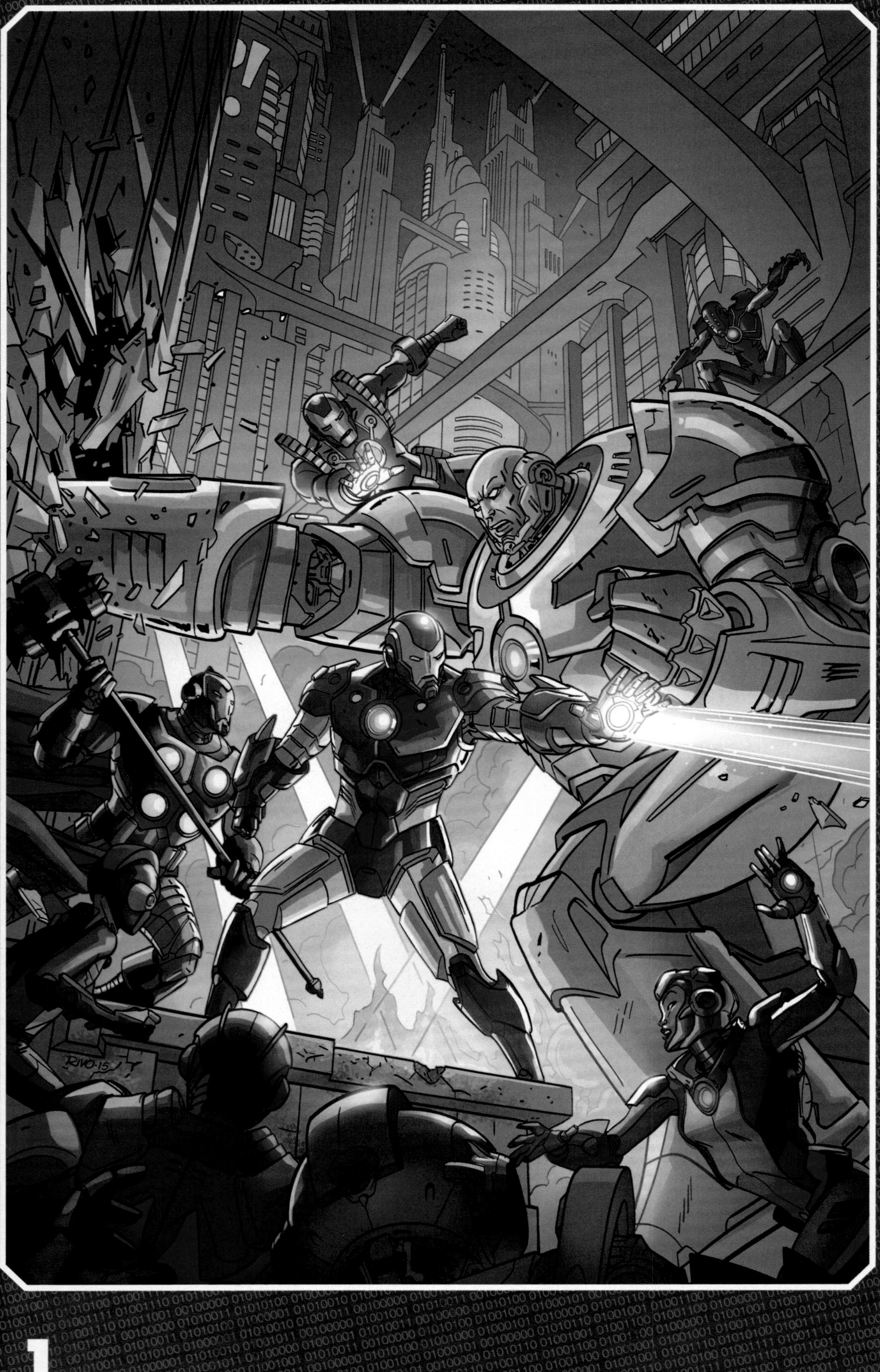
RIVO-15

1

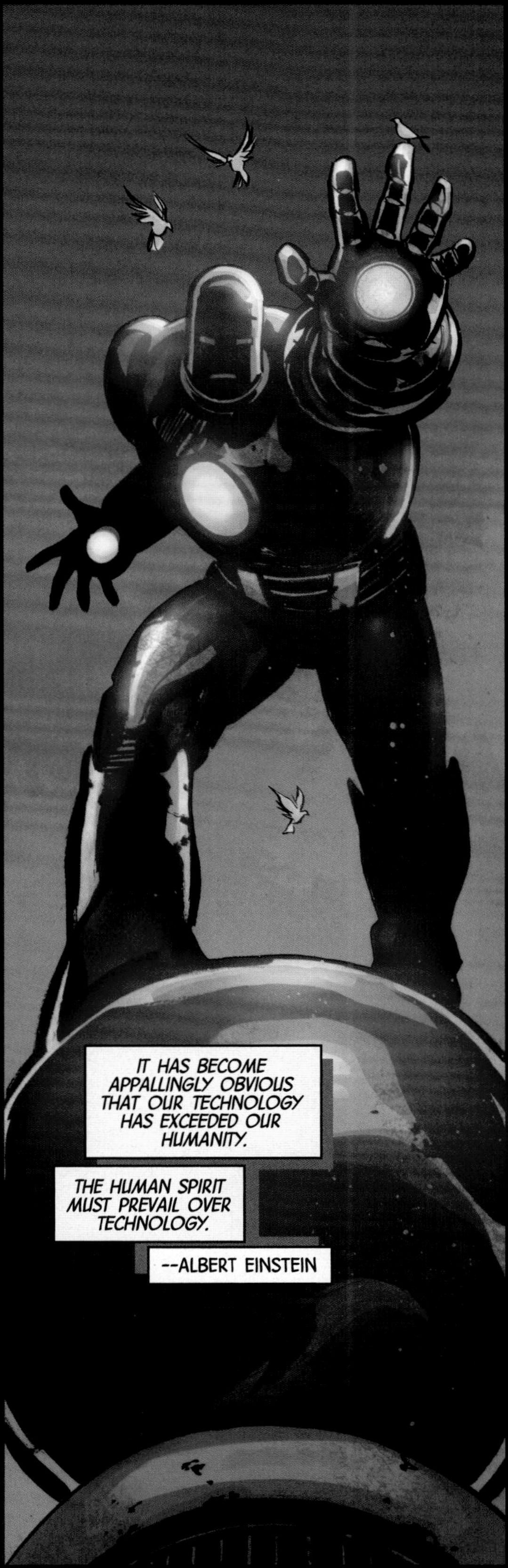
IT HAS BECOME APPALLINGLY OBVIOUS THAT OUR TECHNOLOGY HAS EXCEEDED OUR HUMANITY.
THE HUMAN SPIRIT MUST PREVAIL OVER TECHNOLOGY.
--ALBERT EINSTEIN

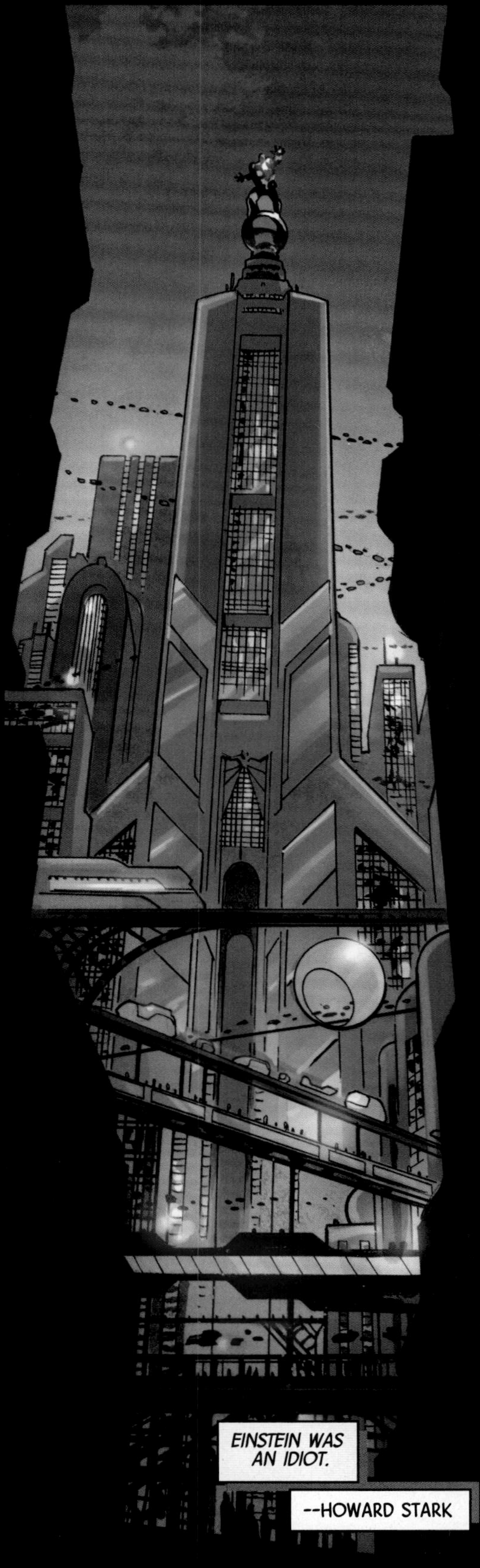
EINSTEIN WAS AN IDIOT.
--HOWARD STARK

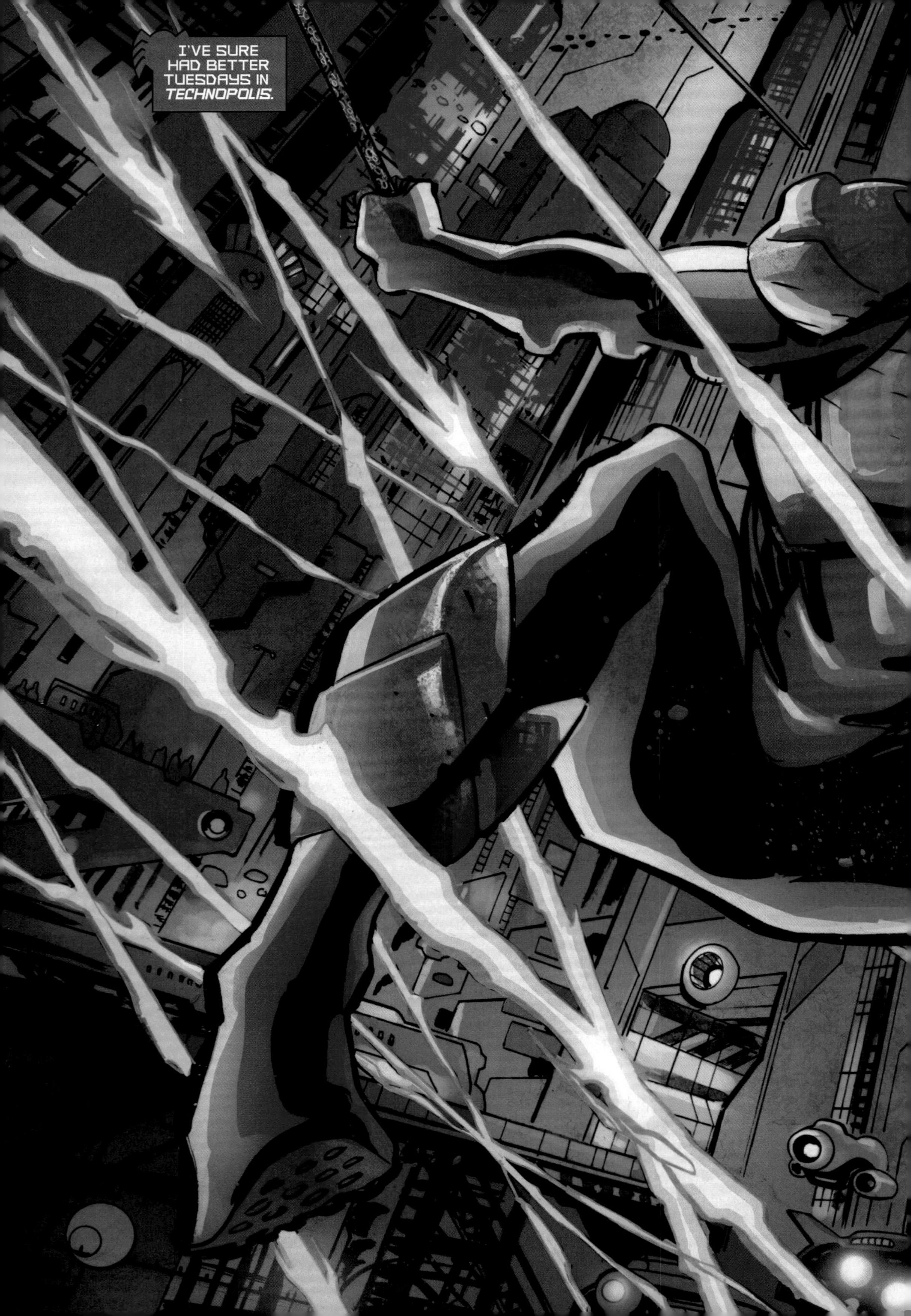
I'VE SURE HAD BETTER TUESDAYS IN *TECHNOPOLIS.*

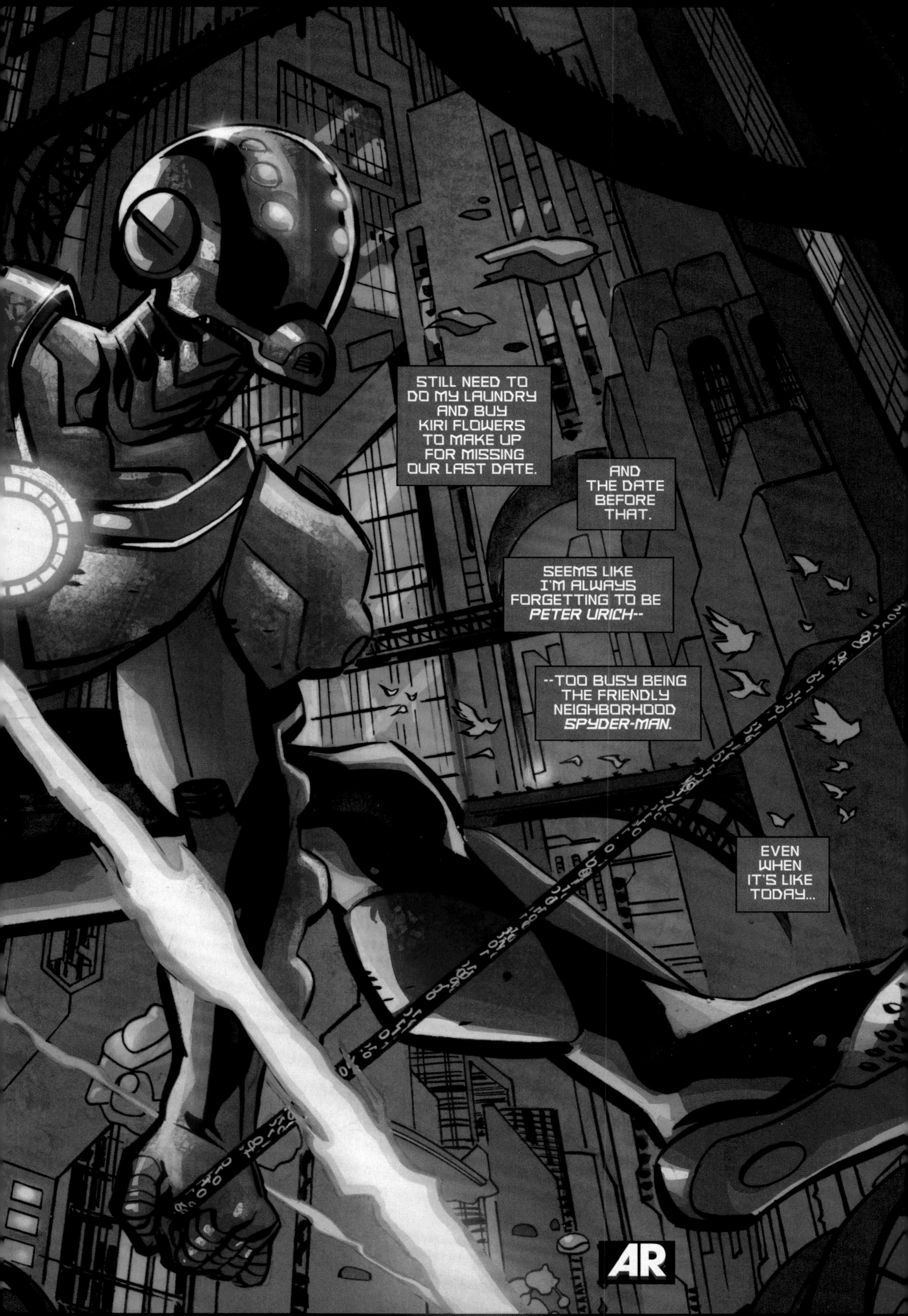
STILL NEED TO DO MY LAUNDRY AND BUY KIRI FLOWERS TO MAKE UP FOR MISSING OUR LAST DATE.
AND THE DATE BEFORE THAT.
SEEMS LIKE I'M ALWAYS FORGETTING TO BE *PETER URICH*--
--TOO BUSY BEING THE FRIENDLY NEIGHBORHOOD *SPYDER-MAN*.
EVEN WHEN IT'S LIKE TODAY...

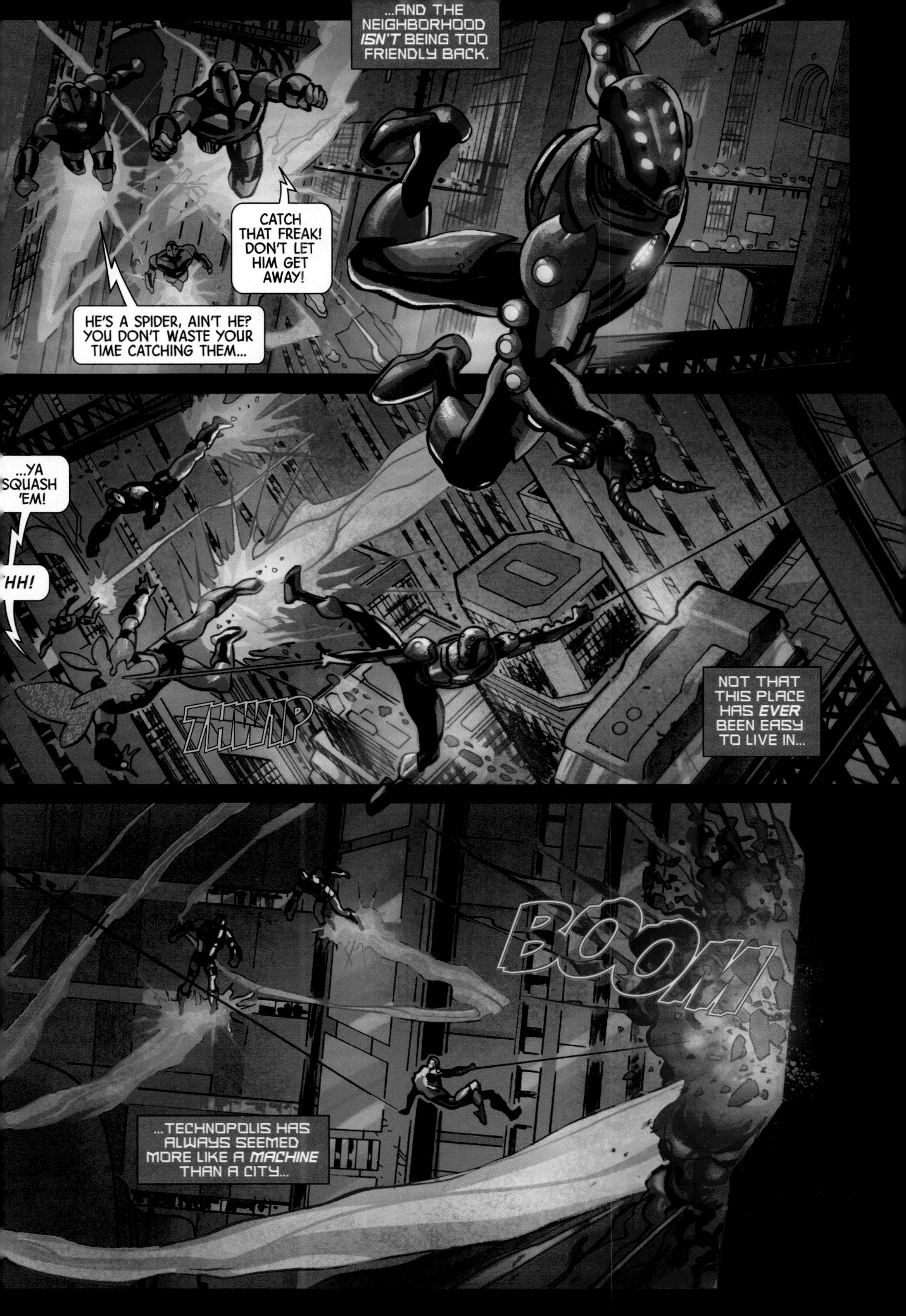
...AND THE NEIGHBORHOOD ISN'T BEING TOO FRIENDLY BACK.
CATCH THAT FREAK! DON'T LET HIM GET AWAY!
HE'S A SPIDER, AIN'T HE? YOU DON'T WASTE YOUR TIME CATCHING THEM...
...YA SQUASH 'EM!
HH!
THWIP
NOT THAT THIS PLACE HAS EVER BEEN EASY TO LIVE IN...
BOOM
...TECHNOPOLIS HAS ALWAYS SEEMED MORE LIKE A MACHINE THAN A CITY...

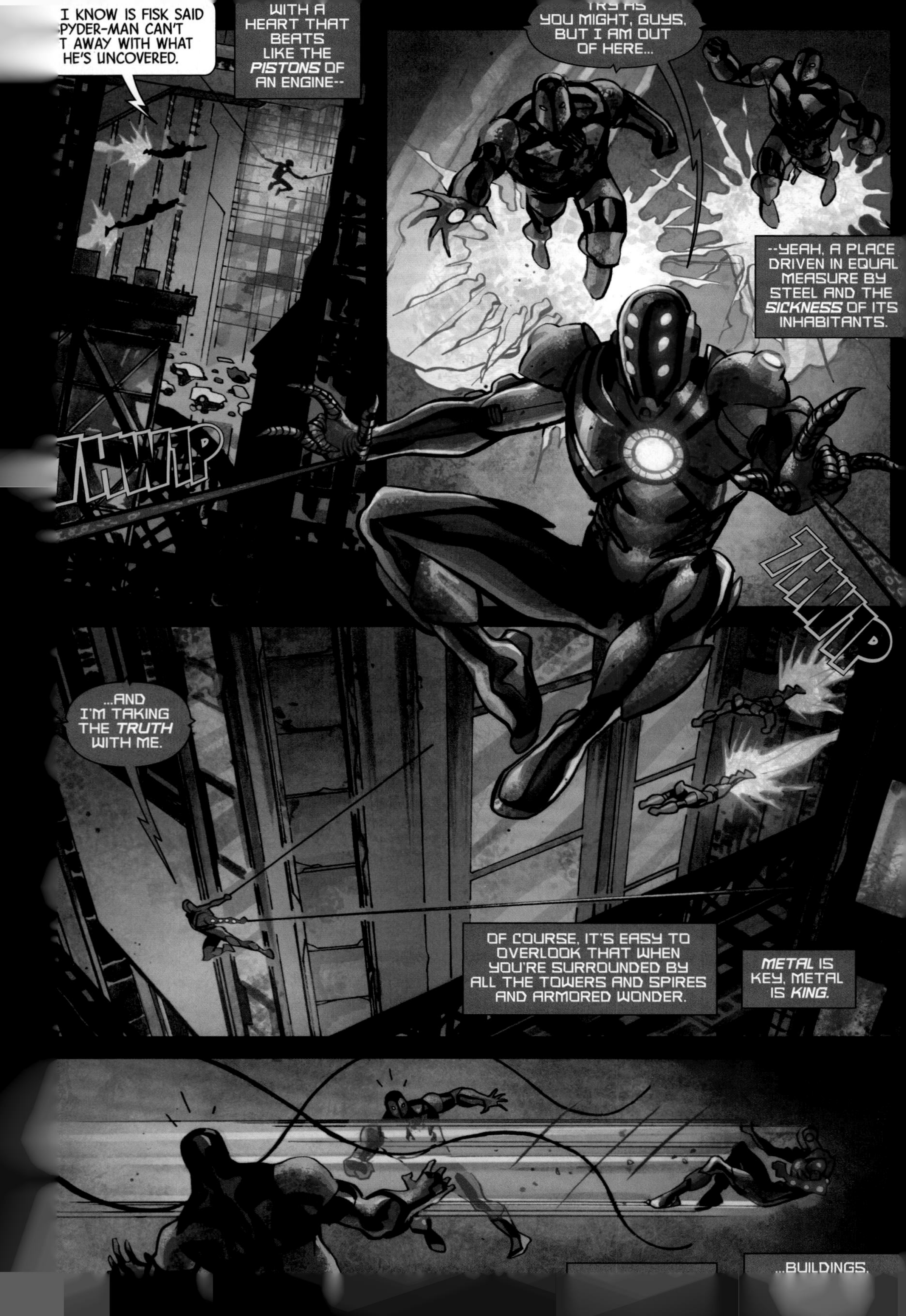

I KNOW IS FISK SAID PYDER-MAN CAN'T T AWAY WITH WHAT HE'S UNCOVERED.
WITH A HEART THAT BEATS LIKE THE PISTONS OF AN ENGINE--
TRY AS YOU MIGHT, GUYS, BUT I AM OUT OF HERE...
--YEAH, A PLACE DRIVEN IN EQUAL MEASURE BY STEEL AND THE SICKNESS OF ITS INHABITANTS.
THWIP
THWIP
...AND I'M TAKING THE TRUTH WITH ME.
OF COURSE, IT'S EASY TO OVERLOOK THAT WHEN YOU'RE SURROUNDED BY ALL THE TOWERS AND SPIRES AND ARMORED WONDER.
METAL IS KEY, METAL IS KING.
...BUILDINGS.

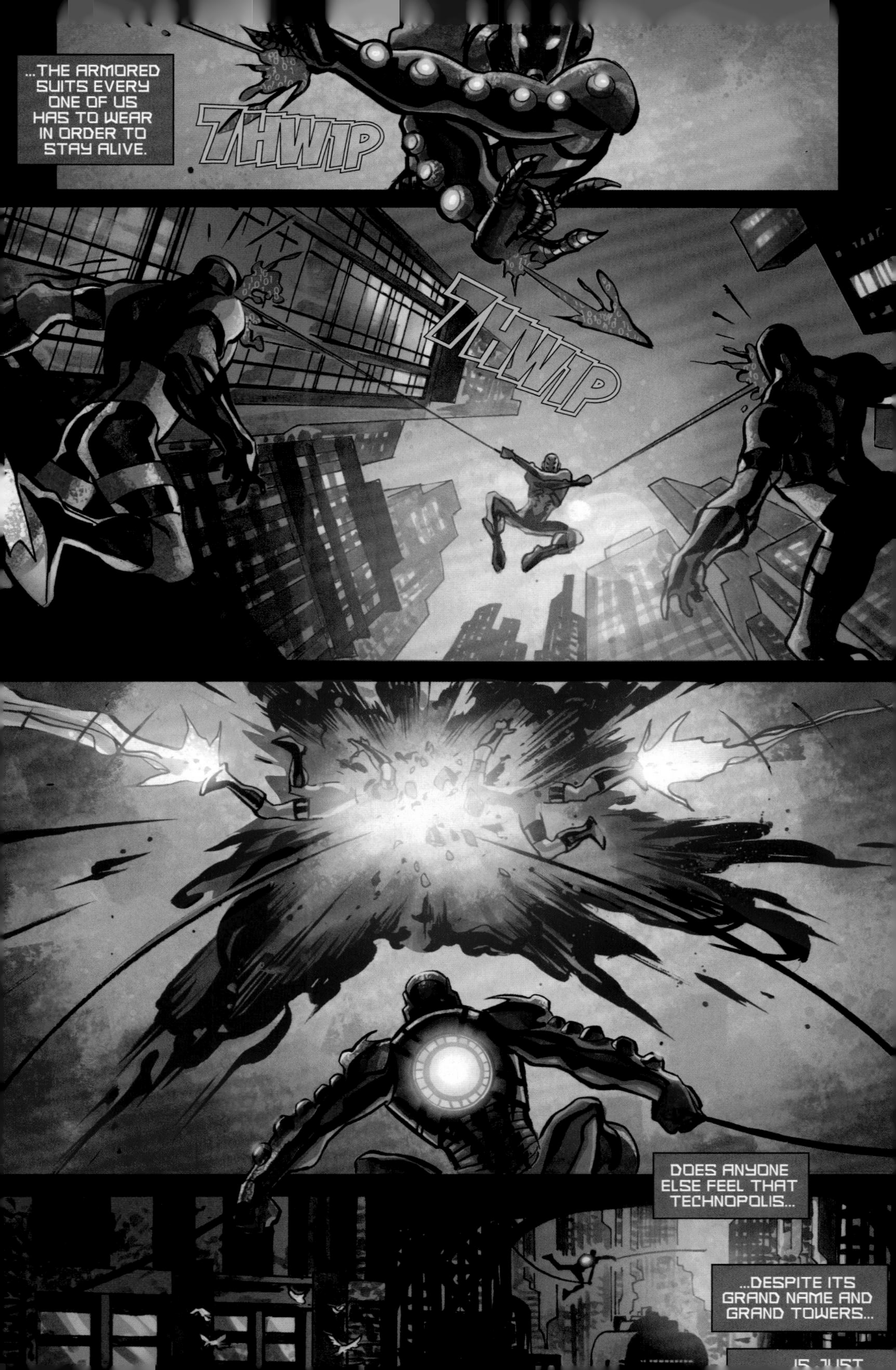
...THE ARMORED SUITS EVERY ONE OF US HAS TO WEAR IN ORDER TO STAY ALIVE.
THWIP
THWIP
DOES ANYONE ELSE FEEL THAT TECHNOPOLIS...
...DESPITE ITS GRAND NAME AND GRAND TOWERS...

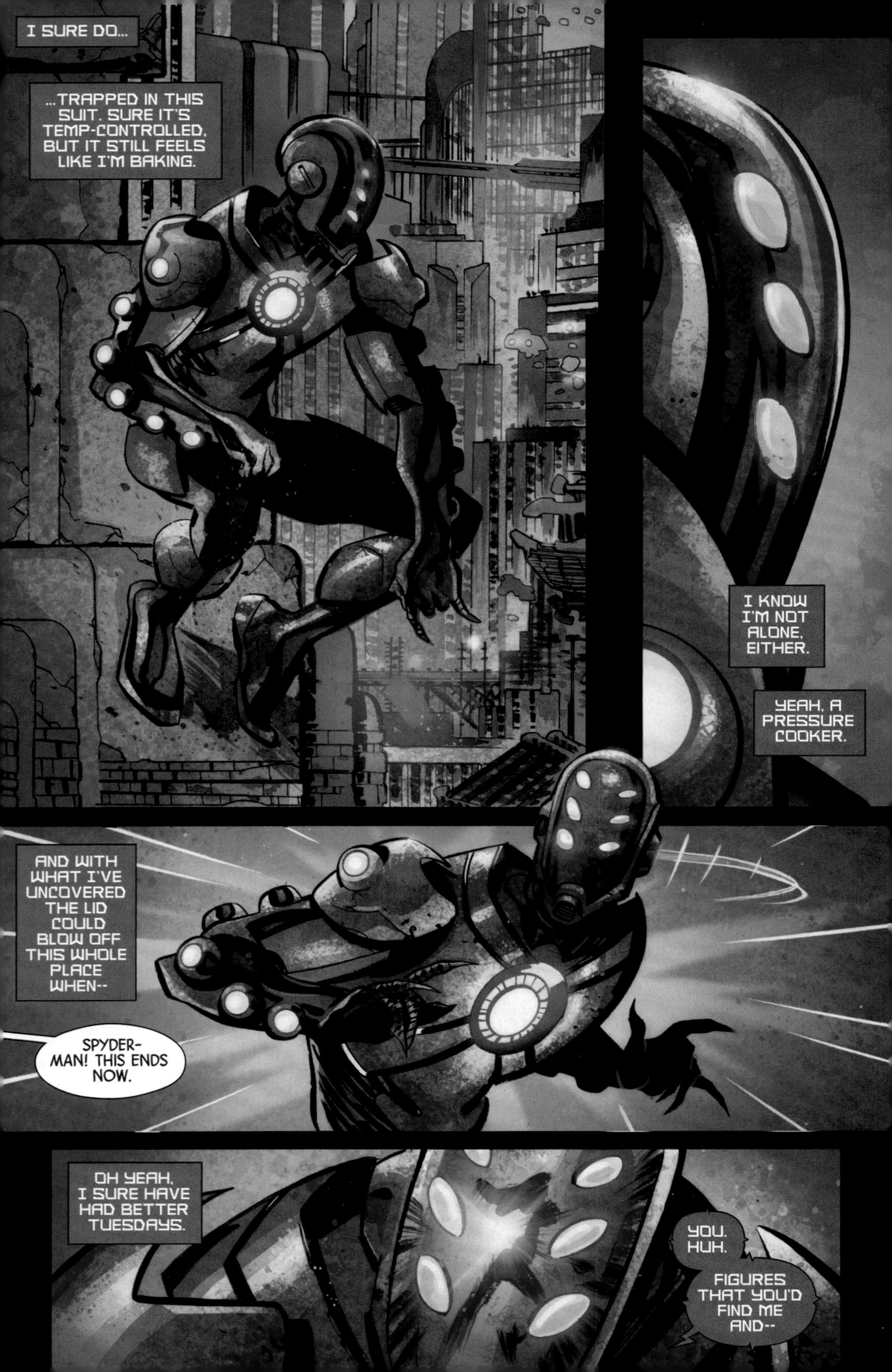
I SURE DO...
...TRAPPED IN THIS SUIT. SURE IT'S TEMP-CONTROLLED, BUT IT STILL FEELS LIKE I'M BAKING.
I KNOW I'M NOT ALONE, EITHER.
YEAH, A PRESSURE COOKER.
AND WITH WHAT I'VE UNCOVERED THE LID COULD BLOW OFF THIS WHOLE PLACE WHEN--
SPYDER-MAN! THIS ENDS NOW.
OH YEAH, I SURE HAVE HAD BETTER TUESDAYS.
YOU. HUH.
FIGURES THAT YOU'D FIND ME AND--

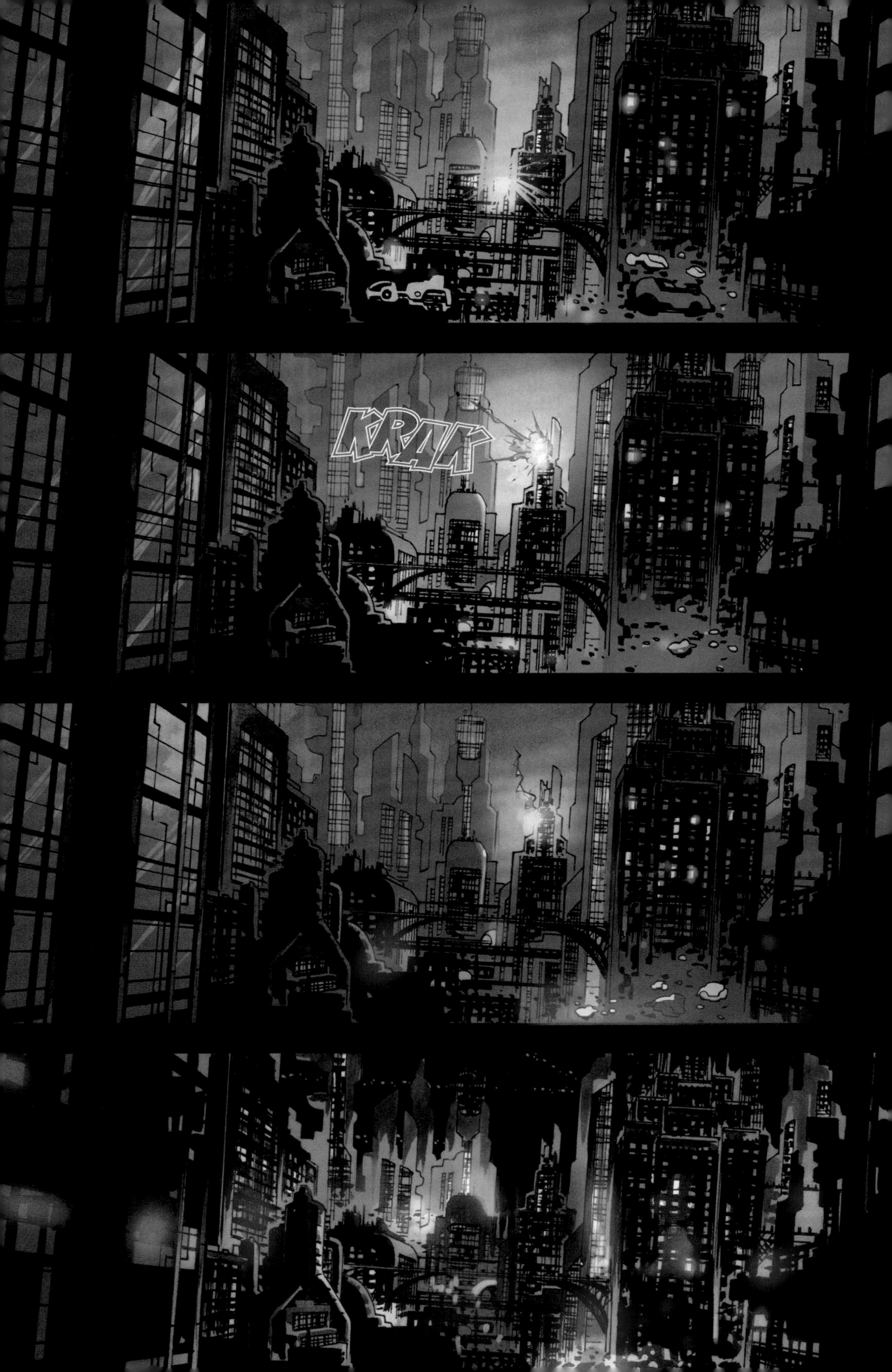
KRAK

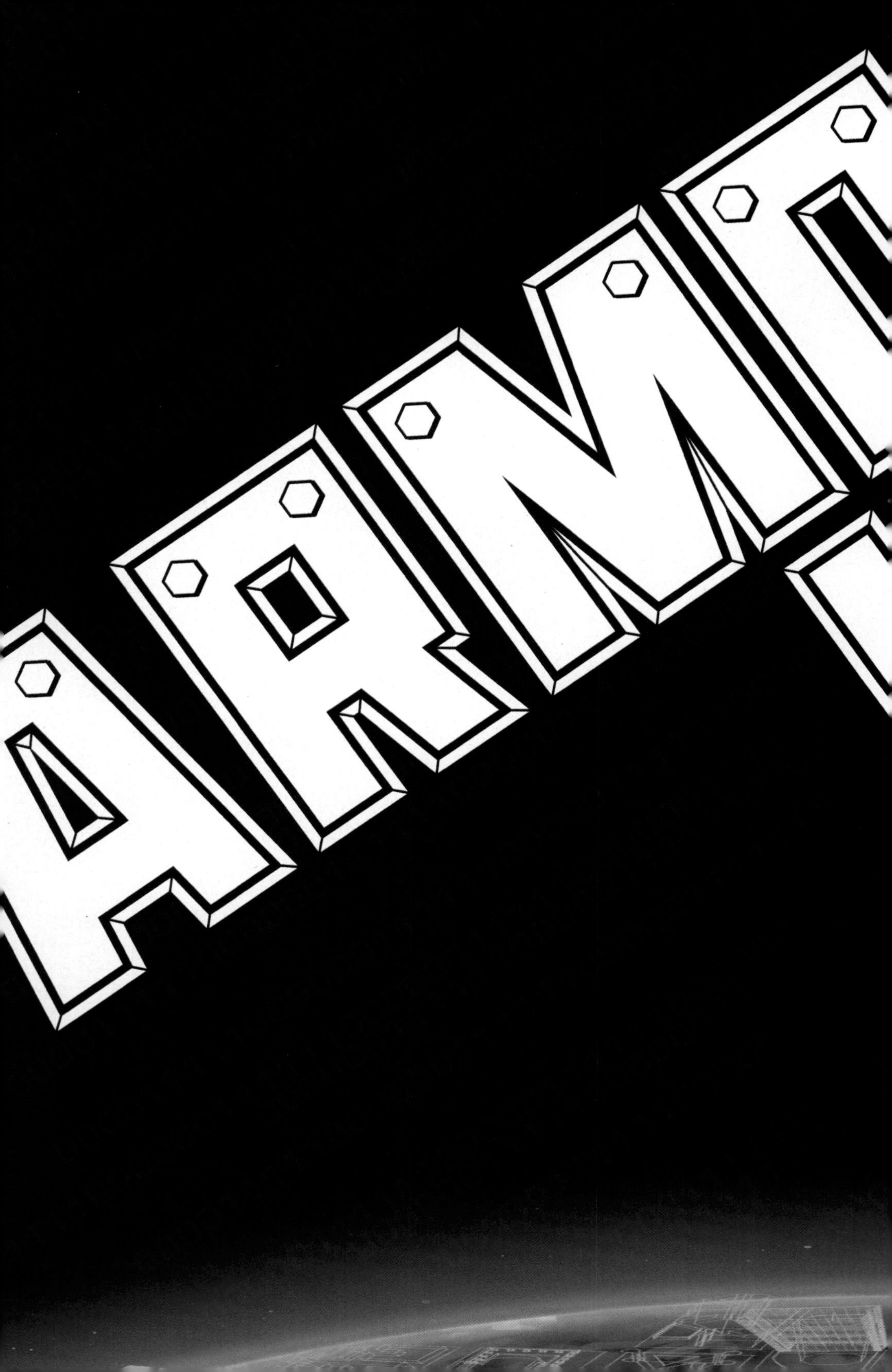
ARM

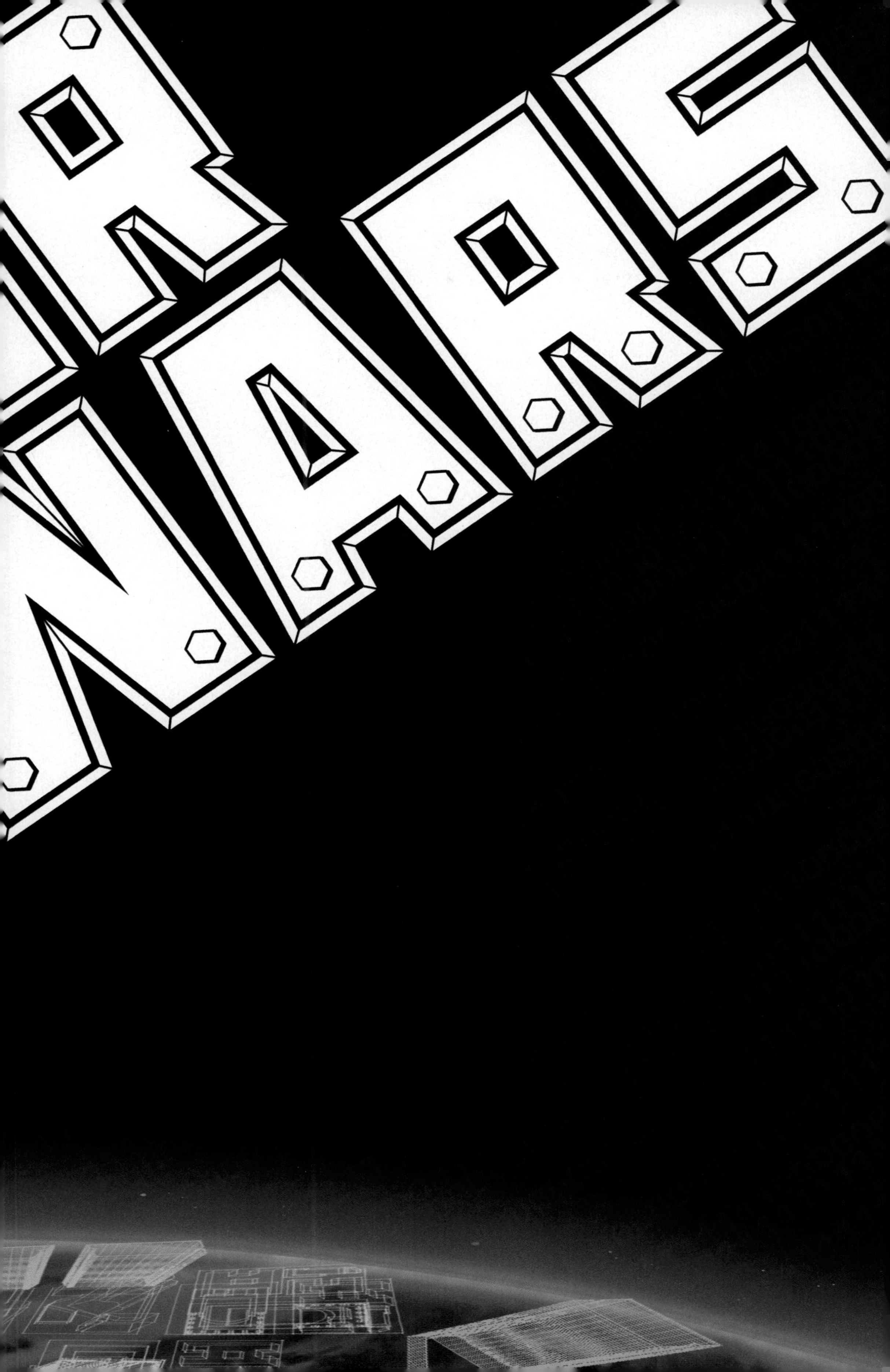

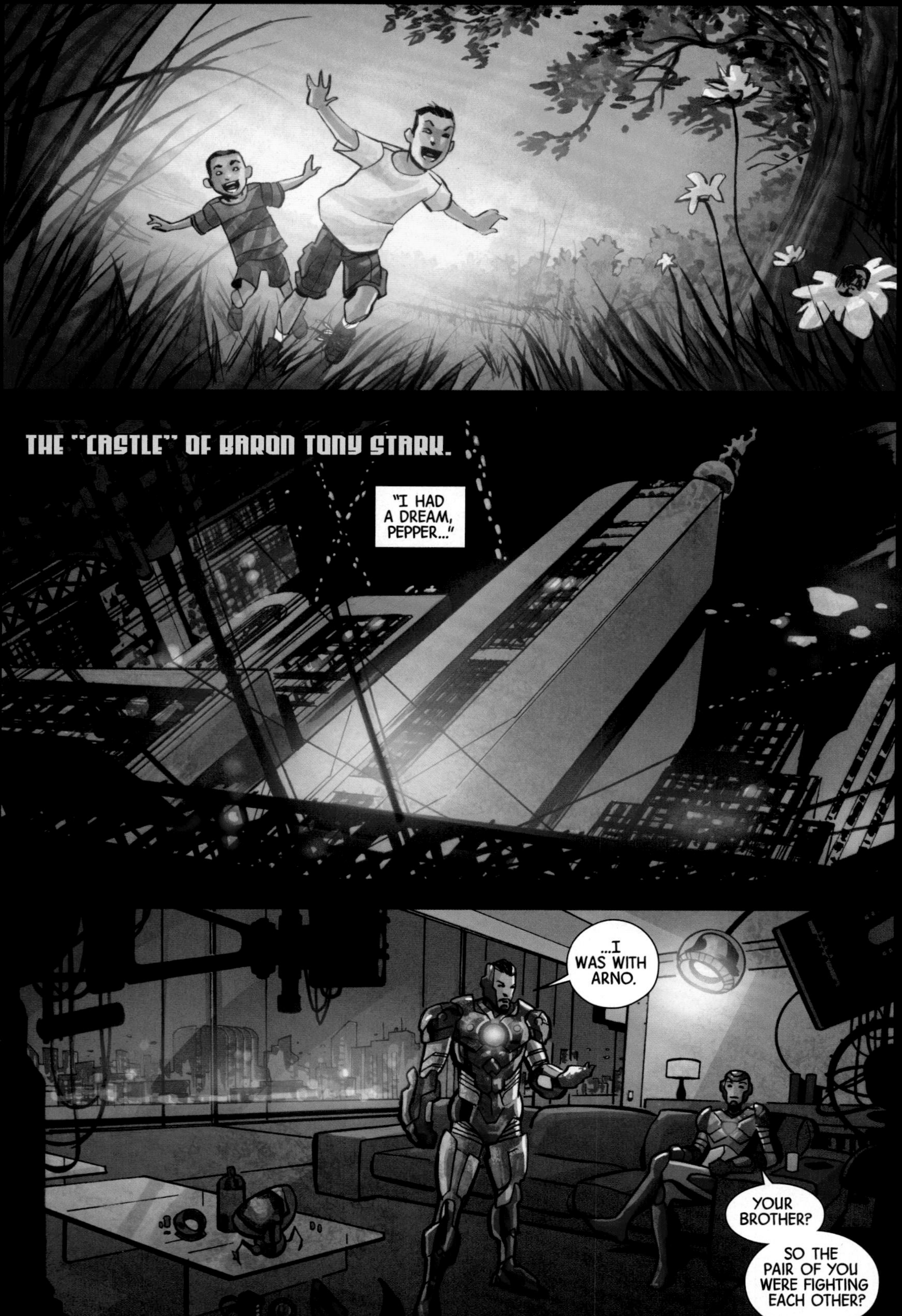
THE "CASTLE" OF BARON TONY STARK.
"I HAD A DREAM, PEPPER..."
...I WAS WITH ARNO.
YOUR BROTHER?
SO THE PAIR OF YOU WERE FIGHTING EACH OTHER?

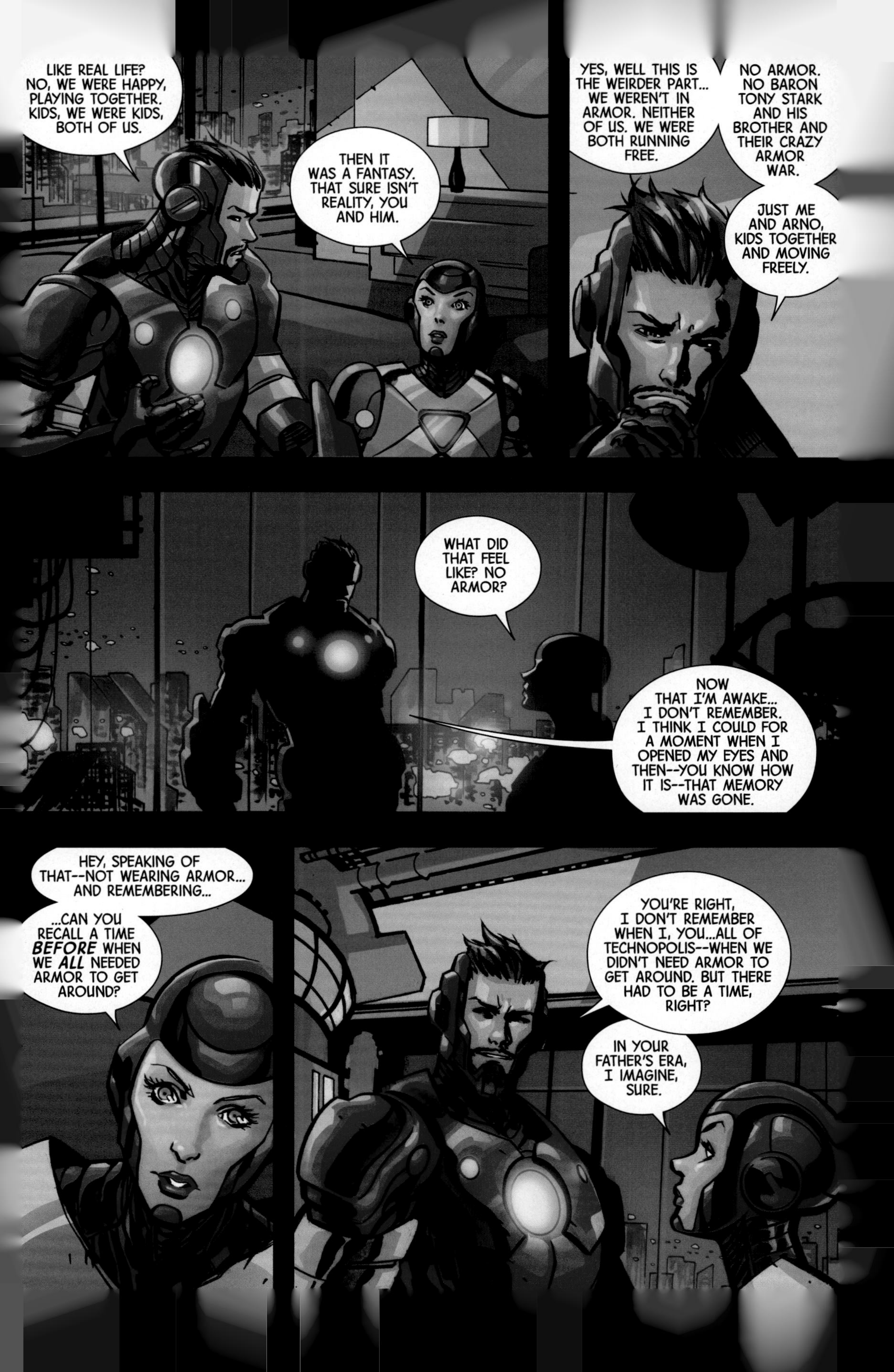
LIKE REAL LIFE? NO, WE WERE HAPPY, PLAYING TOGETHER. KIDS, WE WERE KIDS, BOTH OF US.
THEN IT WAS A FANTASY. THAT SURE ISN'T REALITY, YOU AND HIM.
YES, WELL THIS IS THE WEIRDER PART... WE WEREN'T IN ARMOR. NEITHER OF US. WE WERE BOTH RUNNING FREE.
NO ARMOR. NO BARON TONY STARK AND HIS BROTHER AND THEIR CRAZY ARMOR WAR.
JUST ME AND ARNO, KIDS TOGETHER AND MOVING FREELY.
WHAT DID THAT FEEL LIKE? NO ARMOR?
NOW THAT I'M AWAKE... I DON'T REMEMBER. I THINK I COULD FOR A MOMENT WHEN I OPENED MY EYES AND THEN--YOU KNOW HOW IT IS--THAT MEMORY WAS GONE.
HEY, SPEAKING OF THAT--NOT WEARING ARMOR... AND REMEMBERING...
...CAN YOU RECALL A TIME ***BEFORE*** WHEN WE ***ALL*** NEEDED ARMOR TO GET AROUND?
YOU'RE RIGHT, I DON'T REMEMBER WHEN I, YOU...ALL OF TECHNOPOLIS--WHEN WE DIDN'T NEED ARMOR TO GET AROUND. BUT THERE HAD TO BE A TIME, RIGHT?
IN YOUR FATHER'S ERA, I IMAGINE, SURE.

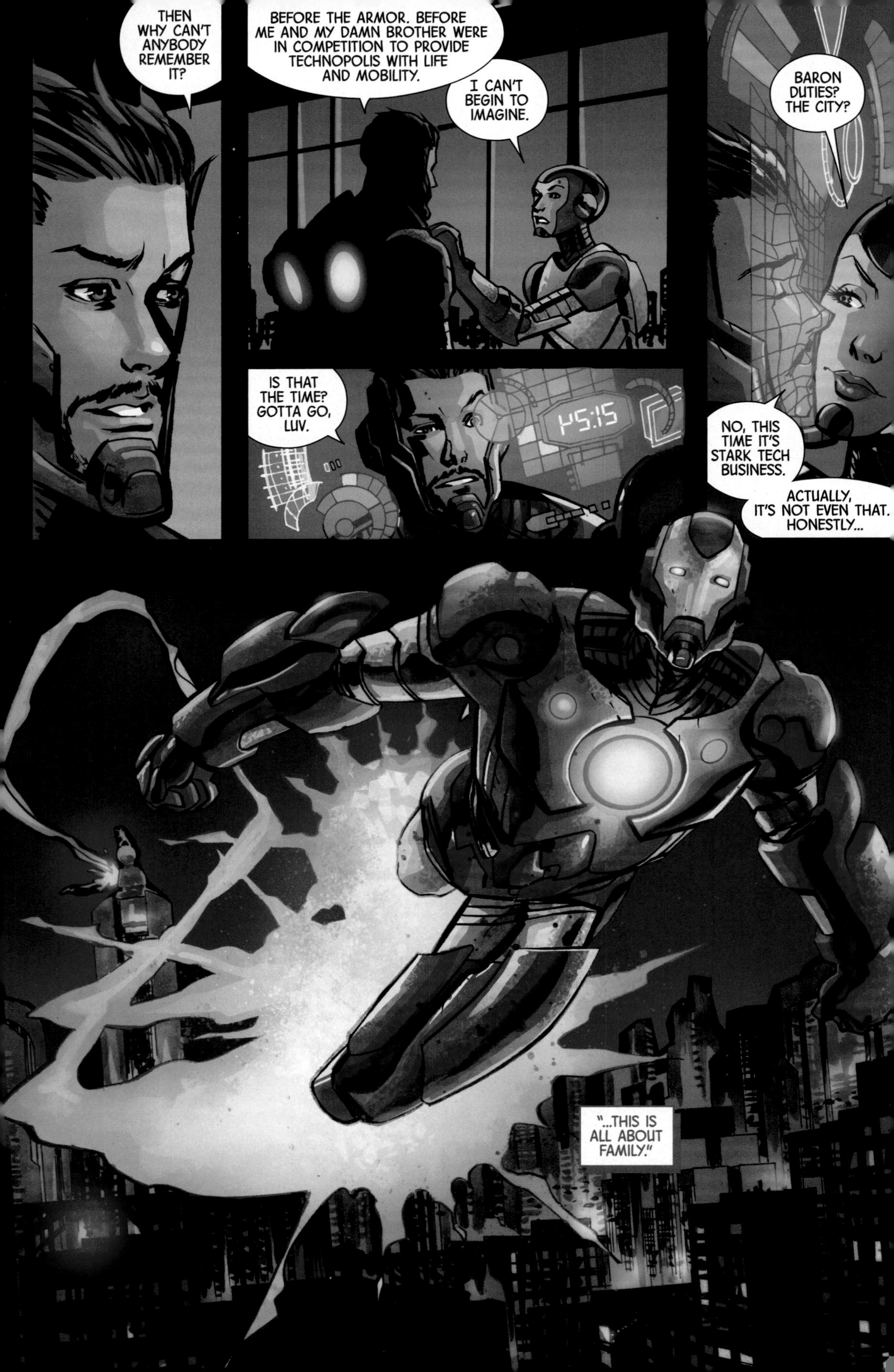
THEN WHY CAN'T ANYBODY REMEMBER IT?
BEFORE THE ARMOR. BEFORE ME AND MY DAMN BROTHER WERE IN COMPETITION TO PROVIDE TECHNOPOLIS WITH LIFE AND MOBILITY.
I CAN'T BEGIN TO IMAGINE.
BARON DUTIES? THE CITY?
IS THAT THE TIME? GOTTA GO, LUV.
14:15
NO, THIS TIME IT'S STARK TECH BUSINESS.
ACTUALLY, IT'S NOT EVEN THAT. HONESTLY...
"...THIS IS ALL ABOUT FAMILY."

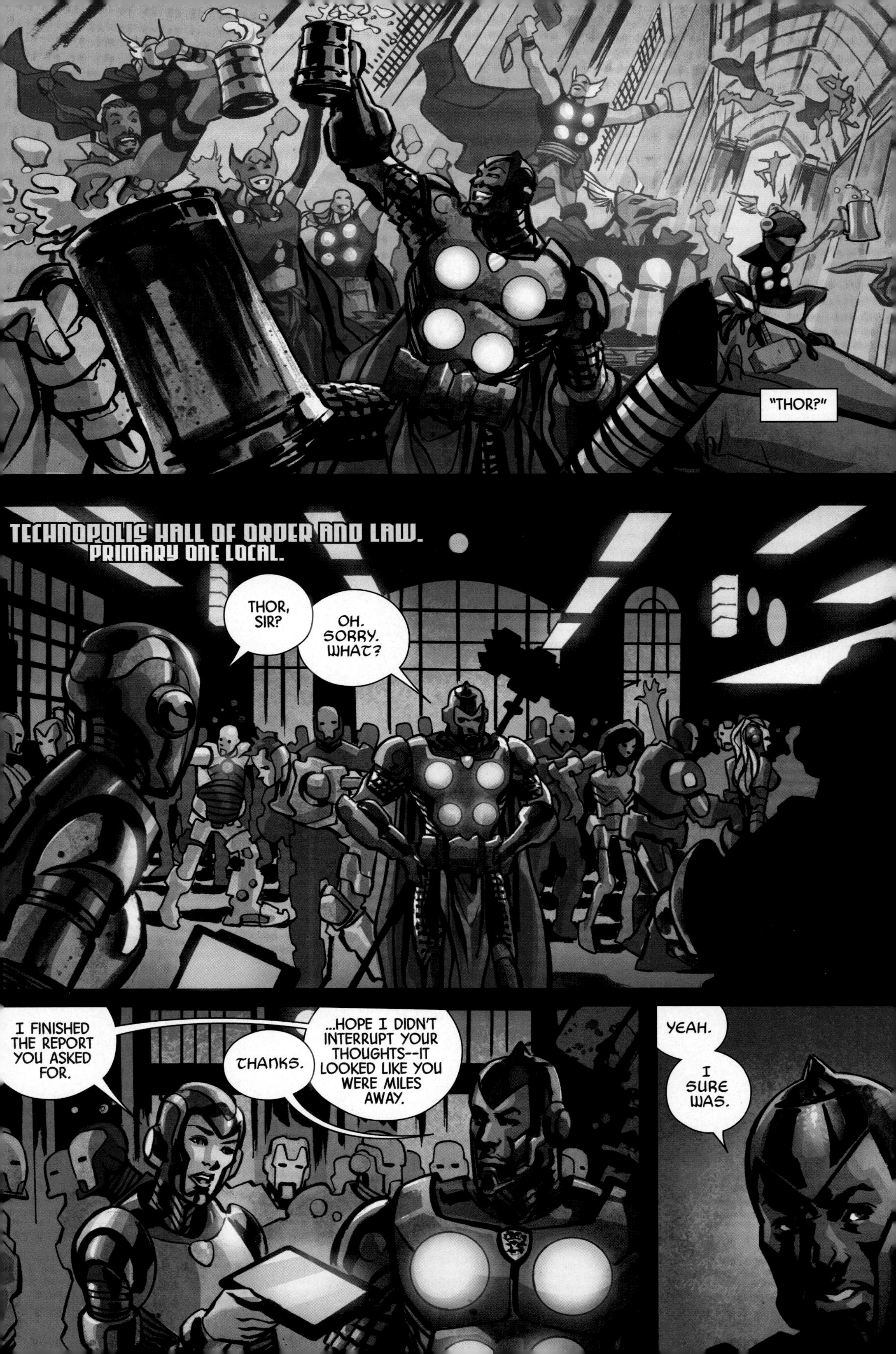
"THOR?"
TECHNOPOLIS HALL OF ORDER AND LAW. PRIMARY ONE LOCAL.
THOR, SIR?
OH. SORRY. WHAT?
I FINISHED THE REPORT YOU ASKED FOR.
THANKS.
...HOPE I DIDN'T INTERRUPT YOUR THOUGHTS--IT LOOKED LIKE YOU WERE MILES AWAY.
YEAH.
I SURE WAS.

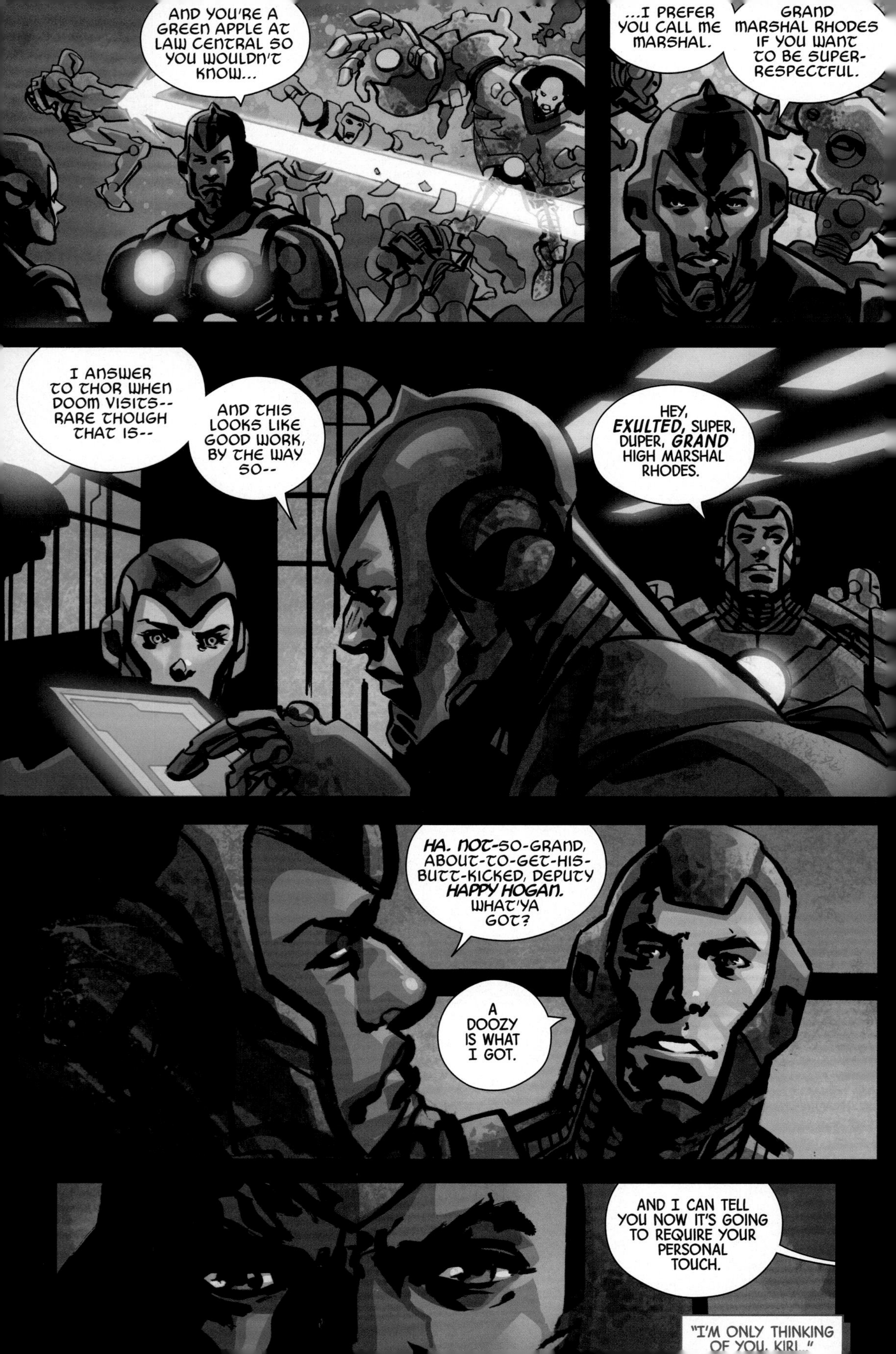
AND YOU'RE A GREEN APPLE AT LAW CENTRAL SO YOU WOULDN'T KNOW...
...I PREFER YOU CALL ME MARSHAL.
GRAND MARSHAL RHODES IF YOU WANT TO BE SUPER-RESPECTFUL.
I ANSWER TO THOR WHEN DOOM VISITS-- RARE THOUGH THAT IS--
AND THIS LOOKS LIKE GOOD WORK, BY THE WAY SO--
HEY, EXULTED, SUPER, DUPER, GRAND HIGH MARSHAL RHODES.
HA. NOT-SO-GRAND, ABOUT-TO-GET-HIS-BUTT-KICKED, DEPUTY HAPPY HOGAN. WHAT'YA GOT?
A DOOZY IS WHAT I GOT.
AND I CAN TELL YOU NOW IT'S GOING TO REQUIRE YOUR PERSONAL TOUCH.
"I'M ONLY THINKING OF YOU, KIRI..."

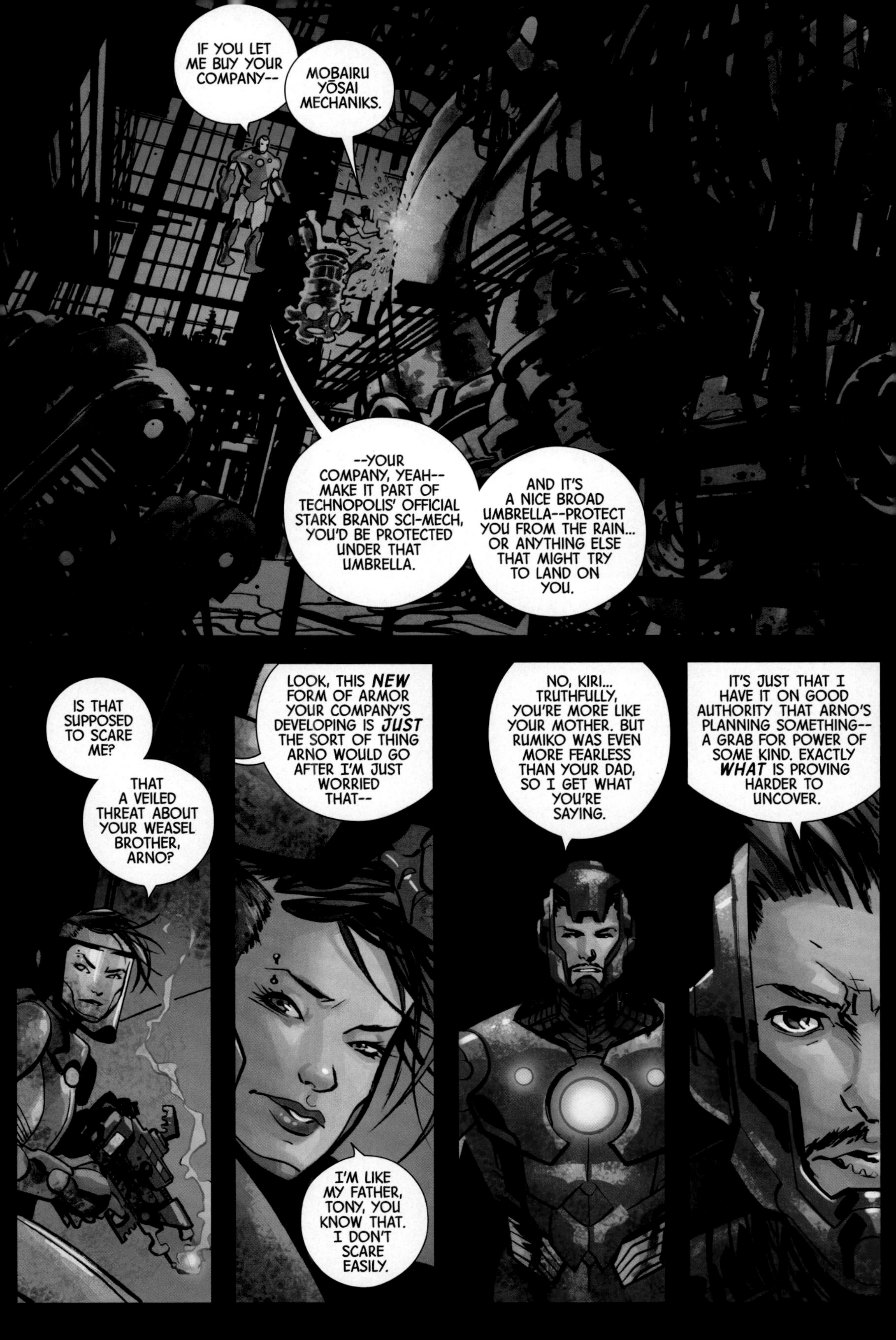
IF YOU LET ME BUY YOUR COMPANY--
MOBAIRU YŌSAI MECHANIKS.
--YOUR COMPANY, YEAH-- MAKE IT PART OF TECHNOPOLIS' OFFICIAL STARK BRAND SCI-MECH, YOU'D BE PROTECTED UNDER THAT UMBRELLA.
AND IT'S A NICE BROAD UMBRELLA--PROTECT YOU FROM THE RAIN... OR ANYTHING ELSE THAT MIGHT TRY TO LAND ON YOU.
IS THAT SUPPOSED TO SCARE ME?
THAT A VEILED THREAT ABOUT YOUR WEASEL BROTHER, ARNO?
LOOK, THIS NEW FORM OF ARMOR YOUR COMPANY'S DEVELOPING IS JUST THE SORT OF THING ARNO WOULD GO AFTER I'M JUST WORRIED THAT--
I'M LIKE MY FATHER, TONY, YOU KNOW THAT. I DON'T SCARE EASILY.
NO, KIRI... TRUTHFULLY, YOU'RE MORE LIKE YOUR MOTHER. BUT RUMIKO WAS EVEN MORE FEARLESS THAN YOUR DAD, SO I GET WHAT YOU'RE SAYING.
IT'S JUST THAT I HAVE IT ON GOOD AUTHORITY THAT ARNO'S PLANNING SOMETHING-- A GRAB FOR POWER OF SOME KIND. EXACTLY WHAT IS PROVING HARDER TO UNCOVER.

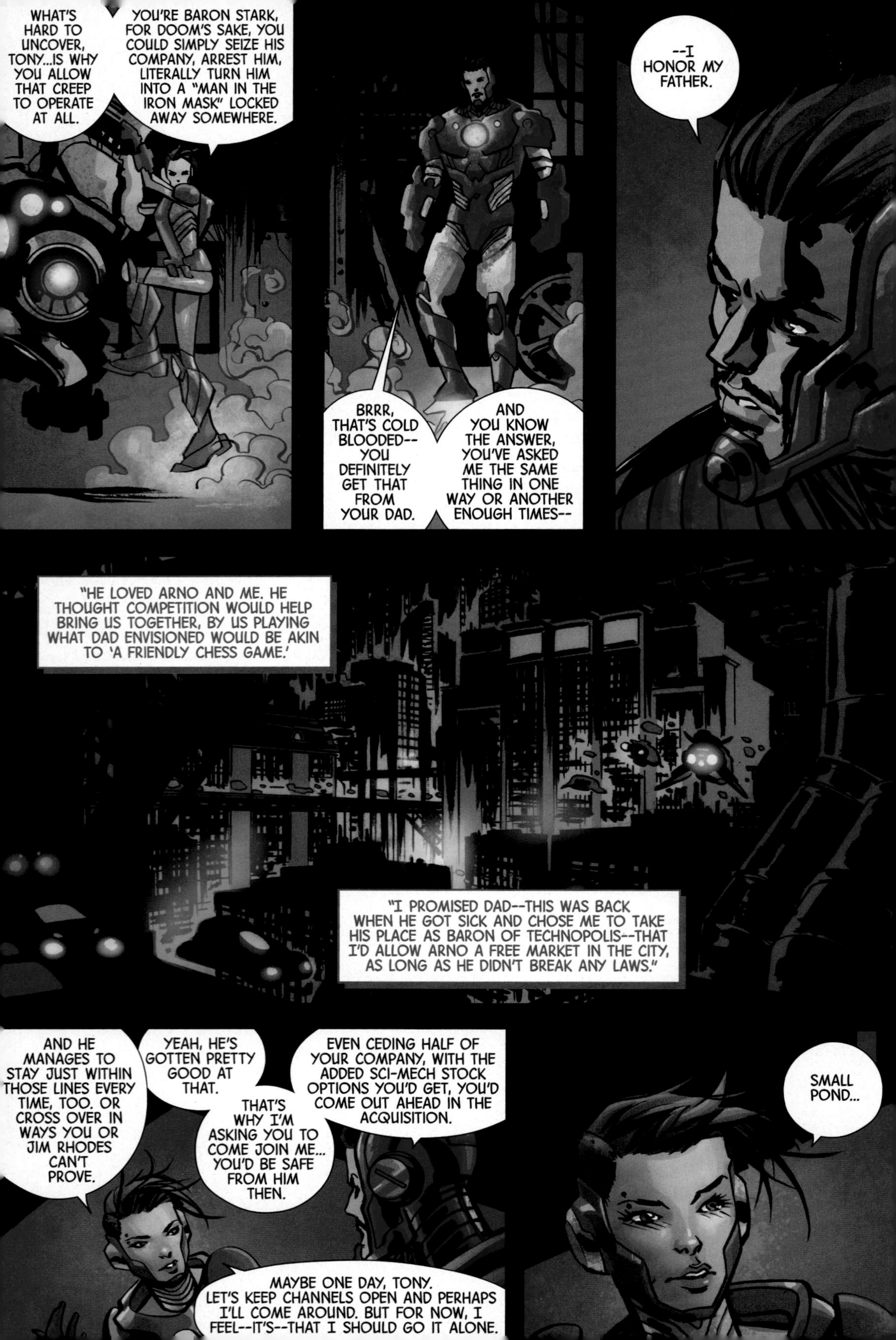
WHAT'S HARD TO UNCOVER, TONY...IS WHY YOU ALLOW THAT CREEP TO OPERATE AT ALL.
YOU'RE BARON STARK, FOR DOOM'S SAKE, YOU COULD SIMPLY SEIZE HIS COMPANY, ARREST HIM, LITERALLY TURN HIM INTO A "MAN IN THE IRON MASK" LOCKED AWAY SOMEWHERE.
BRRR, THAT'S COLD BLOODED--YOU DEFINITELY GET THAT FROM YOUR DAD.
AND YOU KNOW THE ANSWER, YOU'VE ASKED ME THE SAME THING IN ONE WAY OR ANOTHER ENOUGH TIMES--
--I HONOR MY FATHER.
"HE LOVED ARNO AND ME. HE THOUGHT COMPETITION WOULD HELP BRING US TOGETHER, BY US PLAYING WHAT DAD ENVISIONED WOULD BE AKIN TO 'A FRIENDLY CHESS GAME.'
"I PROMISED DAD--THIS WAS BACK WHEN HE GOT SICK AND CHOSE ME TO TAKE HIS PLACE AS BARON OF TECHNOPOLIS--THAT I'D ALLOW ARNO A FREE MARKET IN THE CITY, AS LONG AS HE DIDN'T BREAK ANY LAWS."
AND HE MANAGES TO STAY JUST WITHIN THOSE LINES EVERY TIME, TOO. OR CROSS OVER IN WAYS YOU OR JIM RHODES CAN'T PROVE.
YEAH, HE'S GOTTEN PRETTY GOOD AT THAT.
THAT'S WHY I'M ASKING YOU TO COME JOIN ME... YOU'D BE SAFE FROM HIM THEN.
EVEN CEDING HALF OF YOUR COMPANY, WITH THE ADDED SCI-MECH STOCK OPTIONS YOU'D GET, YOU'D COME OUT AHEAD IN THE ACQUISITION.
MAYBE ONE DAY, TONY. LET'S KEEP CHANNELS OPEN AND PERHAPS I'LL COME AROUND. BUT FOR NOW, I FEEL--IT'S--THAT I SHOULD GO IT ALONE.
SMALL POND...

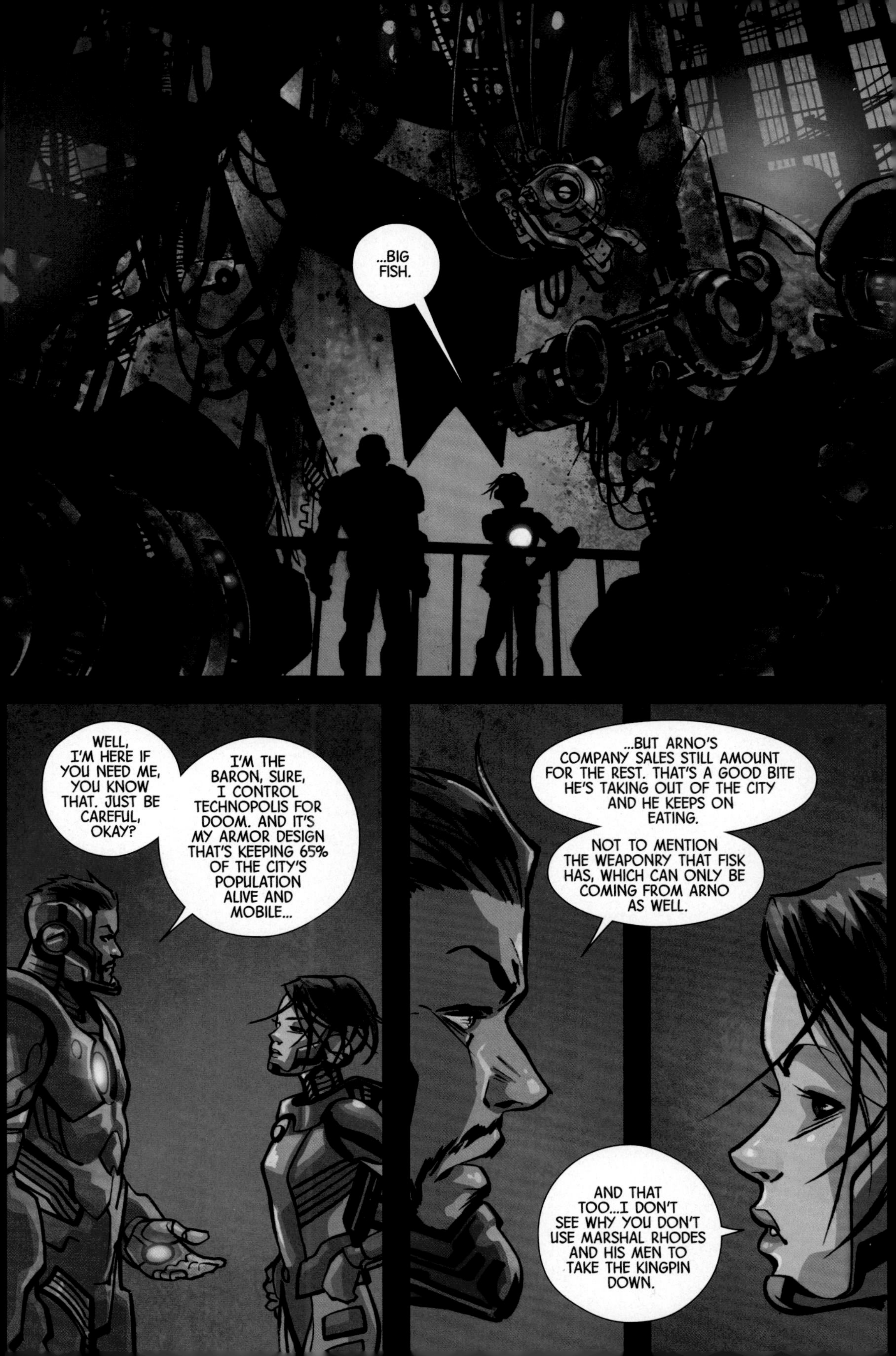
...BIG FISH.
WELL, I'M HERE IF YOU NEED ME, YOU KNOW THAT. JUST BE CAREFUL, OKAY?
I'M THE BARON, SURE, I CONTROL TECHNOPOLIS FOR DOOM. AND IT'S MY ARMOR DESIGN THAT'S KEEPING 65% OF THE CITY'S POPULATION ALIVE AND MOBILE...
...BUT ARNO'S COMPANY SALES STILL AMOUNT FOR THE REST. THAT'S A GOOD BITE HE'S TAKING OUT OF THE CITY AND HE KEEPS ON EATING.
NOT TO MENTION THE WEAPONRY THAT FISK HAS, WHICH CAN ONLY BE COMING FROM ARNO AS WELL.
AND THAT TOO...I DON'T SEE WHY YOU DON'T USE MARSHAL RHODES AND HIS MEN TO TAKE THE KINGPIN DOWN.

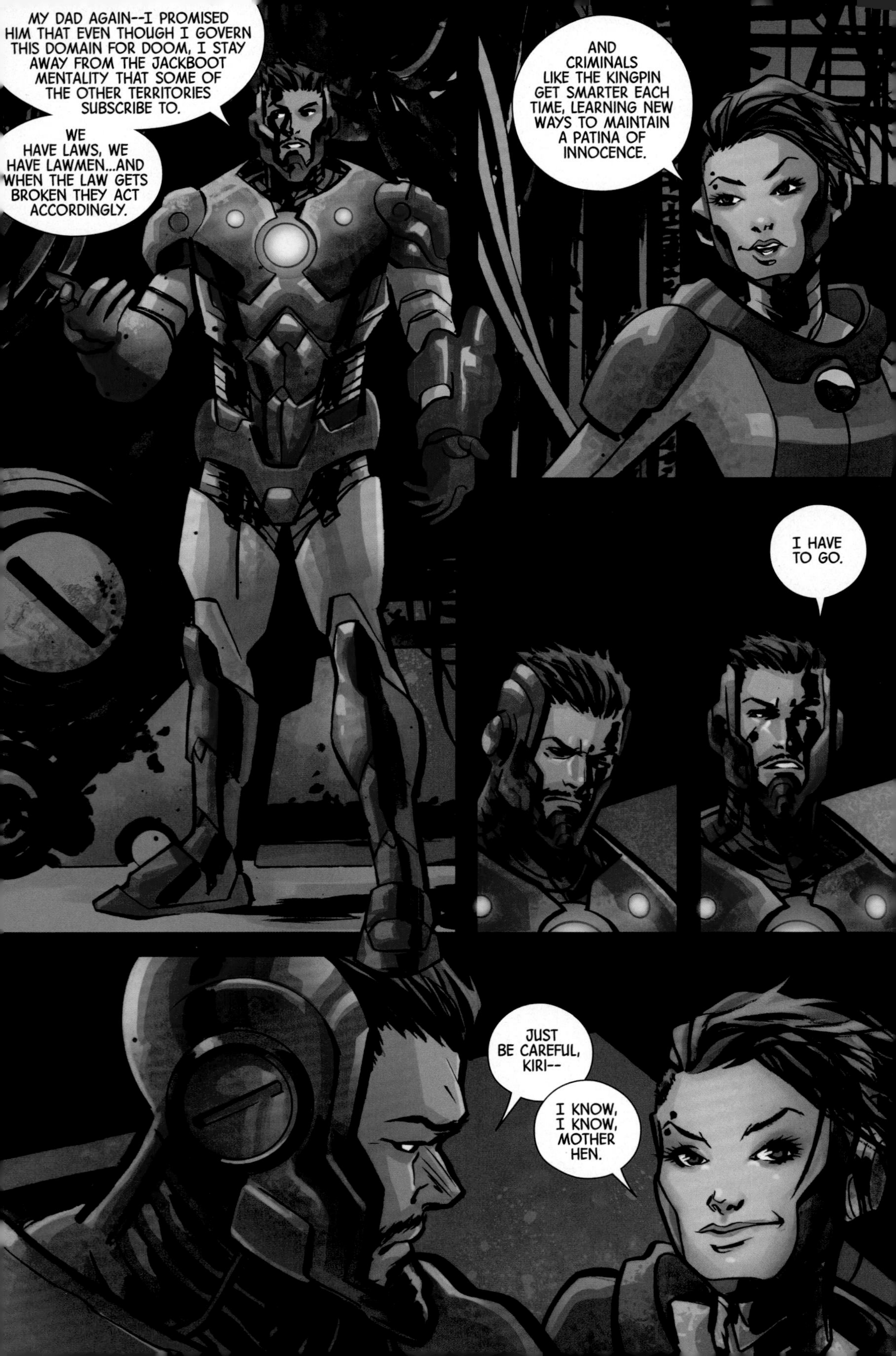

MY DAD AGAIN--I PROMISED HIM THAT EVEN THOUGH I GOVERN THIS DOMAIN FOR DOOM, I STAY AWAY FROM THE JACKBOOT MENTALITY THAT SOME OF THE OTHER TERRITORIES SUBSCRIBE TO.
WE HAVE LAWS, WE HAVE LAWMEN...AND WHEN THE LAW GETS BROKEN THEY ACT ACCORDINGLY.
AND CRIMINALS LIKE THE KINGPIN GET SMARTER EACH TIME, LEARNING NEW WAYS TO MAINTAIN A PATINA OF INNOCENCE.
I HAVE TO GO.
JUST BE CAREFUL, KIRI--
I KNOW, I KNOW, MOTHER HEN.

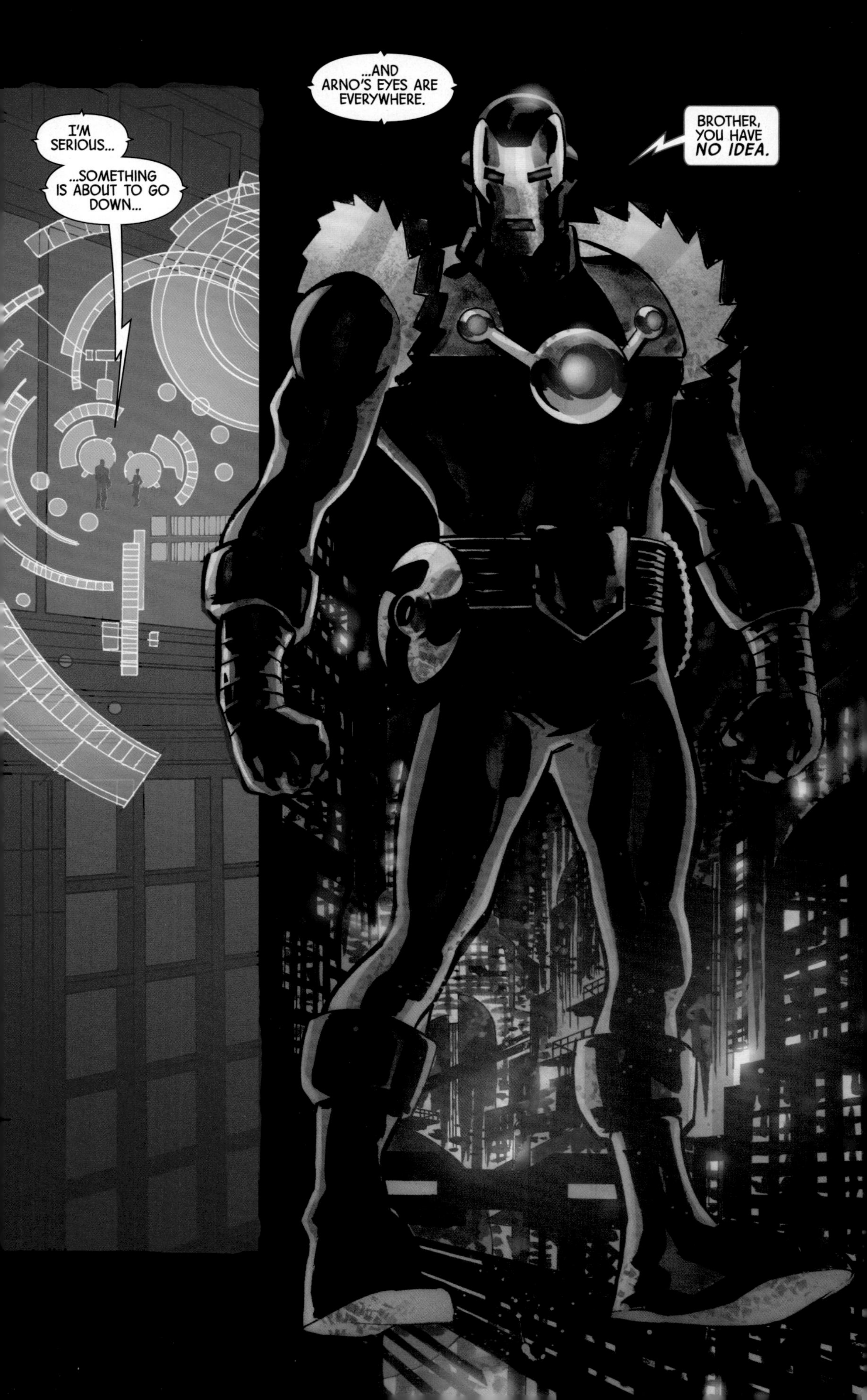
I'M SERIOUS...
...SOMETHING IS ABOUT TO GO DOWN...
...AND ARNO'S EYES ARE EVERYWHERE.
BROTHER, YOU HAVE *NO IDEA.*

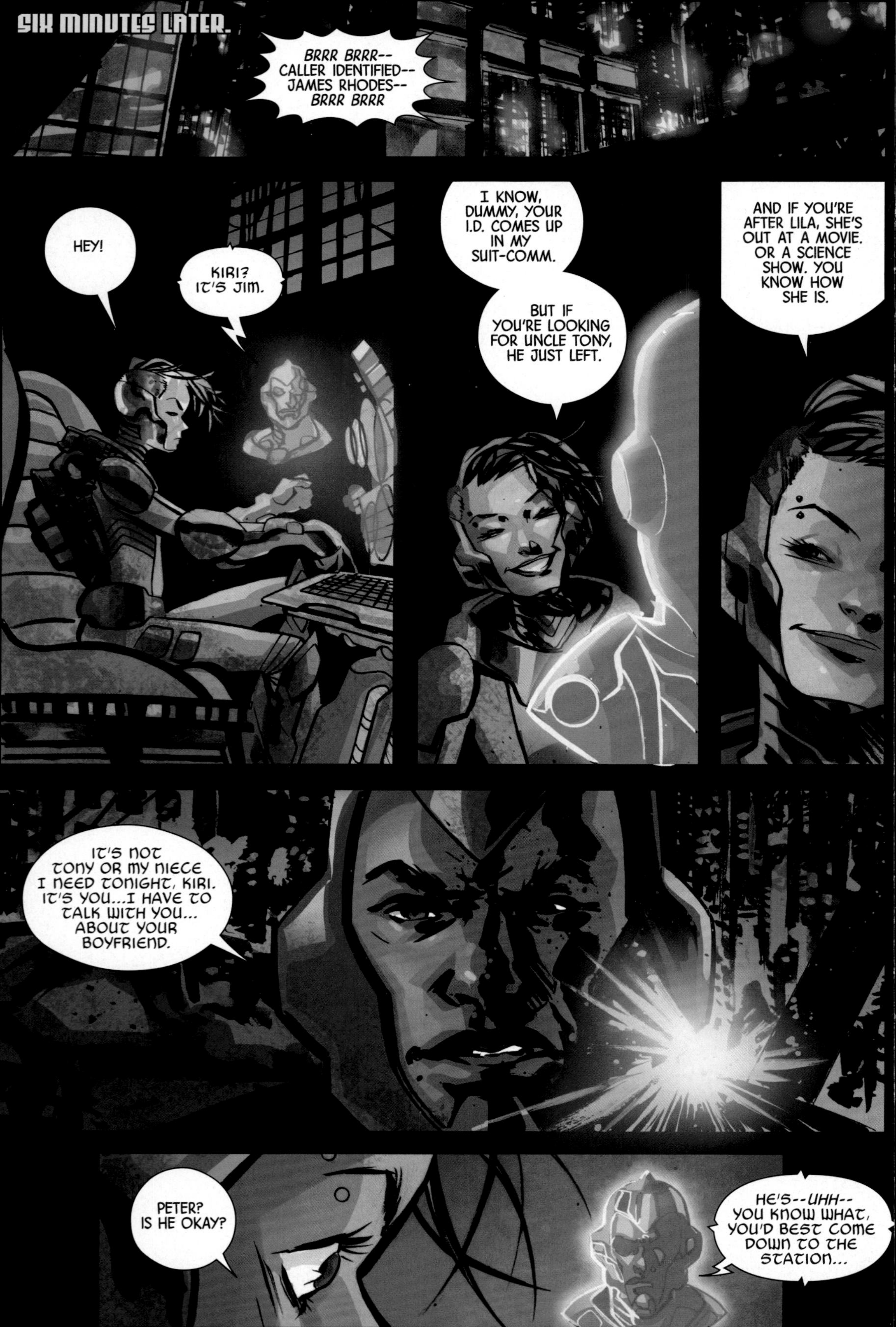
SIX MINUTES LATER.
BRRR BRRR-- CALLER IDENTIFIED-- JAMES RHODES-- BRRR BRRR
HEY!
KIRI? IT'S JIM.
I KNOW, DUMMY, YOUR I.D. COMES UP IN MY SUIT-COMM.
BUT IF YOU'RE LOOKING FOR UNCLE TONY, HE JUST LEFT.
AND IF YOU'RE AFTER LILA, SHE'S OUT AT A MOVIE. OR A SCIENCE SHOW. YOU KNOW HOW SHE IS.
IT'S NOT TONY OR MY NIECE I NEED TONIGHT, KIRI. IT'S YOU...I HAVE TO TALK WITH YOU... ABOUT YOUR BOYFRIEND.
PETER? IS HE OKAY?
HE'S--UHH-- YOU KNOW WHAT, YOU'D BEST COME DOWN TO THE STATION...

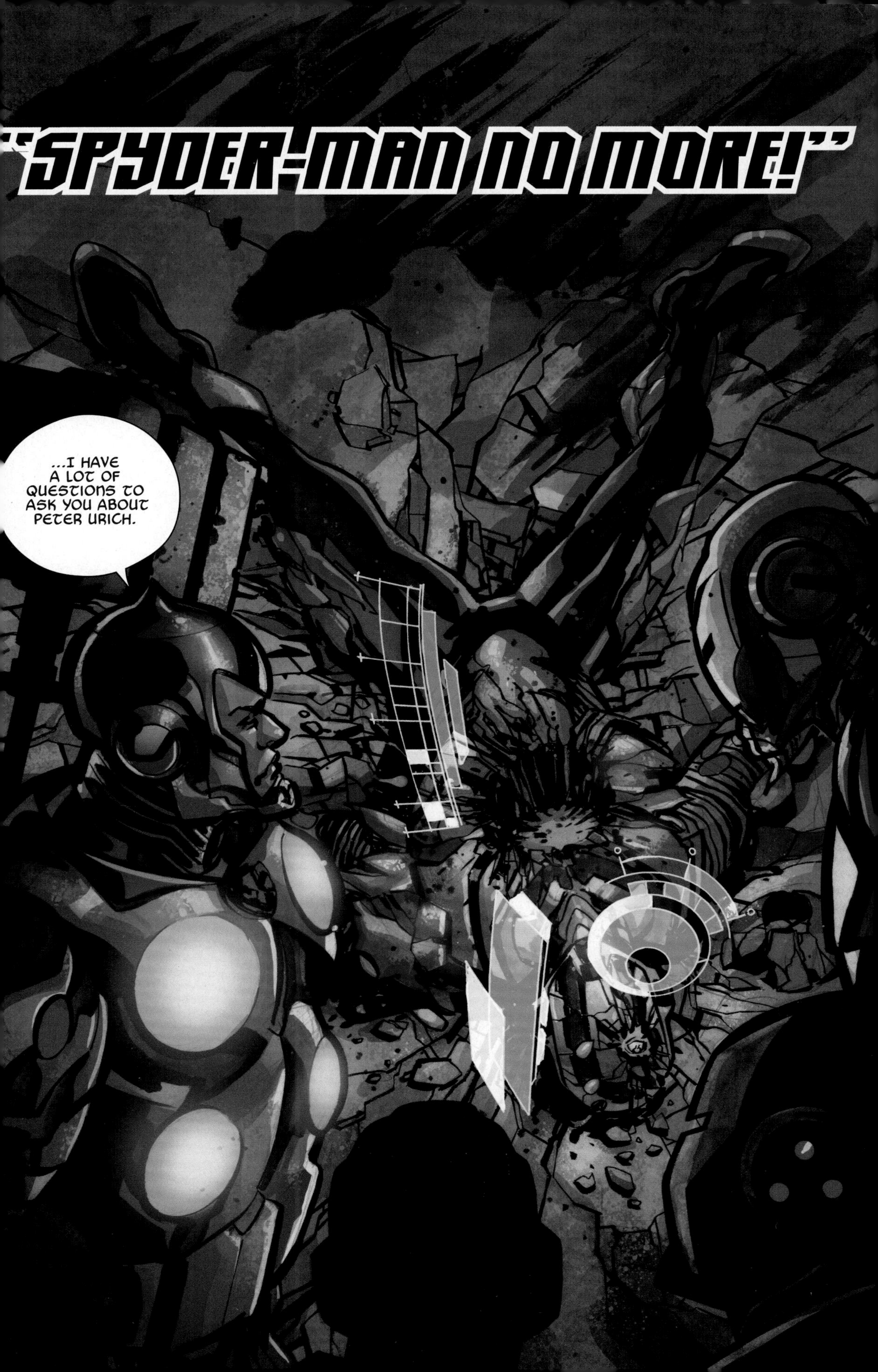
"SPYDER-MAN NO MORE!"
...I HAVE A LOT OF QUESTIONS TO ASK YOU ABOUT PETER URICH.

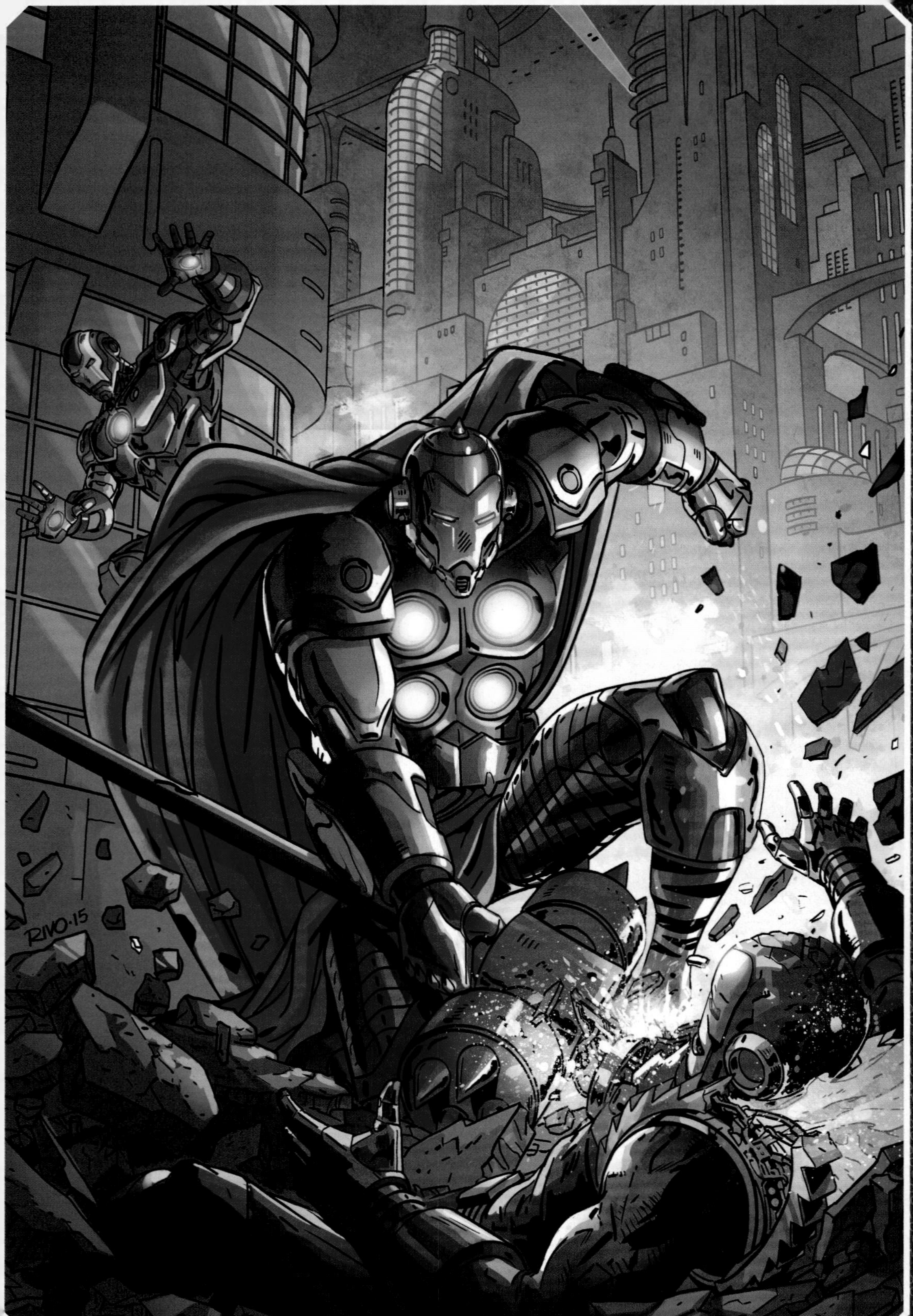
RIVO·15

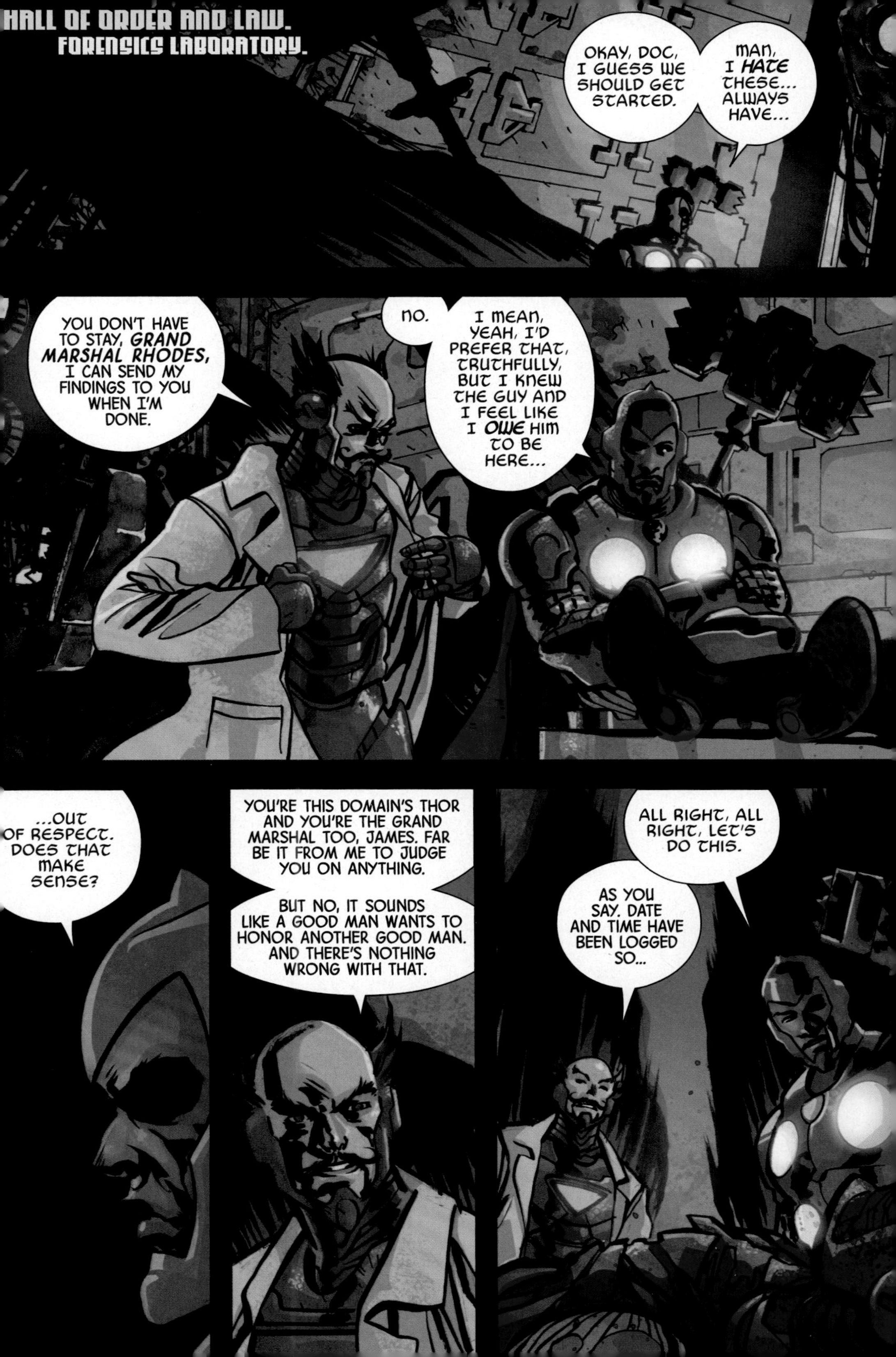
HALL OF ORDER AND LAW. FORENSICS LABORATORY.
OKAY, DOC, I GUESS WE SHOULD GET STARTED.
MAN, I HATE THESE... ALWAYS HAVE...
YOU DON'T HAVE TO STAY, GRAND MARSHAL RHODES, I CAN SEND MY FINDINGS TO YOU WHEN I'M DONE.
NO.
I MEAN, YEAH, I'D PREFER THAT, TRUTHFULLY, BUT I KNEW THE GUY AND I FEEL LIKE I OWE HIM TO BE HERE...
...OUT OF RESPECT. DOES THAT MAKE SENSE?
YOU'RE THIS DOMAIN'S THOR AND YOU'RE THE GRAND MARSHAL TOO, JAMES. FAR BE IT FROM ME TO JUDGE YOU ON ANYTHING.
BUT NO, IT SOUNDS LIKE A GOOD MAN WANTS TO HONOR ANOTHER GOOD MAN. AND THERE'S NOTHING WRONG WITH THAT.
ALL RIGHT, ALL RIGHT, LET'S DO THIS.
AS YOU SAY. DATE AND TIME HAVE BEEN LOGGED SO...

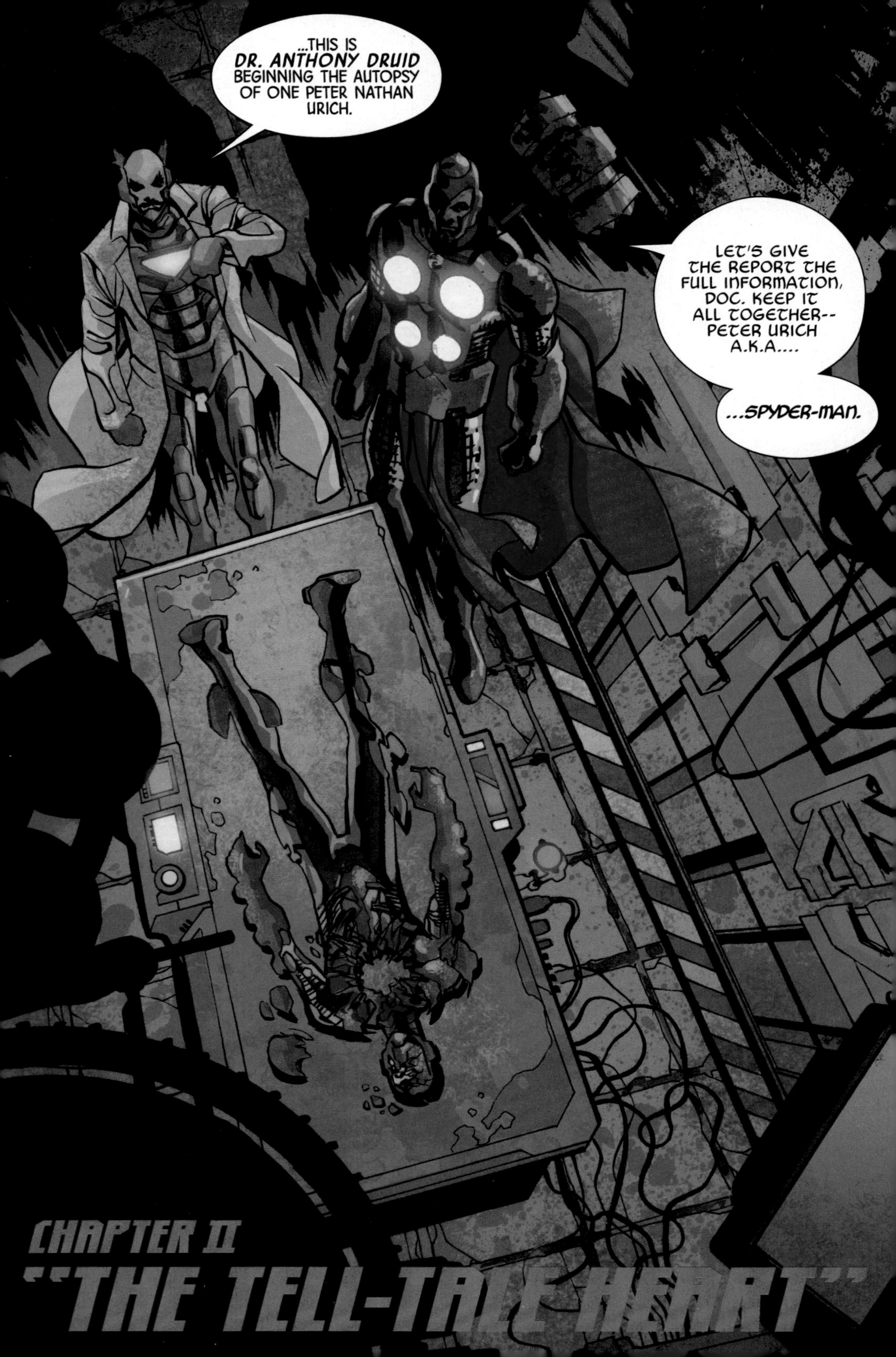
...THIS IS DR. ANTHONY DRUID BEGINNING THE AUTOPSY OF ONE PETER NATHAN URICH.
LET'S GIVE THE REPORT THE FULL INFORMATION, DOC. KEEP IT ALL TOGETHER-- PETER URICH A.K.A....
...SPYDER-MAN.
CHAPTER II
"THE TELL-TALE HEART"

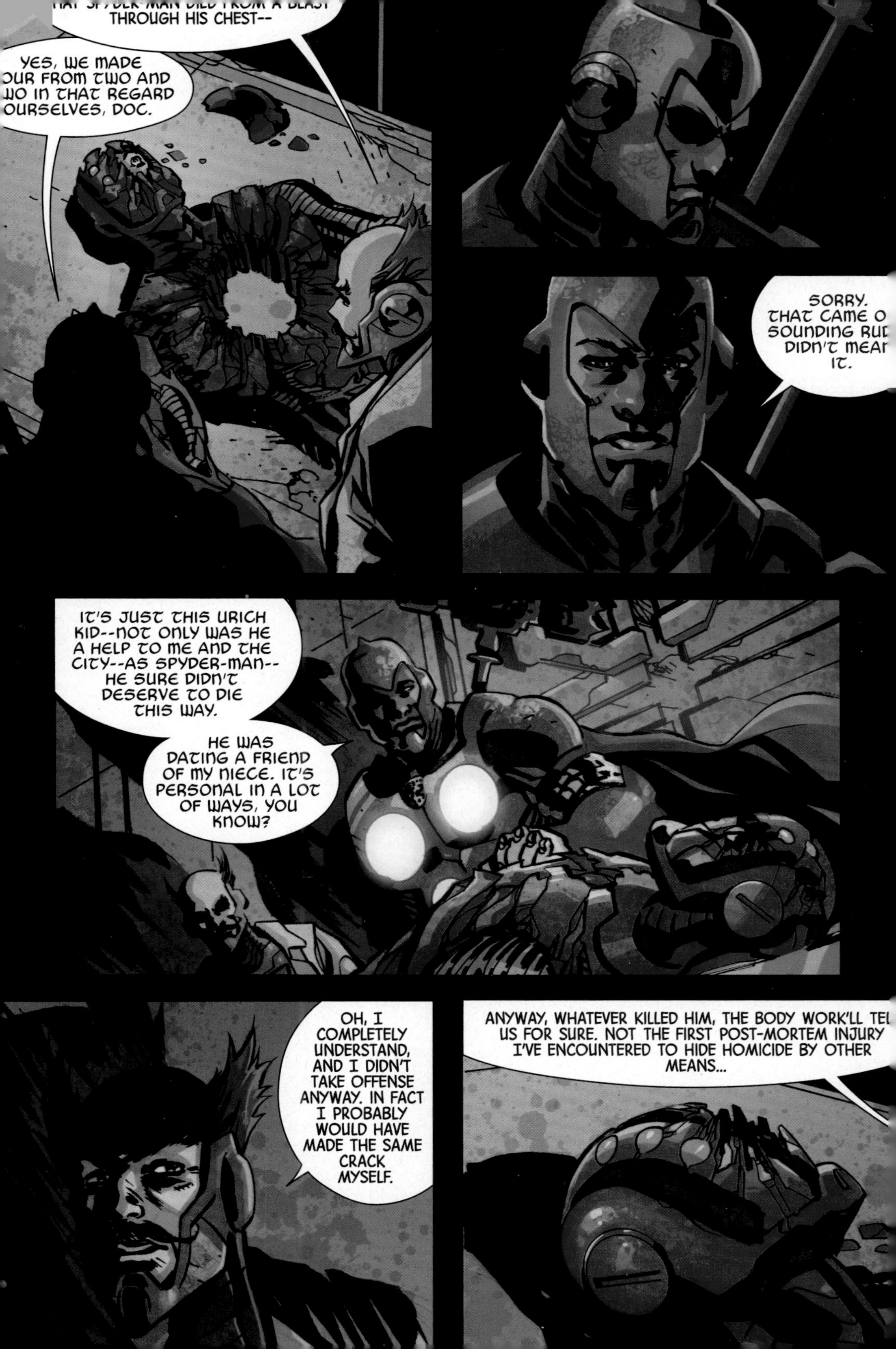
THROUGH HIS CHEST--
YES, WE MADE OUR FROM TWO AND WO IN THAT REGARD OURSELVES, DOC.
SORRY. THAT CAME O SOUNDING RUD DIDN'T MEAN IT.
IT'S JUST THIS URICH KID--NOT ONLY WAS HE A HELP TO ME AND THE CITY--AS SPYDER-MAN--HE SURE DIDN'T DESERVE TO DIE THIS WAY.
HE WAS DATING A FRIEND OF MY NIECE. IT'S PERSONAL IN A LOT OF WAYS, YOU KNOW?
OH, I COMPLETELY UNDERSTAND, AND I DIDN'T TAKE OFFENSE ANYWAY. IN FACT I PROBABLY WOULD HAVE MADE THE SAME CRACK MYSELF.
ANYWAY, WHATEVER KILLED HIM, THE BODY WORK'LL TEL US FOR SURE. NOT THE FIRST POST-MORTEM INJURY I'VE ENCOUNTERED TO HIDE HOMICIDE BY OTHER MEANS...

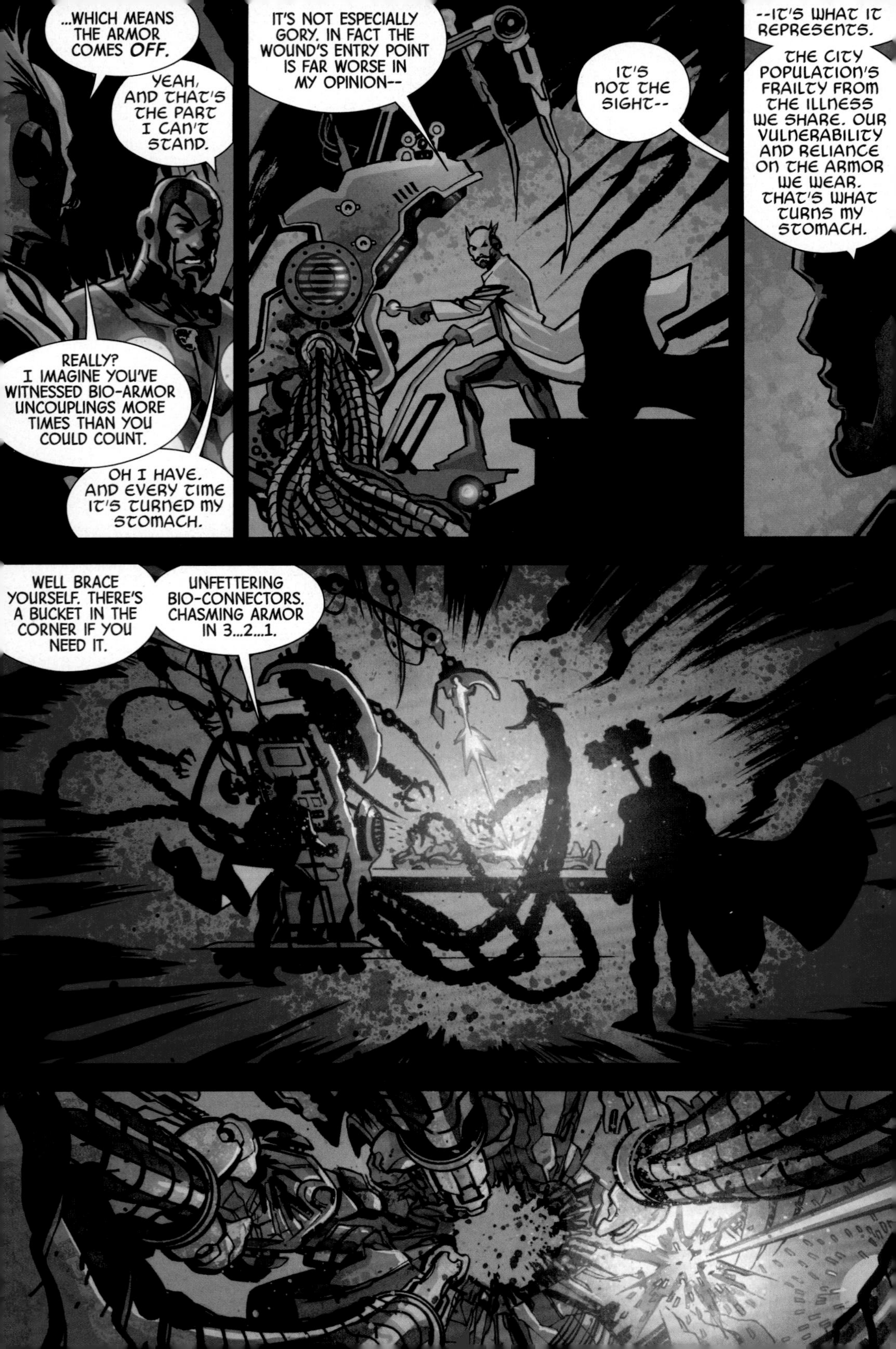
...WHICH MEANS THE ARMOR COMES *OFF*.
YEAH, AND THAT'S THE PART I CAN'T STAND.
REALLY? I IMAGINE YOU'VE WITNESSED BIO-ARMOR UNCOUPLINGS MORE TIMES THAN YOU COULD COUNT.
OH I HAVE. AND EVERY TIME IT'S TURNED MY STOMACH.
IT'S NOT ESPECIALLY GORY. IN FACT THE WOUND'S ENTRY POINT IS FAR WORSE IN MY OPINION--
IT'S NOT THE SIGHT--
--IT'S WHAT IT REPRESENTS.
THE CITY POPULATION'S FRAILTY FROM THE ILLNESS WE SHARE. OUR VULNERABILITY AND RELIANCE ON THE ARMOR WE WEAR. THAT'S WHAT TURNS MY STOMACH.
WELL BRACE YOURSELF. THERE'S A BUCKET IN THE CORNER IF YOU NEED IT.
UNFETTERING BIO-CONNECTORS. CHASMING ARMOR IN 3...2...1.

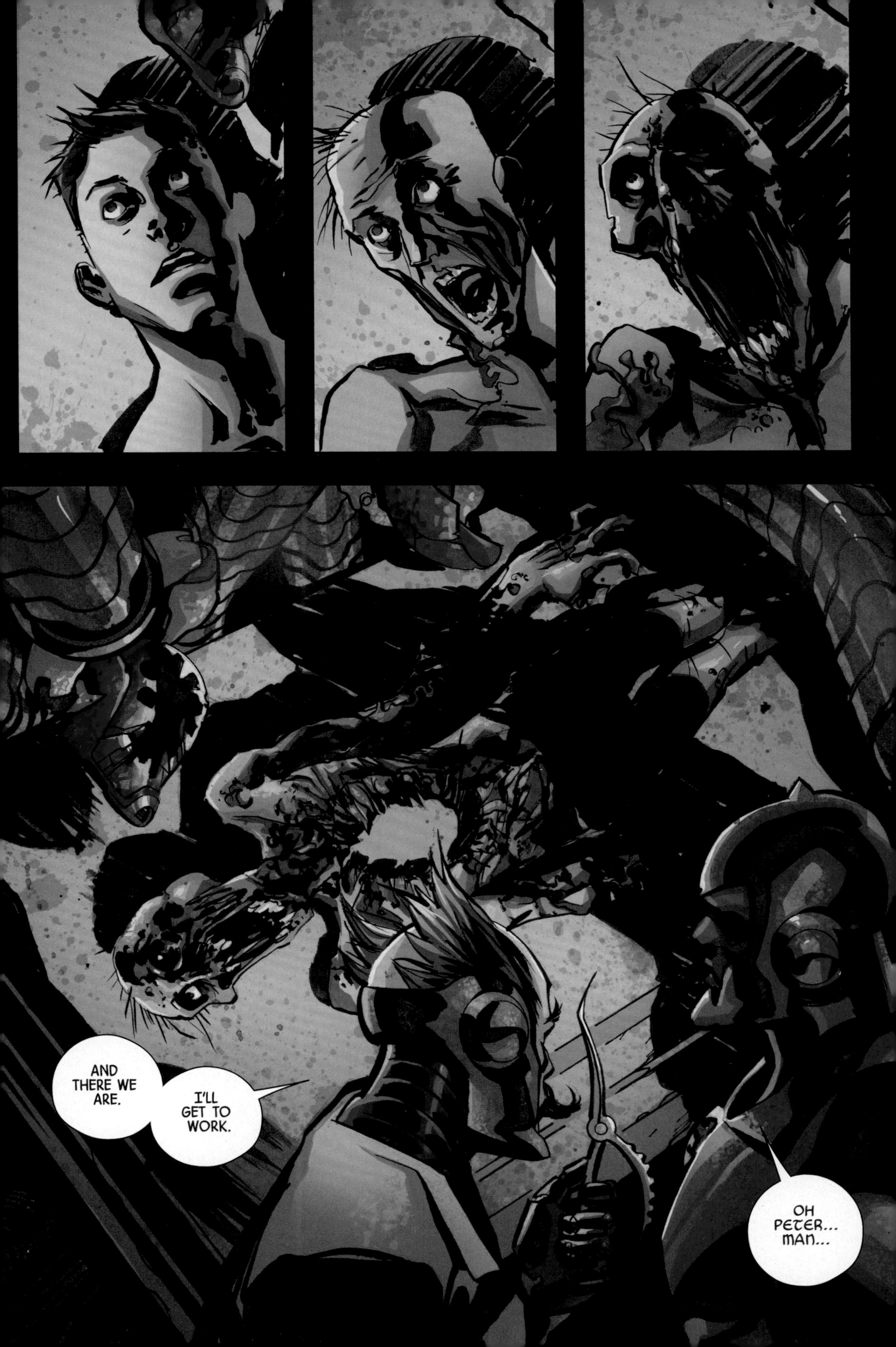
AND THERE WE ARE.
I'LL GET TO WORK.
OH PETER... MAN...

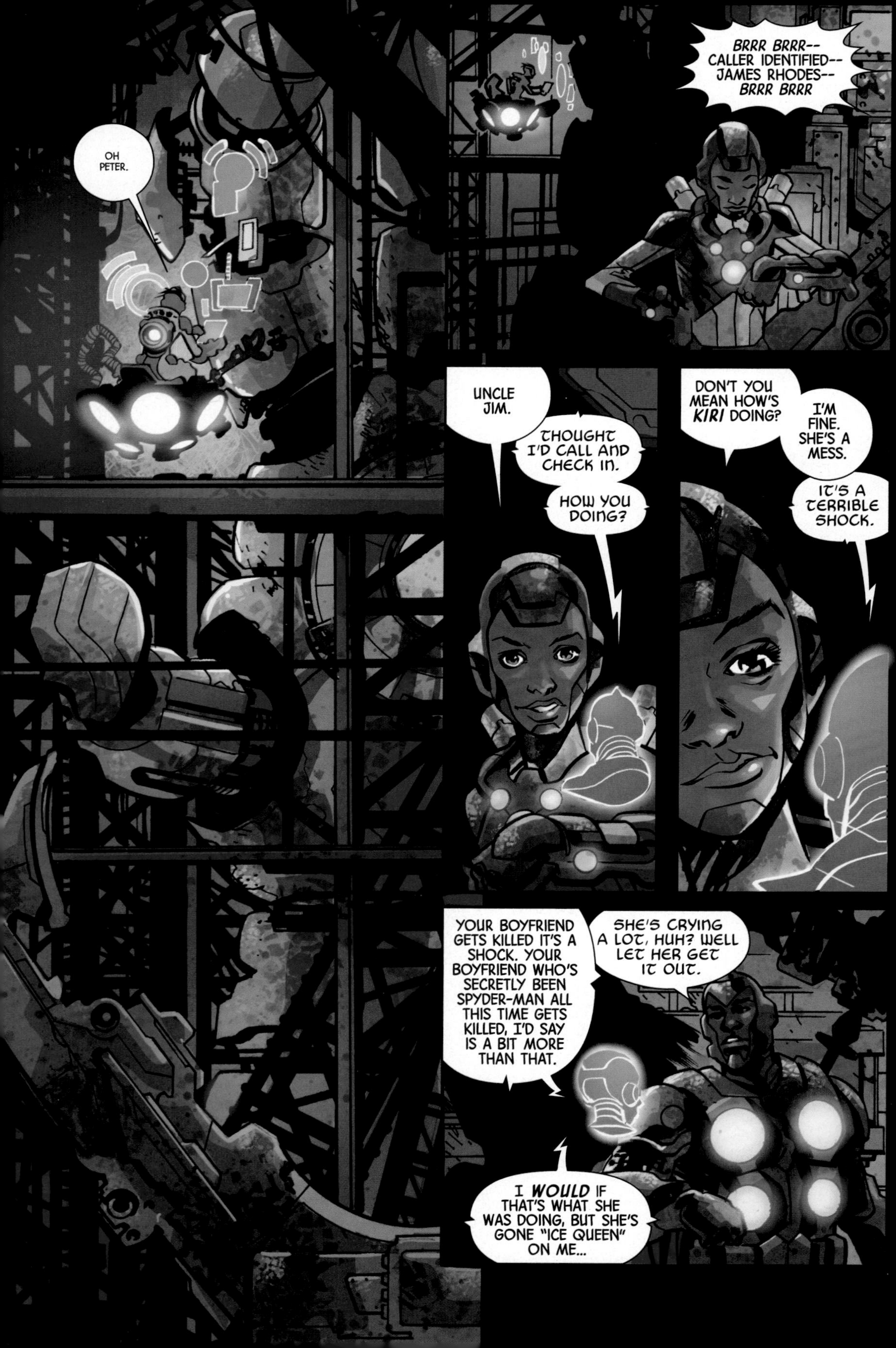
OH PETER.
BRRR BRRR-- CALLER IDENTIFIED-- JAMES RHODES-- BRRR BRRR
UNCLE JIM.
THOUGHT I'D CALL AND CHECK IN.
HOW YOU DOING?
DON'T YOU MEAN HOW'S KIRI DOING?
I'M FINE. SHE'S A MESS.
IT'S A TERRIBLE SHOCK.
YOUR BOYFRIEND GETS KILLED IT'S A SHOCK. YOUR BOYFRIEND WHO'S SECRETLY BEEN SPYDER-MAN ALL THIS TIME GETS KILLED, I'D SAY IS A BIT MORE THAN THAT.
SHE'S CRYING A LOT, HUH? WELL LET HER GET IT OUT.
I WOULD IF THAT'S WHAT SHE WAS DOING, BUT SHE'S GONE "ICE QUEEN" ON ME...

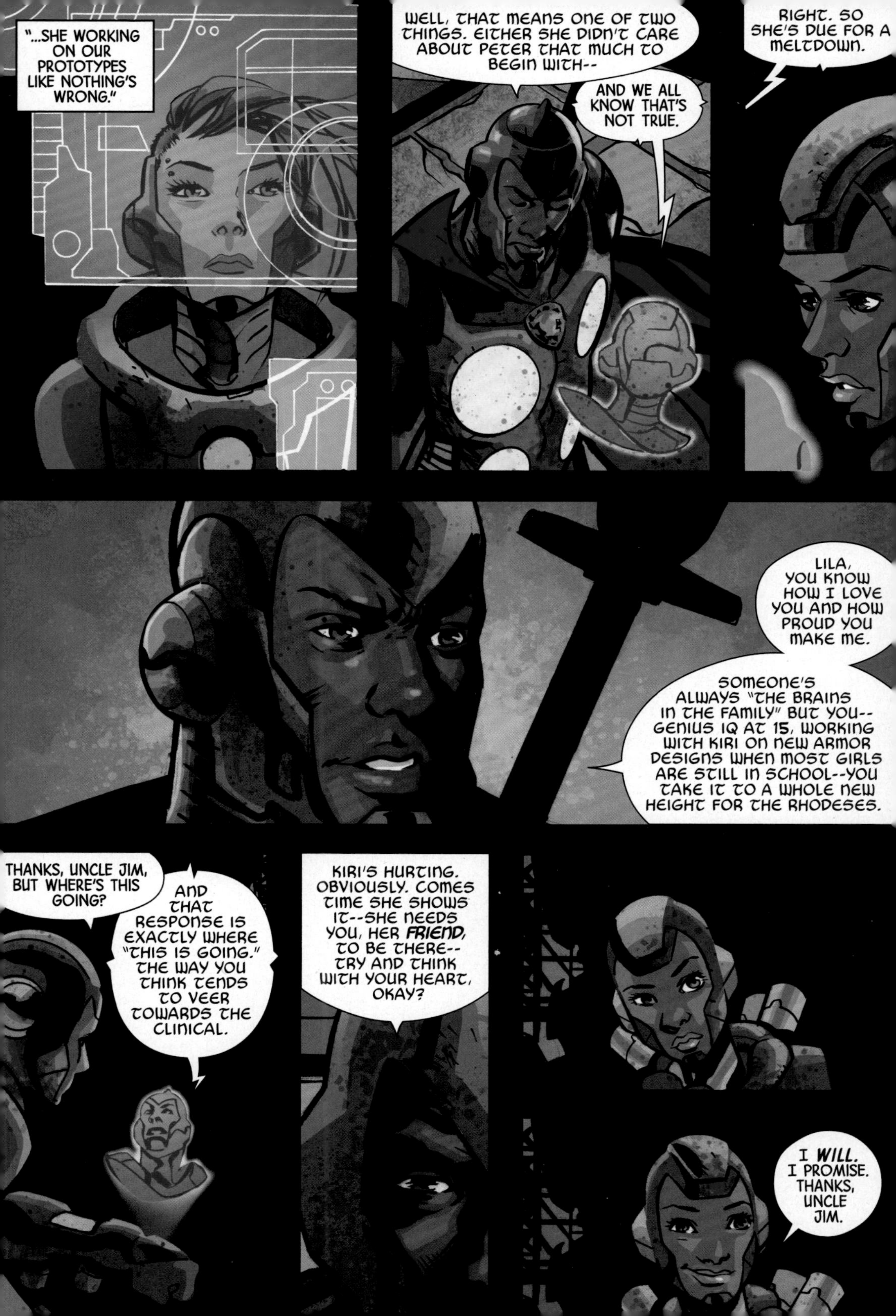
"...SHE WORKING ON OUR PROTOTYPES LIKE NOTHING'S WRONG."
WELL, THAT MEANS ONE OF TWO THINGS. EITHER SHE DIDN'T CARE ABOUT PETER THAT MUCH TO BEGIN WITH--
AND WE ALL KNOW THAT'S NOT TRUE.
RIGHT. SO SHE'S DUE FOR A MELTDOWN.
LILA, YOU KNOW HOW I LOVE YOU AND HOW PROUD YOU MAKE ME.
SOMEONE'S ALWAYS "THE BRAINS IN THE FAMILY" BUT YOU--GENIUS IQ AT 15, WORKING WITH KIRI ON NEW ARMOR DESIGNS WHEN MOST GIRLS ARE STILL IN SCHOOL--YOU TAKE IT TO A WHOLE NEW HEIGHT FOR THE RHODESES.
THANKS, UNCLE JIM, BUT WHERE'S THIS GOING?
AND THAT RESPONSE IS EXACTLY WHERE "THIS IS GOING." THE WAY YOU THINK TENDS TO VEER TOWARDS THE CLINICAL.
KIRI'S HURTING. OBVIOUSLY. COMES TIME SHE SHOWS IT--SHE NEEDS YOU, HER *FRIEND*, TO BE THERE--TRY AND THINK WITH YOUR HEART, OKAY?
I *WILL*. I PROMISE. THANKS, UNCLE JIM.

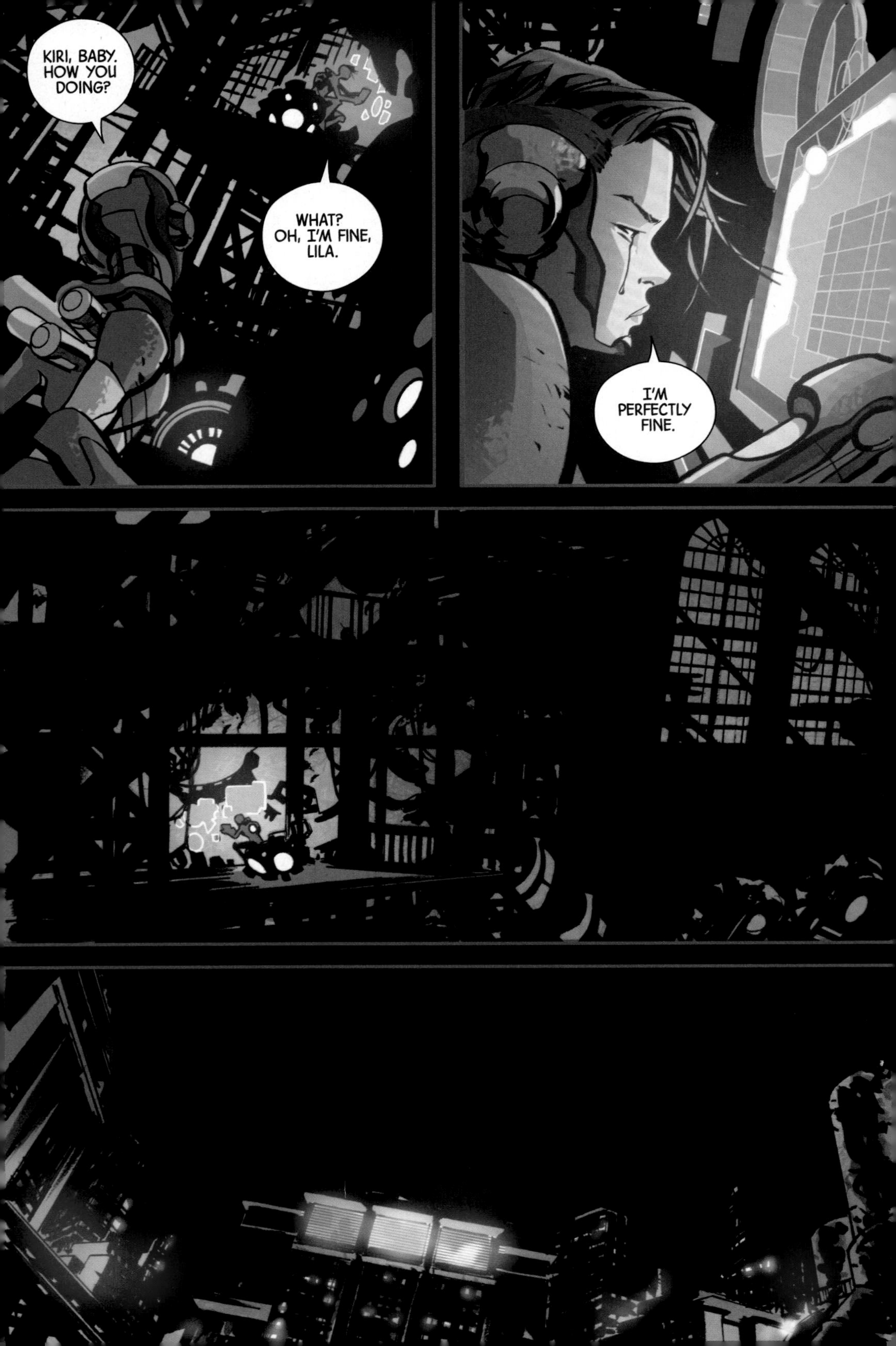
KIRI, BABY. HOW YOU DOING?
WHAT? OH, I'M FINE, LILA.
I'M PERFECTLY FINE.

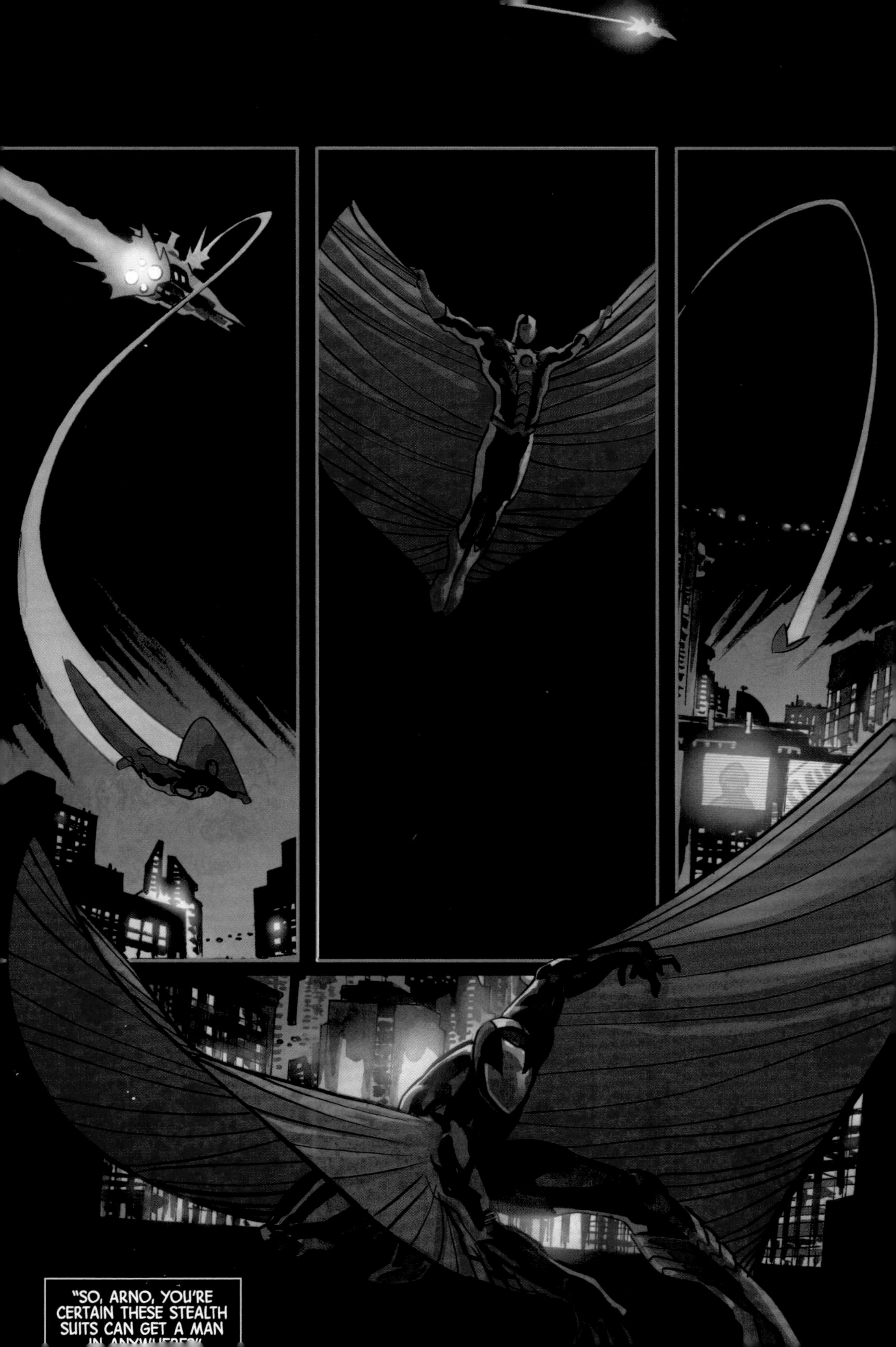
"SO, ARNO, YOU'RE CERTAIN THESE STEALTH SUITS CAN GET A MAN

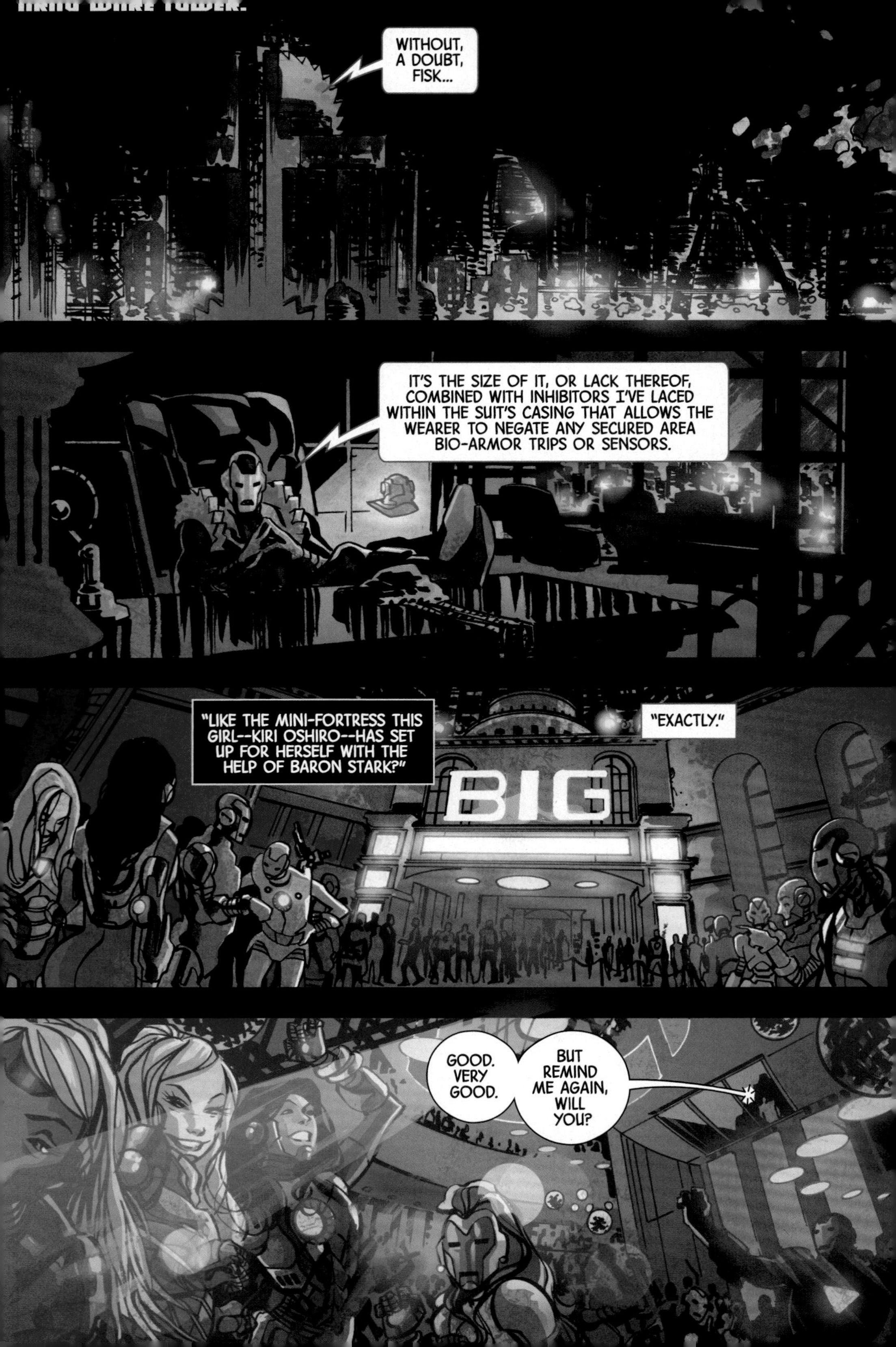
WITHOUT, A DOUBT, FISK...
IT'S THE SIZE OF IT, OR LACK THEREOF, COMBINED WITH INHIBITORS I'VE LACED WITHIN THE SUIT'S CASING THAT ALLOWS THE WEARER TO NEGATE ANY SECURED AREA BIO-ARMOR TRIPS OR SENSORS.
"LIKE THE MINI-FORTRESS THIS GIRL--KIRI OSHIRO--HAS SET UP FOR HERSELF WITH THE HELP OF BARON STARK?"
"EXACTLY."
BIG
GOOD. VERY GOOD.
BUT REMIND ME AGAIN, WILL YOU?

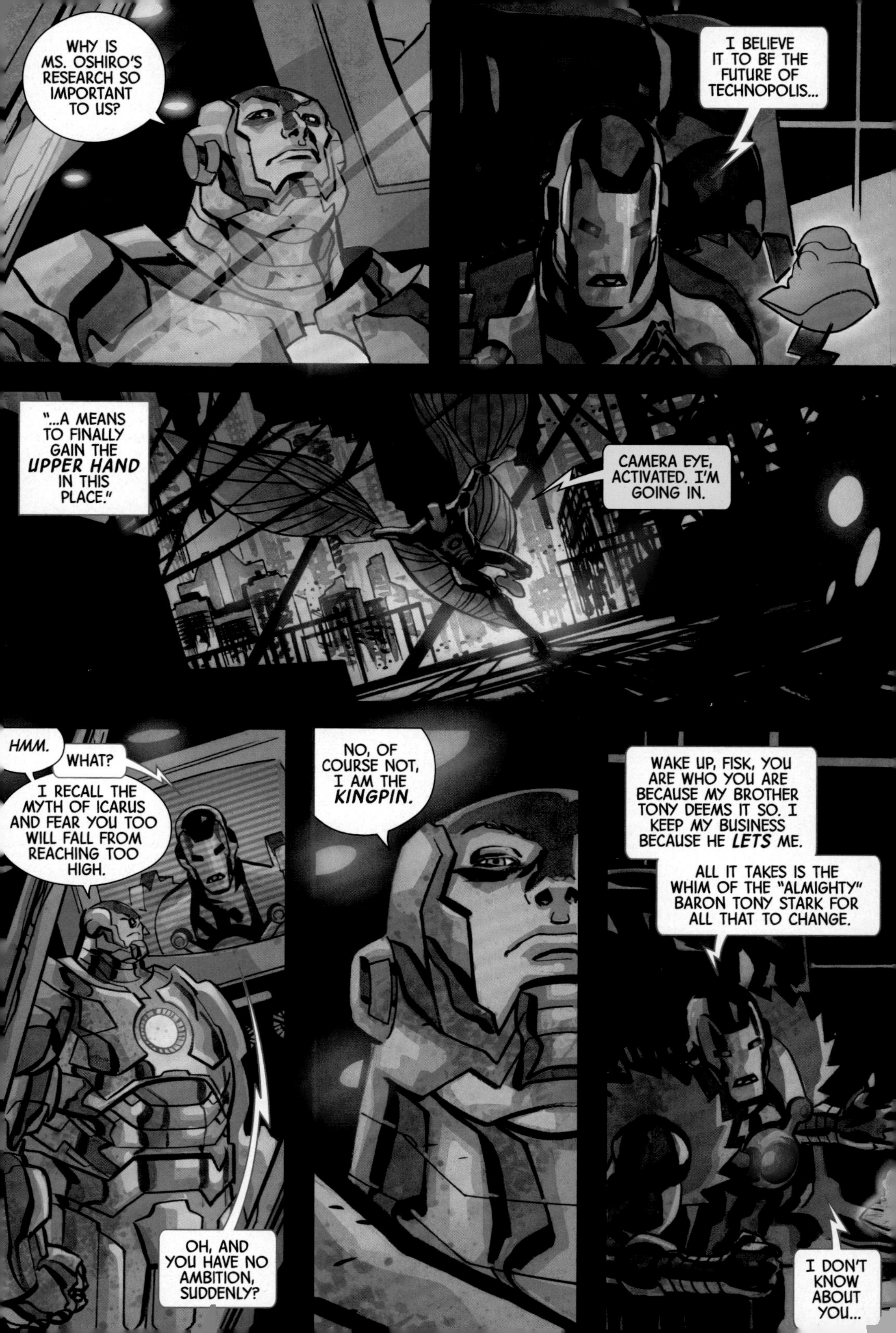
WHY IS MS. OSHIRO'S RESEARCH SO IMPORTANT TO US?
I BELIEVE IT TO BE THE FUTURE OF TECHNOPOLIS...
"...A MEANS TO FINALLY GAIN THE UPPER HAND IN THIS PLACE."
CAMERA EYE, ACTIVATED. I'M GOING IN.
HMM.
WHAT?
I RECALL THE MYTH OF ICARUS AND FEAR YOU TOO WILL FALL FROM REACHING TOO HIGH.
OH, AND YOU HAVE NO AMBITION, SUDDENLY?
NO, OF COURSE NOT, I AM THE KINGPIN.
WAKE UP, FISK, YOU ARE WHO YOU ARE BECAUSE MY BROTHER TONY DEEMS IT SO. I KEEP MY BUSINESS BECAUSE HE LETS ME.
ALL IT TAKES IS THE WHIM OF THE "ALMIGHTY" BARON TONY STARK FOR ALL THAT TO CHANGE.
I DON'T KNOW ABOUT YOU...

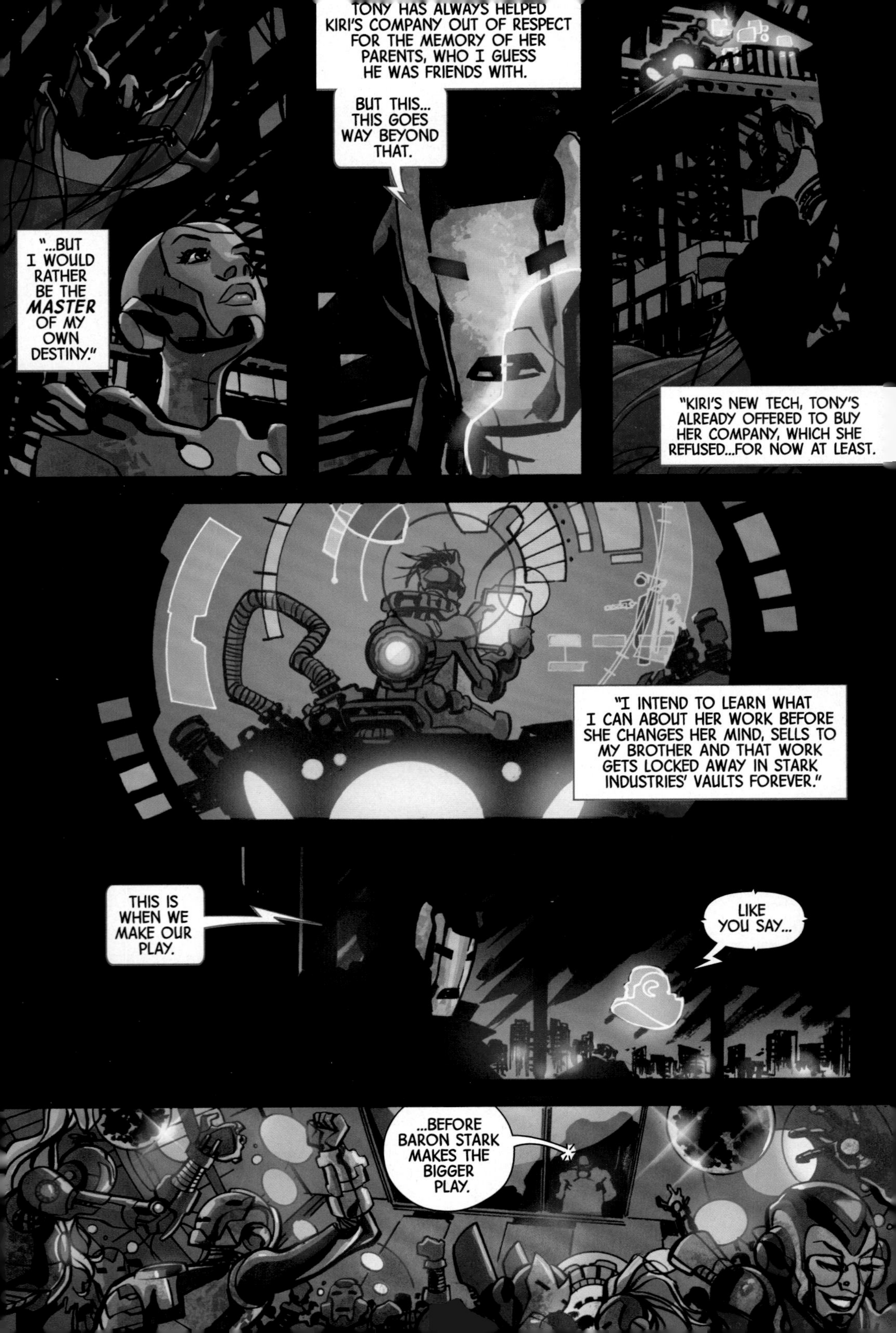

TONY HAS ALWAYS HELPED KIRI'S COMPANY OUT OF RESPECT FOR THE MEMORY OF HER PARENTS, WHO I GUESS HE WAS FRIENDS WITH.
BUT THIS... THIS GOES WAY BEYOND THAT.
"...BUT I WOULD RATHER BE THE ***MASTER*** OF MY OWN DESTINY."
"KIRI'S NEW TECH, TONY'S ALREADY OFFERED TO BUY HER COMPANY, WHICH SHE REFUSED...FOR NOW AT LEAST.
"I INTEND TO LEARN WHAT I CAN ABOUT HER WORK BEFORE SHE CHANGES HER MIND, SELLS TO MY BROTHER AND THAT WORK GETS LOCKED AWAY IN STARK INDUSTRIES' VAULTS FOREVER."
THIS IS WHEN WE MAKE OUR PLAY.
LIKE YOU SAY...
...BEFORE BARON STARK MAKES THE BIGGER PLAY.

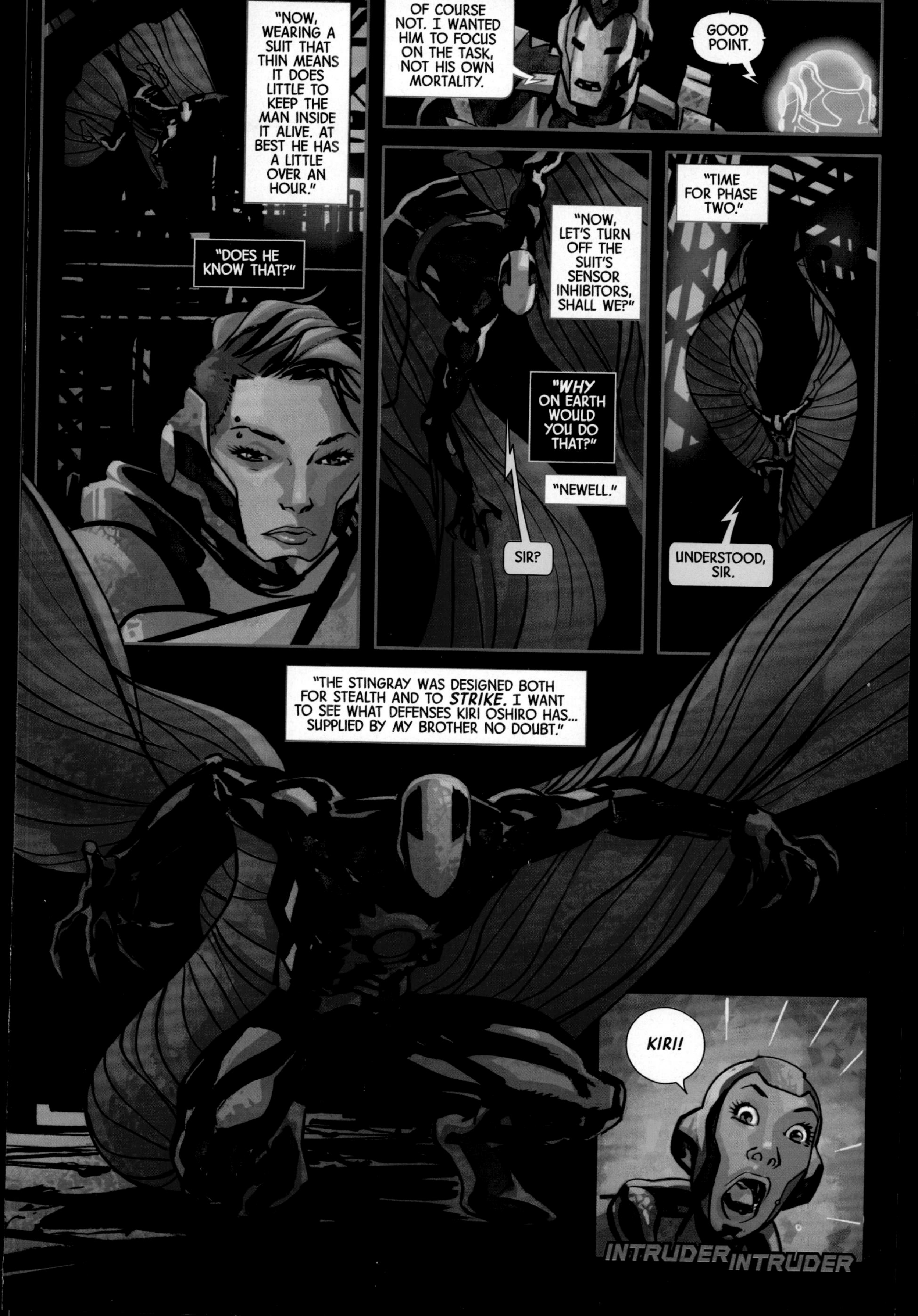
"NOW, WEARING A SUIT THAT THIN MEANS IT DOES LITTLE TO KEEP THE MAN INSIDE IT ALIVE. AT BEST HE HAS A LITTLE OVER AN HOUR."
OF COURSE NOT. I WANTED HIM TO FOCUS ON THE TASK, NOT HIS OWN MORTALITY.
GOOD POINT.
"DOES HE KNOW THAT?"
"NOW, LET'S TURN OFF THE SUIT'S SENSOR INHIBITORS, SHALL WE?"
"WHY ON EARTH WOULD YOU DO THAT?"
"NEWELL."
SIR?
"TIME FOR PHASE TWO."
UNDERSTOOD, SIR.
"THE STINGRAY WAS DESIGNED BOTH FOR STEALTH AND TO STRIKE. I WANT TO SEE WHAT DEFENSES KIRI OSHIRO HAS... SUPPLIED BY MY BROTHER NO DOUBT."
KIRI!
INTRUDER INTRUDER

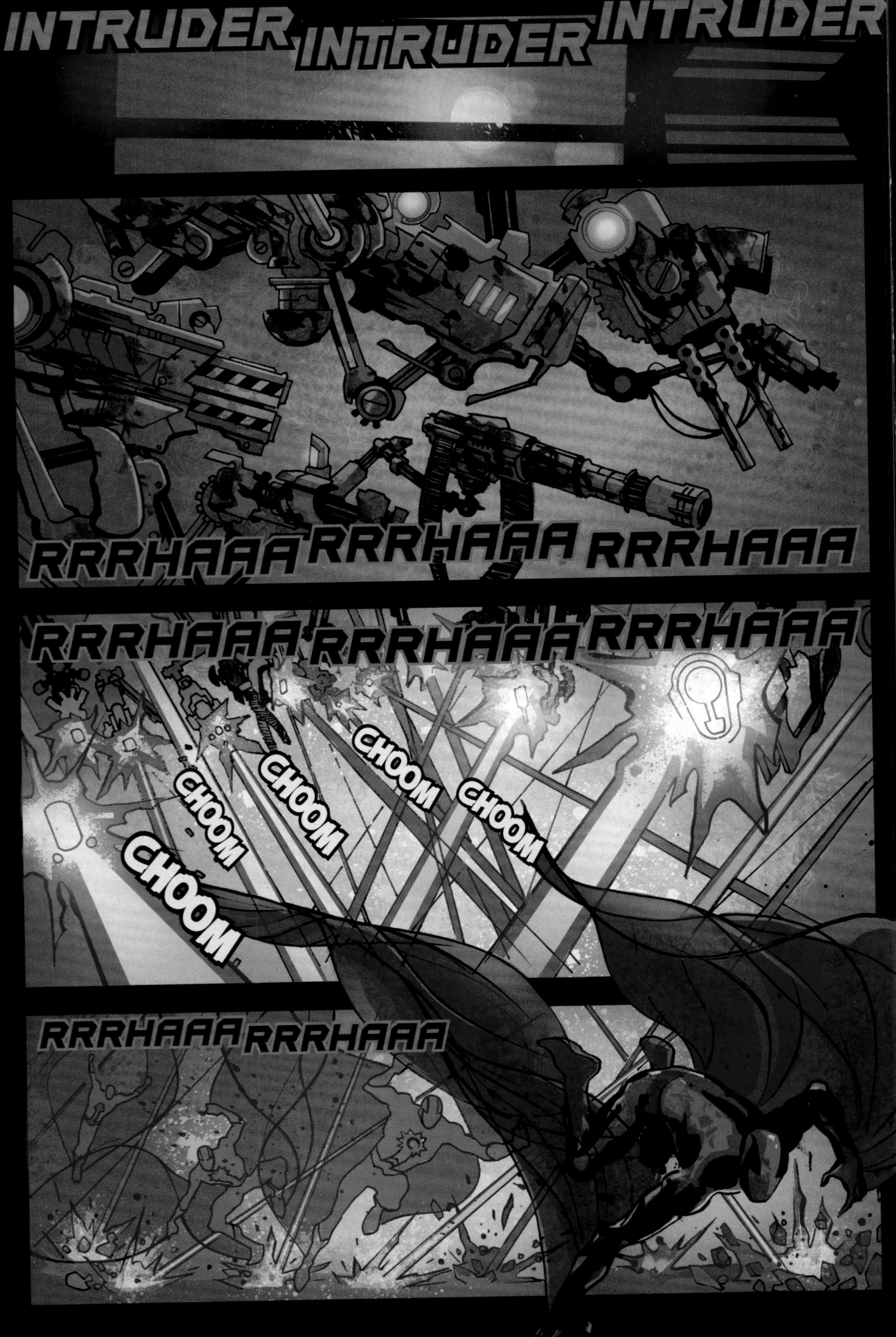
INTRUDER INTRUDER INTRUDER
RRRHAAA RRRHAAA RRRHAAA
RRRHAAA RRRHAAA RRRHAAA
CHOOM
CHOOM
CHOOM
CHOOM
CHOOM
RRRHAAA RRRHAAA

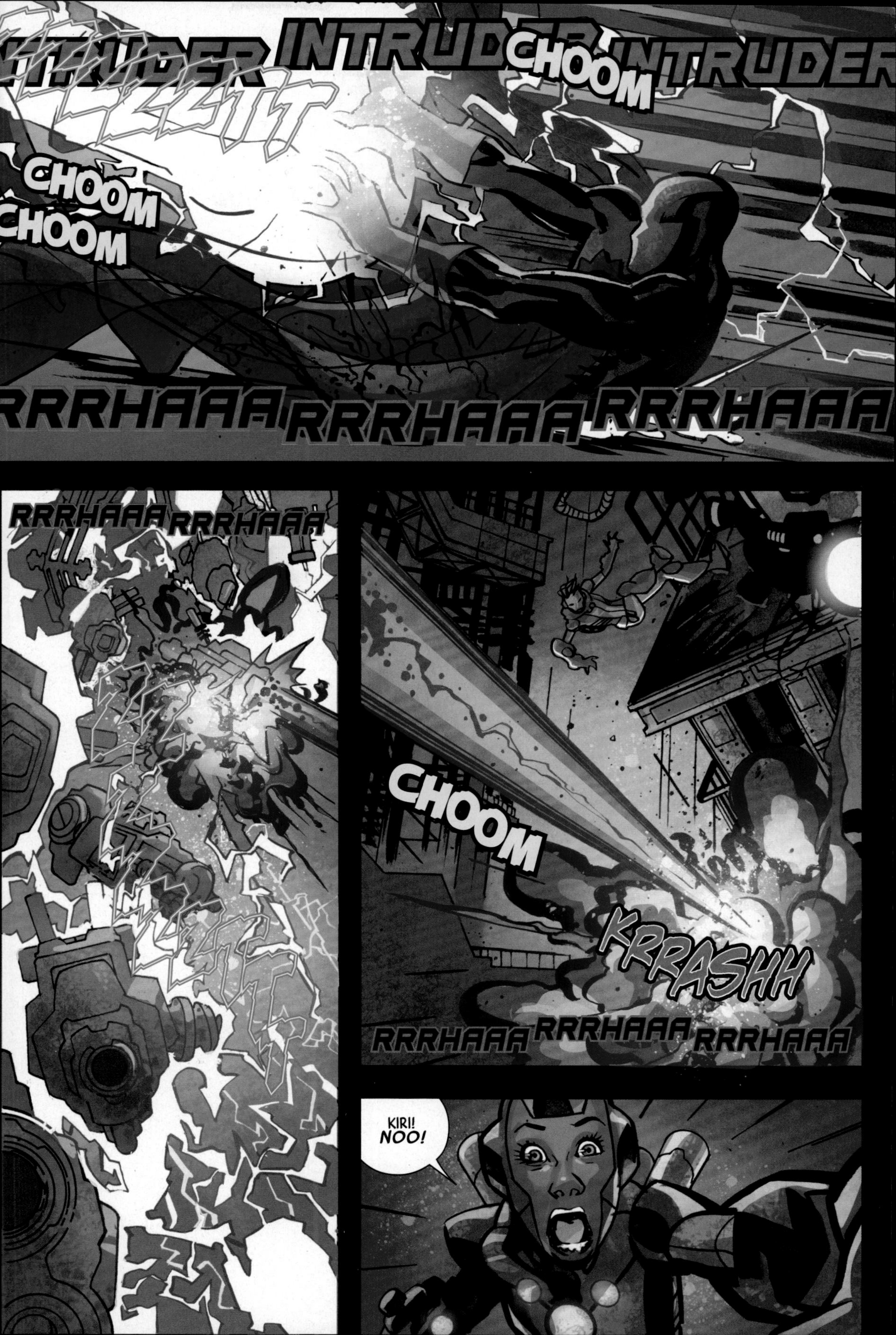
INTRUDER
CHOOM
INTRUDER
CHOOM
CHOOM
RRRHAAA RRRHAAA RRRHAAA
RRRHAAA RRRHAAA
CHOOM
KRRASHH
RRRHAAA RRRHAAA RRRHAAA
KIRI! NOO!

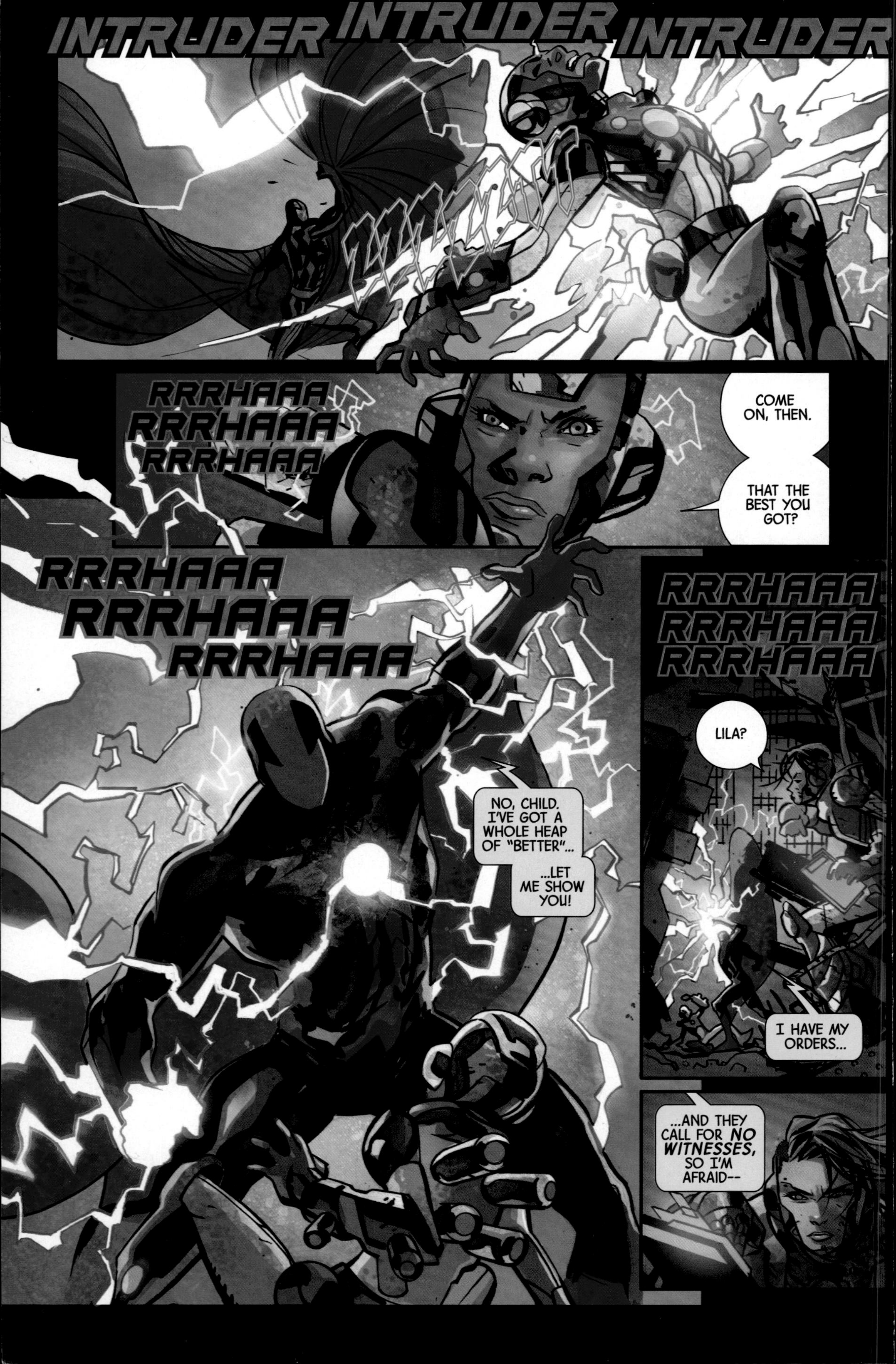
INTRUDER INTRUDER INTRUDER
RRRHAAA RRRHAAA RRRHAAA
COME ON, THEN.
THAT THE BEST YOU GOT?
RRRHAAA RRRHAAA RRRHAAA
NO, CHILD. I'VE GOT A WHOLE HEAP OF "BETTER"...
...LET ME SHOW YOU!
RRRHAAA RRRHAAA RRRHAAA
LILA?
I HAVE MY ORDERS...
...AND THEY CALL FOR NO WITNESSES, SO I'M AFRAID--

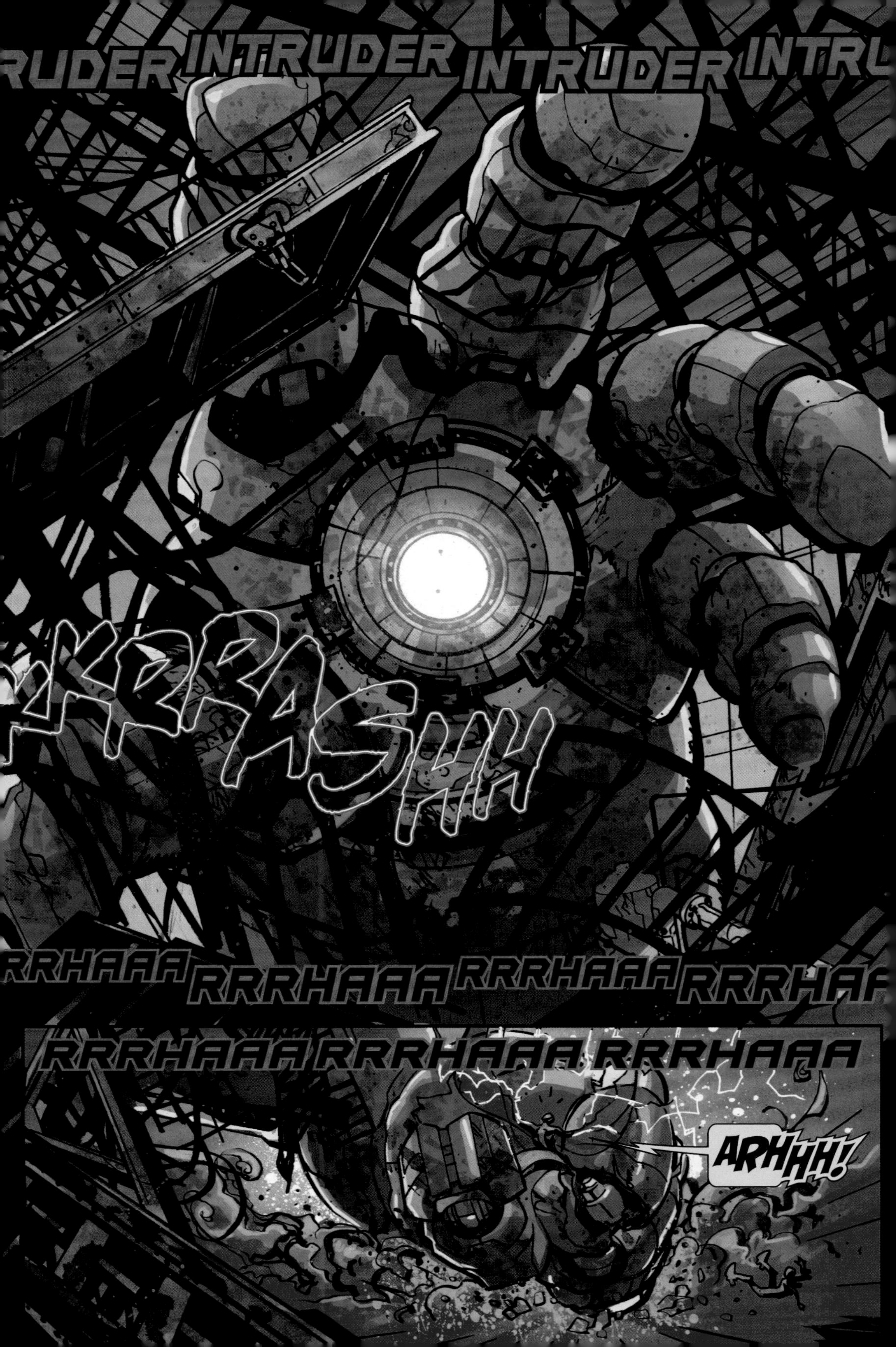
RUDER INTRUDER INTRUDER INTRU
KKRASHH
RRRHAAA RRRHAAA RRRHAAA RRRHAA
RRRHAAA RRRHAAA RRRHAAA
ARHHH!

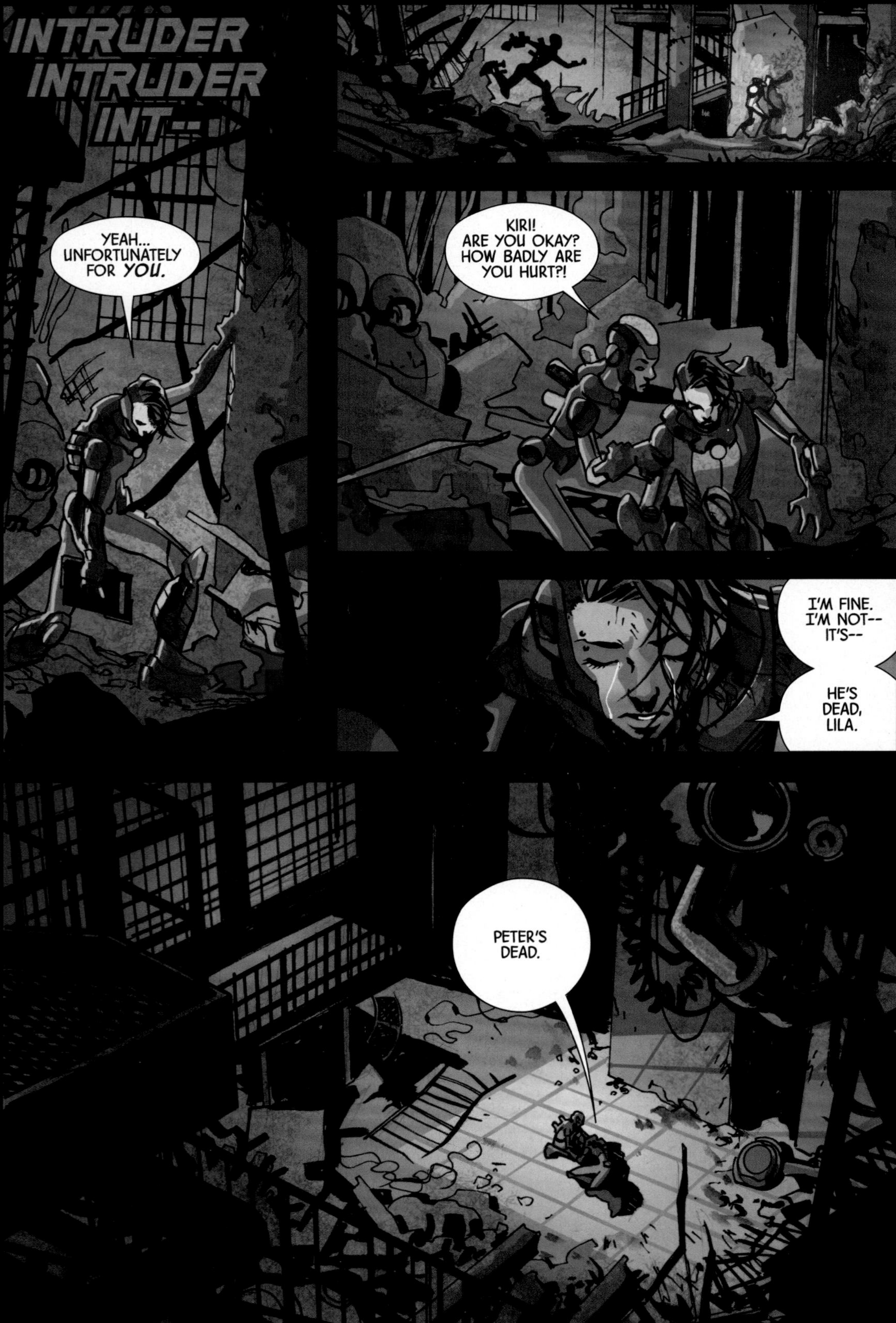
INTRUDER
INTRUDER
INT--
YEAH... UNFORTUNATELY FOR YOU.
KIRI! ARE YOU OKAY? HOW BADLY ARE YOU HURT?!
I'M FINE. I'M NOT-- IT'S--
HE'S DEAD, LILA.
PETER'S DEAD.

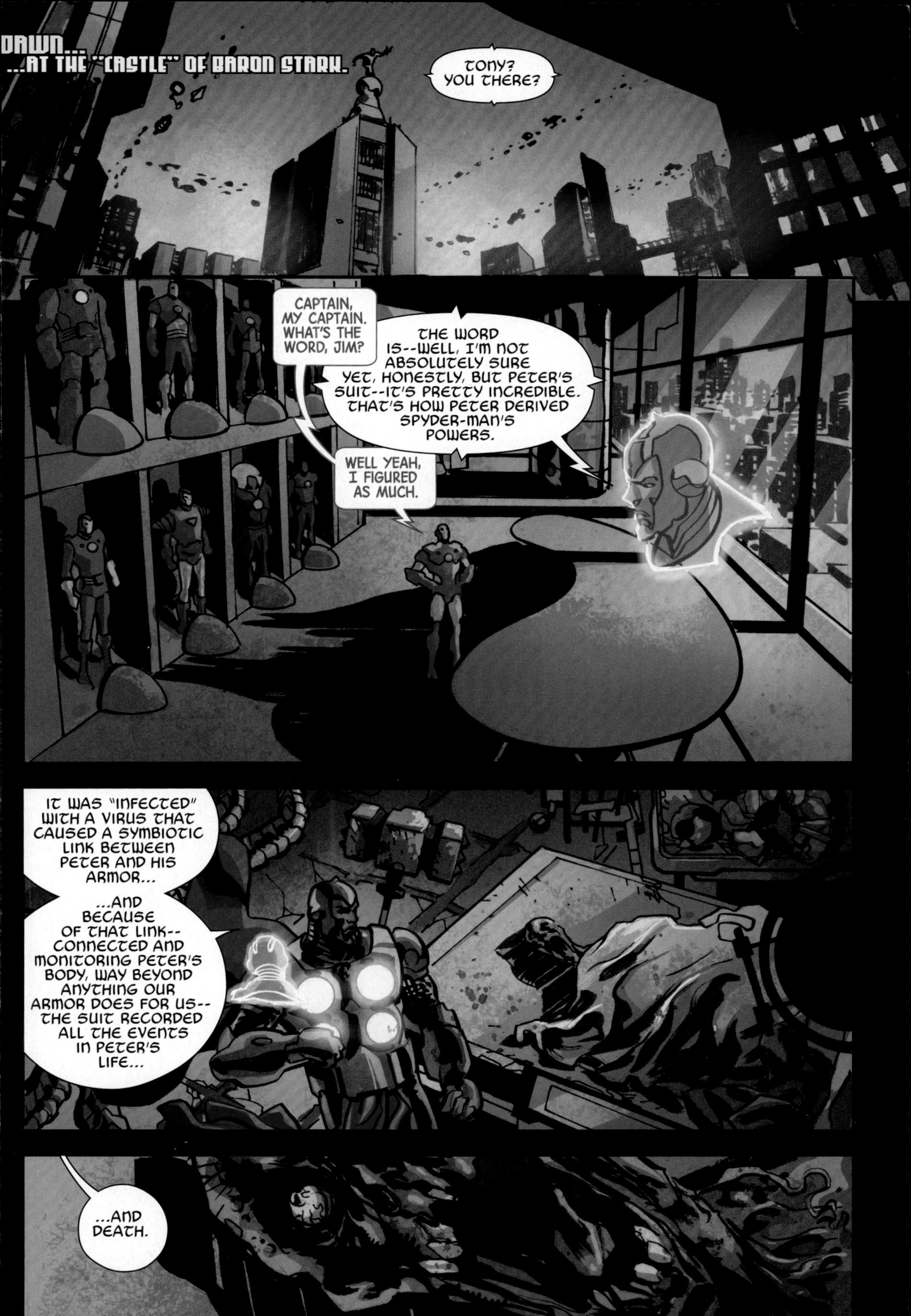
DAWN... ...AT THE "CASTLE" OF BARON STARK.
TONY? YOU THERE?
CAPTAIN, MY CAPTAIN. WHAT'S THE WORD, JIM?
THE WORD IS--WELL, I'M NOT ABSOLUTELY SURE YET, HONESTLY, BUT PETER'S SUIT--IT'S PRETTY INCREDIBLE. THAT'S HOW PETER DERIVED SPYDER-MAN'S POWERS.
WELL YEAH, I FIGURED AS MUCH.
IT WAS "INFECTED" WITH A VIRUS THAT CAUSED A SYMBIOTIC LINK BETWEEN PETER AND HIS ARMOR...
...AND BECAUSE OF THAT LINK--CONNECTED AND MONITORING PETER'S BODY, WAY BEYOND ANYTHING OUR ARMOR DOES FOR US--THE SUIT RECORDED ALL THE EVENTS IN PETER'S LIFE...
...AND DEATH.

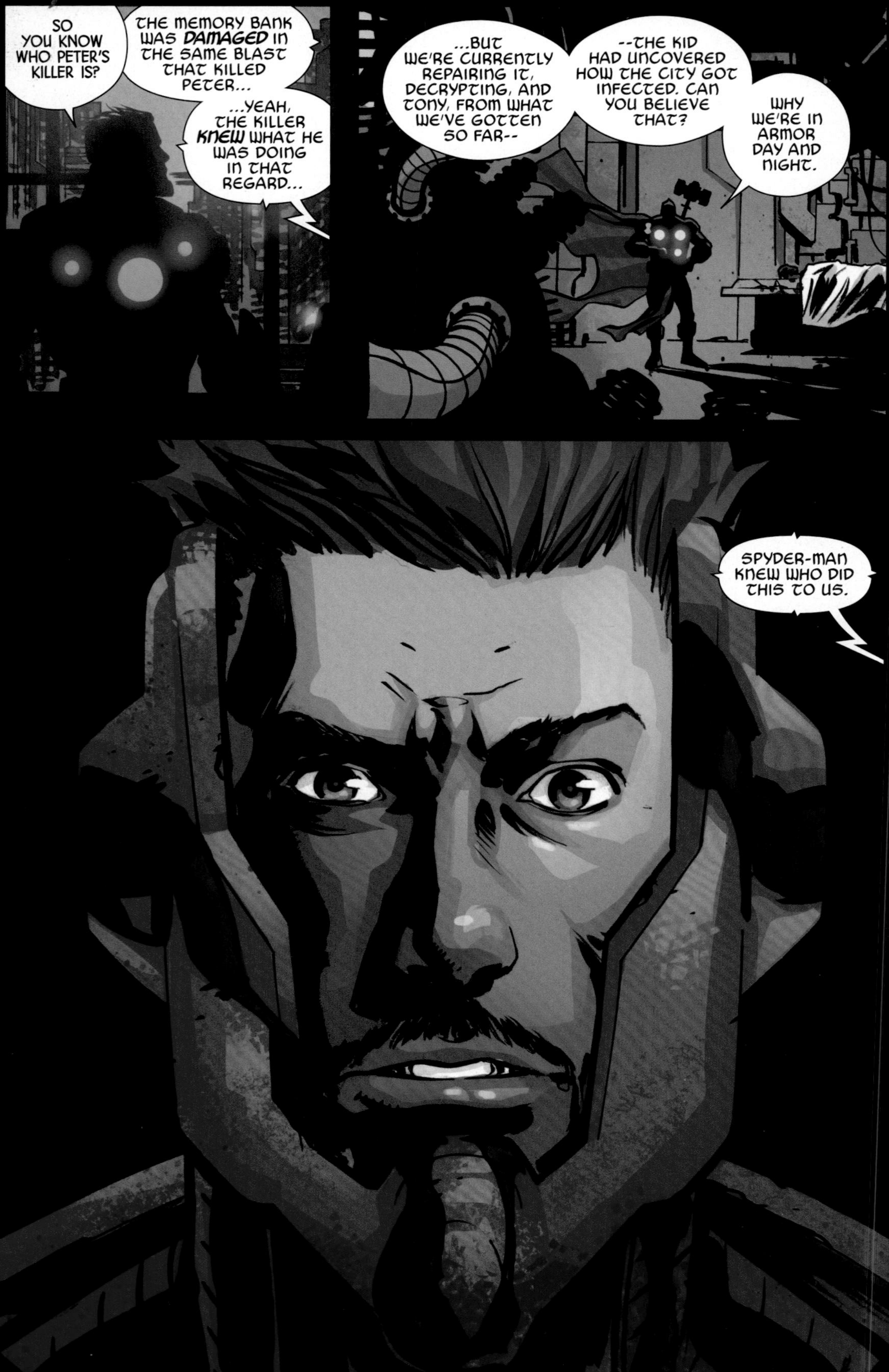
SO YOU KNOW WHO PETER'S KILLER IS?
THE MEMORY BANK WAS **DAMAGED** IN THE SAME BLAST THAT KILLED PETER...
...YEAH, THE KILLER **KNEW** WHAT HE WAS DOING IN THAT REGARD...
...BUT WE'RE CURRENTLY REPAIRING IT, DECRYPTING, AND TONY, FROM WHAT WE'VE GOTTEN SO FAR--
--THE KID HAD UNCOVERED HOW THE CITY GOT INFECTED. CAN YOU BELIEVE THAT?
WHY WE'RE IN ARMOR DAY AND NIGHT.
SPYDER-MAN KNEW WHO DID THIS TO US.

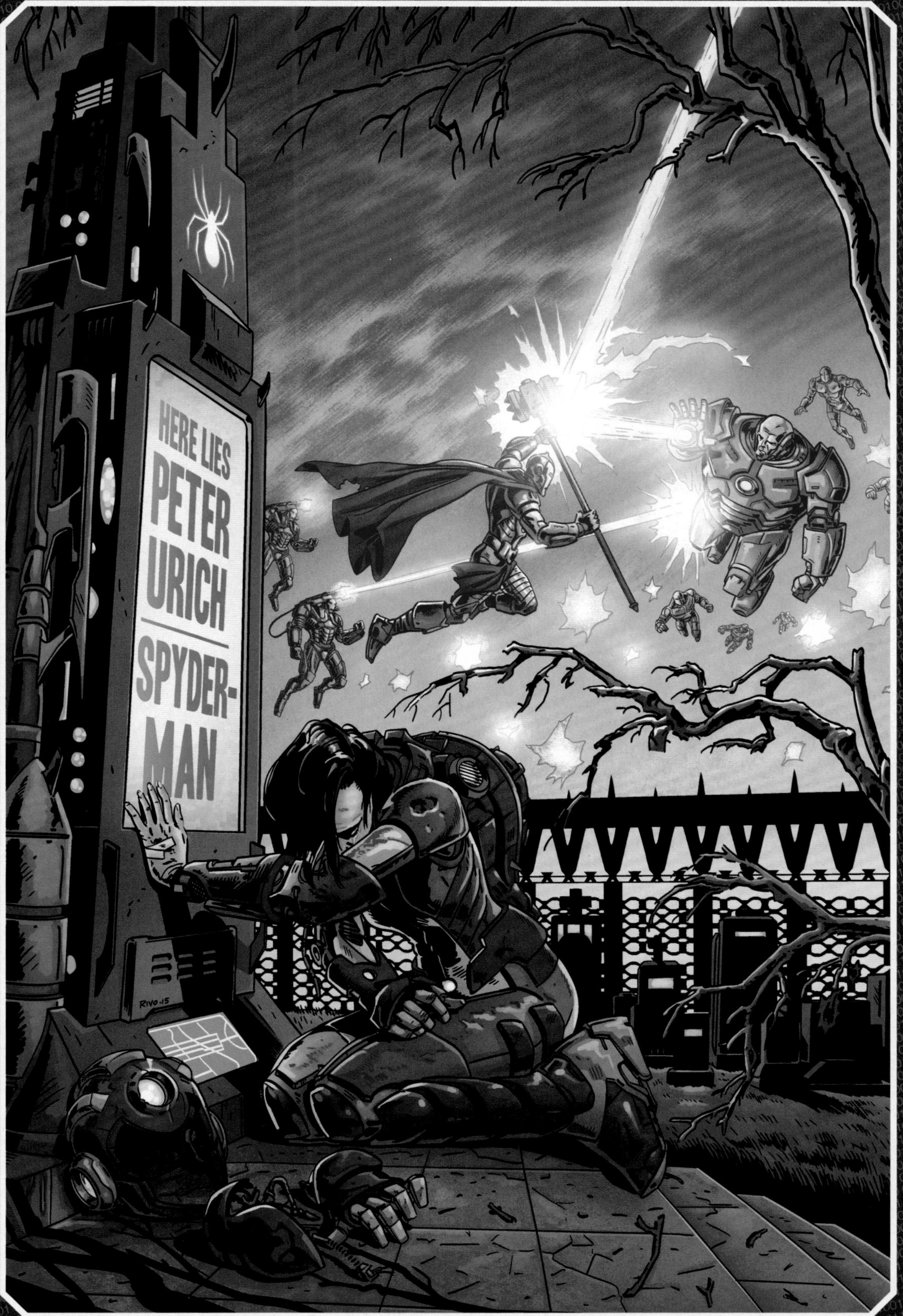
HERE LIES
PETER
URICH
SPYDER-
MAN
RIVO-15

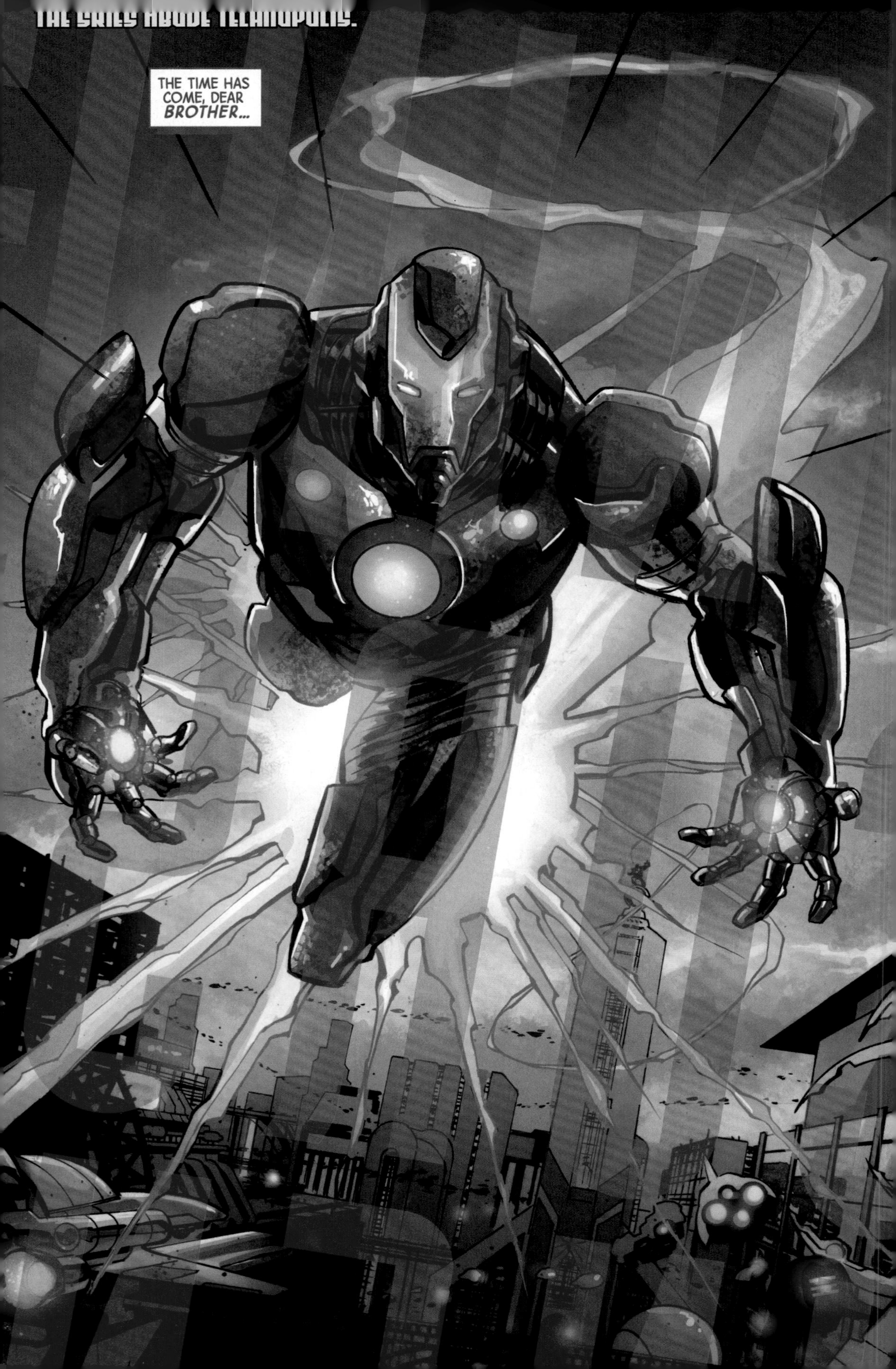
THE SKIES ABOVE TECHNOPOLIS.
THE TIME HAS COME, DEAR *BROTHER*...

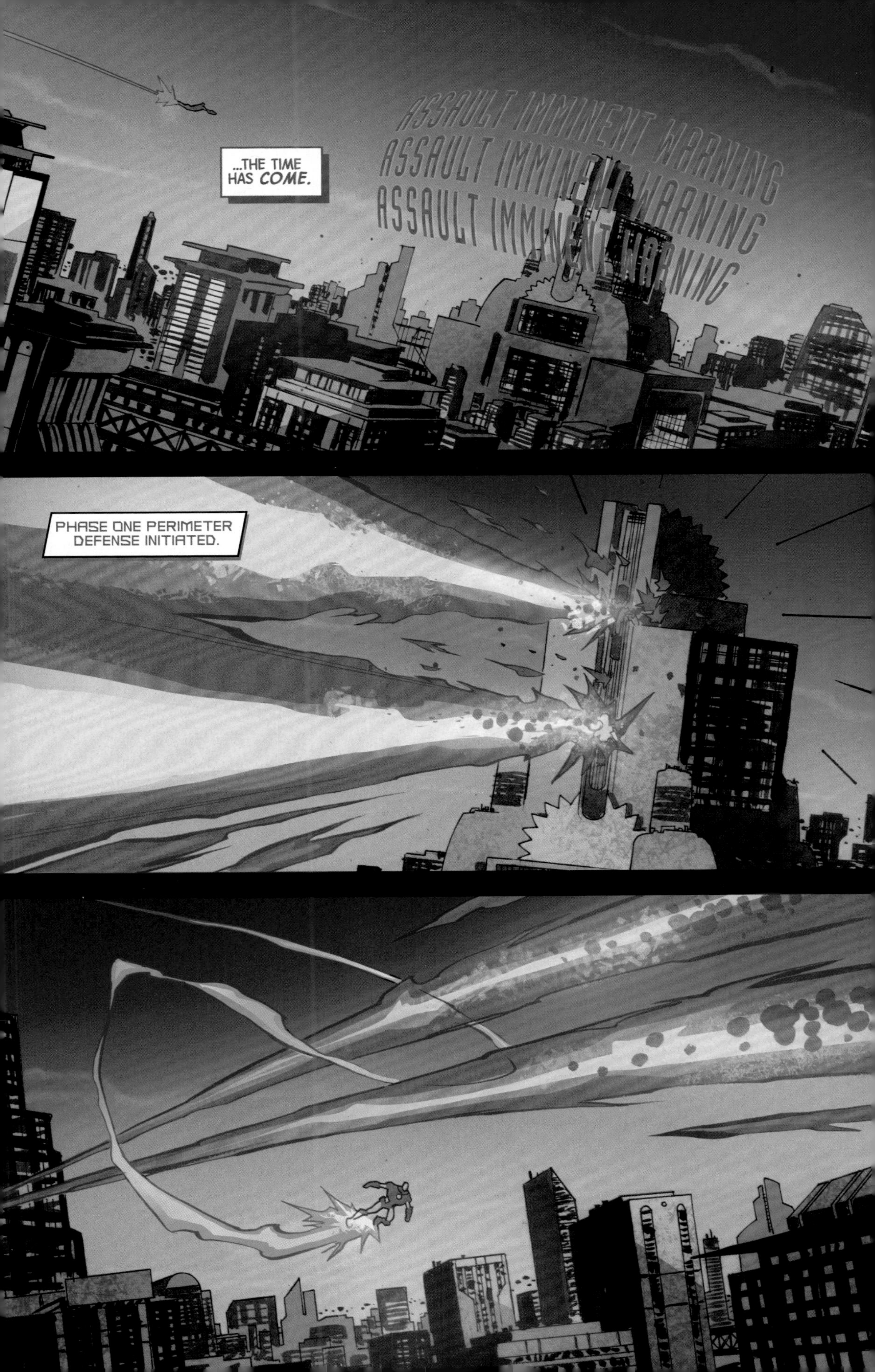

...THE TIME HAS COME.
ASSAULT IMMINENT WARNING
ASSAULT IMMINENT WARNING
ASSAULT IMMINENT WARNING
ASSAULT IMMINENT WARNING
PHASE ONE PERIMETER DEFENSE INITIATED.

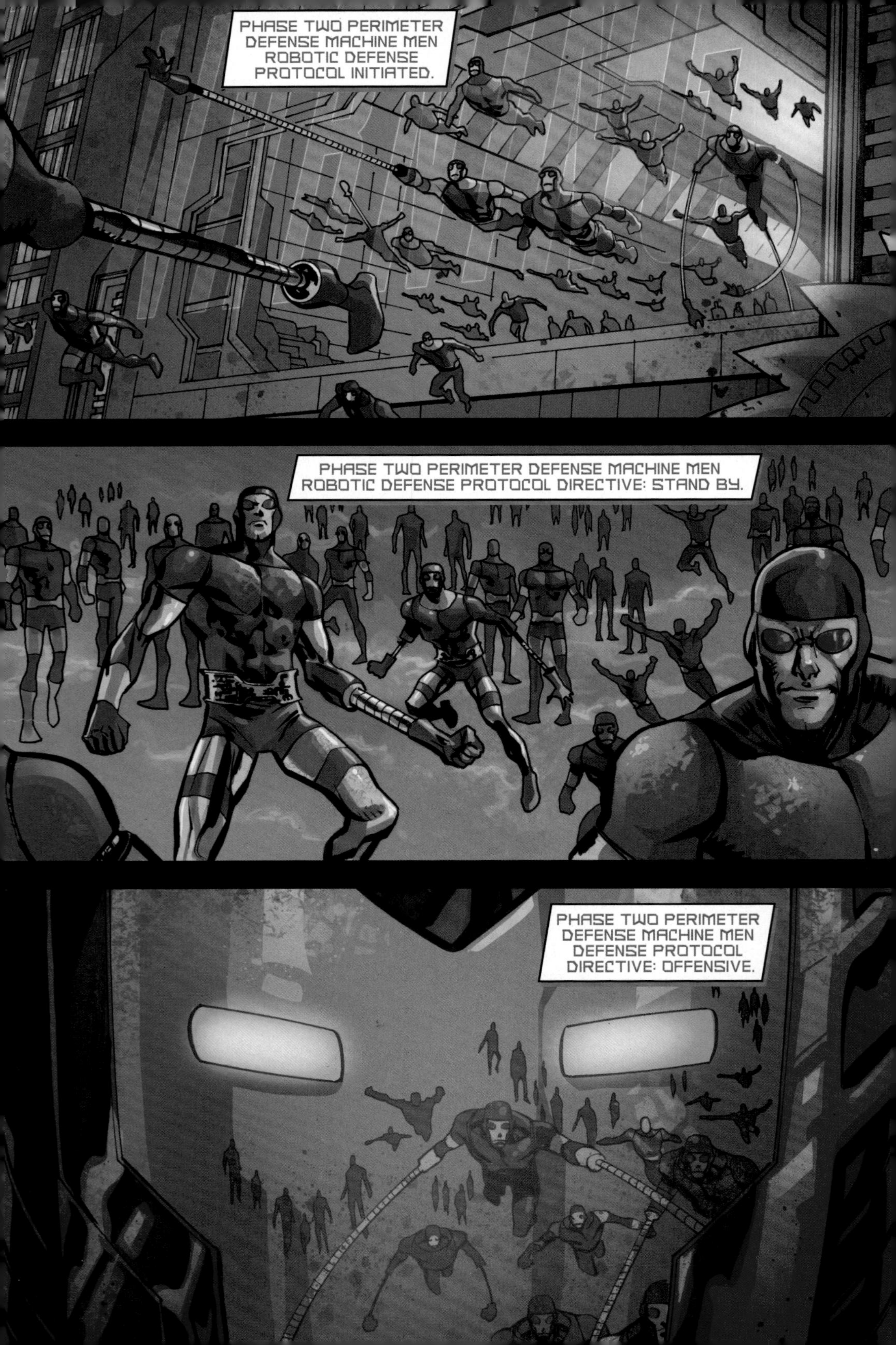
PHASE TWO PERIMETER DEFENSE MACHINE MEN ROBOTIC DEFENSE PROTOCOL INITIATED.
PHASE TWO PERIMETER DEFENSE MACHINE MEN ROBOTIC DEFENSE PROTOCOL DIRECTIVE: STAND BY.
PHASE TWO PERIMETER DEFENSE MACHINE MEN DEFENSE PROTOCOL DIRECTIVE: OFFENSIVE.

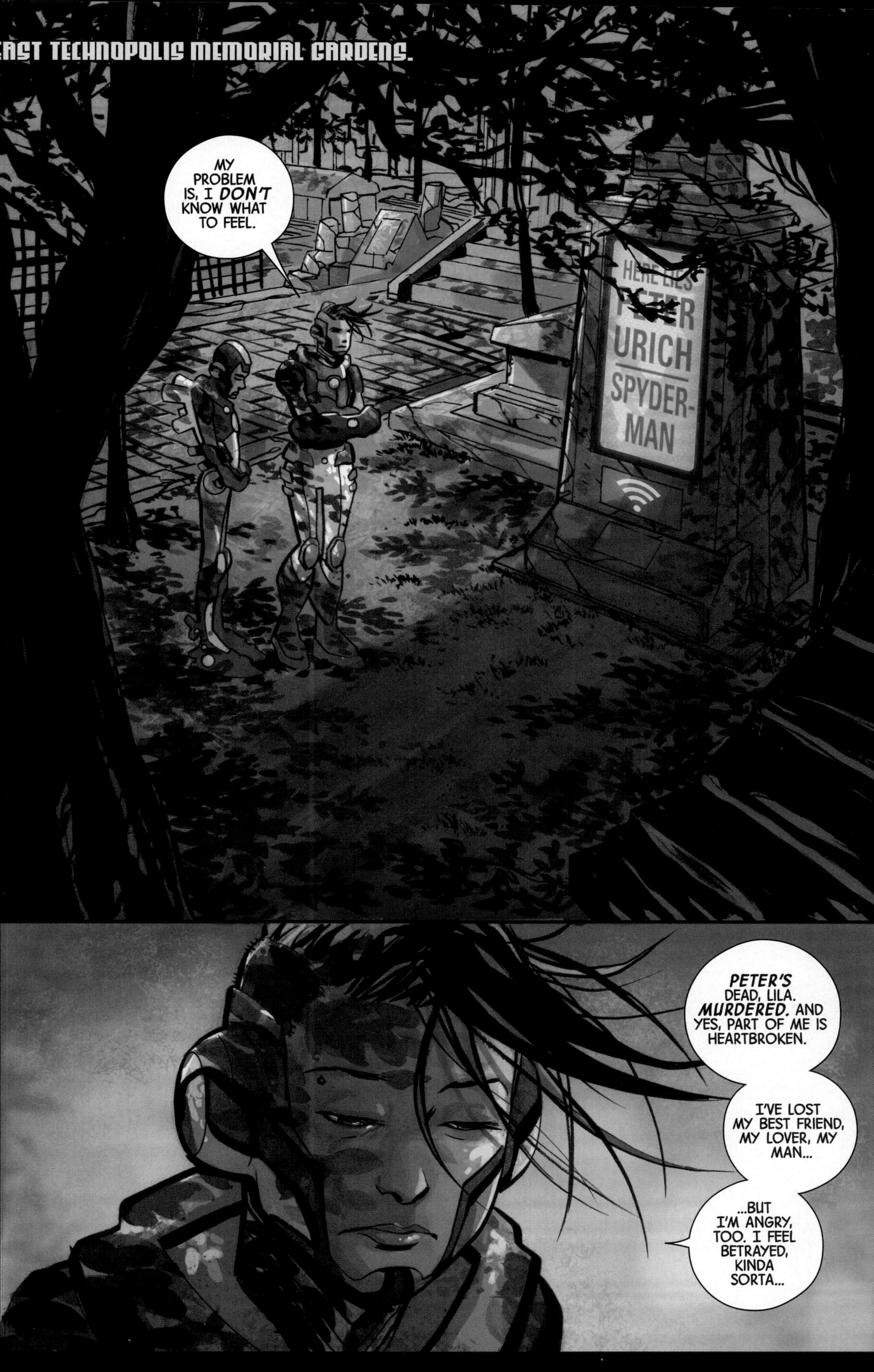
EAST TECHNOPOLIS MEMORIAL GARDENS.
MY PROBLEM IS, I *DON'T* KNOW WHAT TO FEEL.
HERE LIES
URICH
SPYDER-MAN
PETER'S DEAD, LILA. *MURDERED.* AND YES, PART OF ME IS HEARTBROKEN.
I'VE LOST MY BEST FRIEND, MY LOVER, MY MAN...
...BUT I'M ANGRY, TOO. I FEEL BETRAYED, KINDA SORTA...

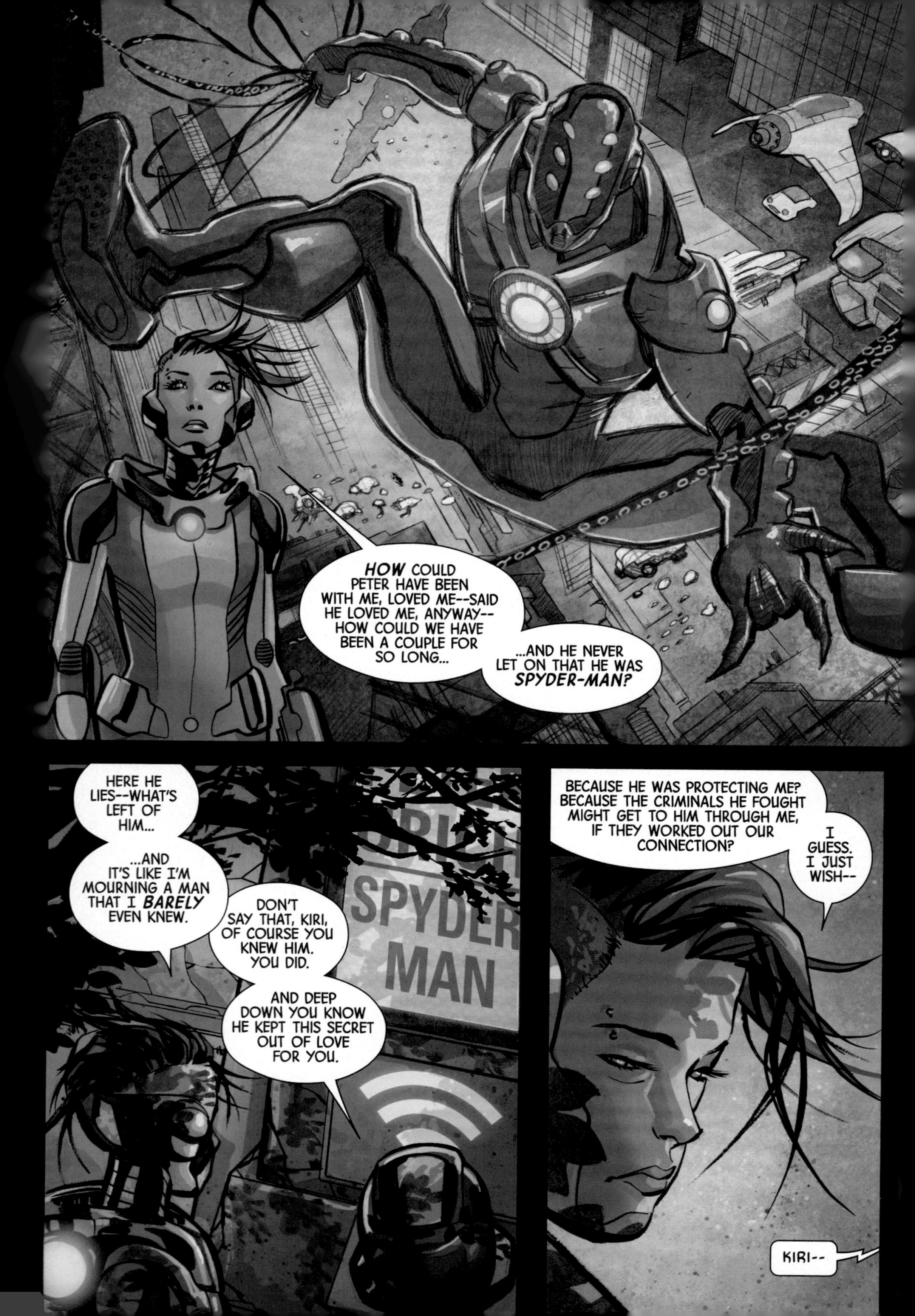
HOW COULD PETER HAVE BEEN WITH ME, LOVED ME--SAID HE LOVED ME, ANYWAY--HOW COULD WE HAVE BEEN A COUPLE FOR SO LONG...
...AND HE NEVER LET ON THAT HE WAS SPYDER-MAN?
HERE HE LIES--WHAT'S LEFT OF HIM...
...AND IT'S LIKE I'M MOURNING A MAN THAT I BARELY EVEN KNEW.
SPYDER MAN
DON'T SAY THAT, KIRI, OF COURSE YOU KNEW HIM. YOU DID.
AND DEEP DOWN YOU KNOW HE KEPT THIS SECRET OUT OF LOVE FOR YOU.
BECAUSE HE WAS PROTECTING ME? BECAUSE THE CRIMINALS HE FOUGHT MIGHT GET TO HIM THROUGH ME, IF THEY WORKED OUT OUR CONNECTION?
I GUESS. I JUST WISH--
KIRI--

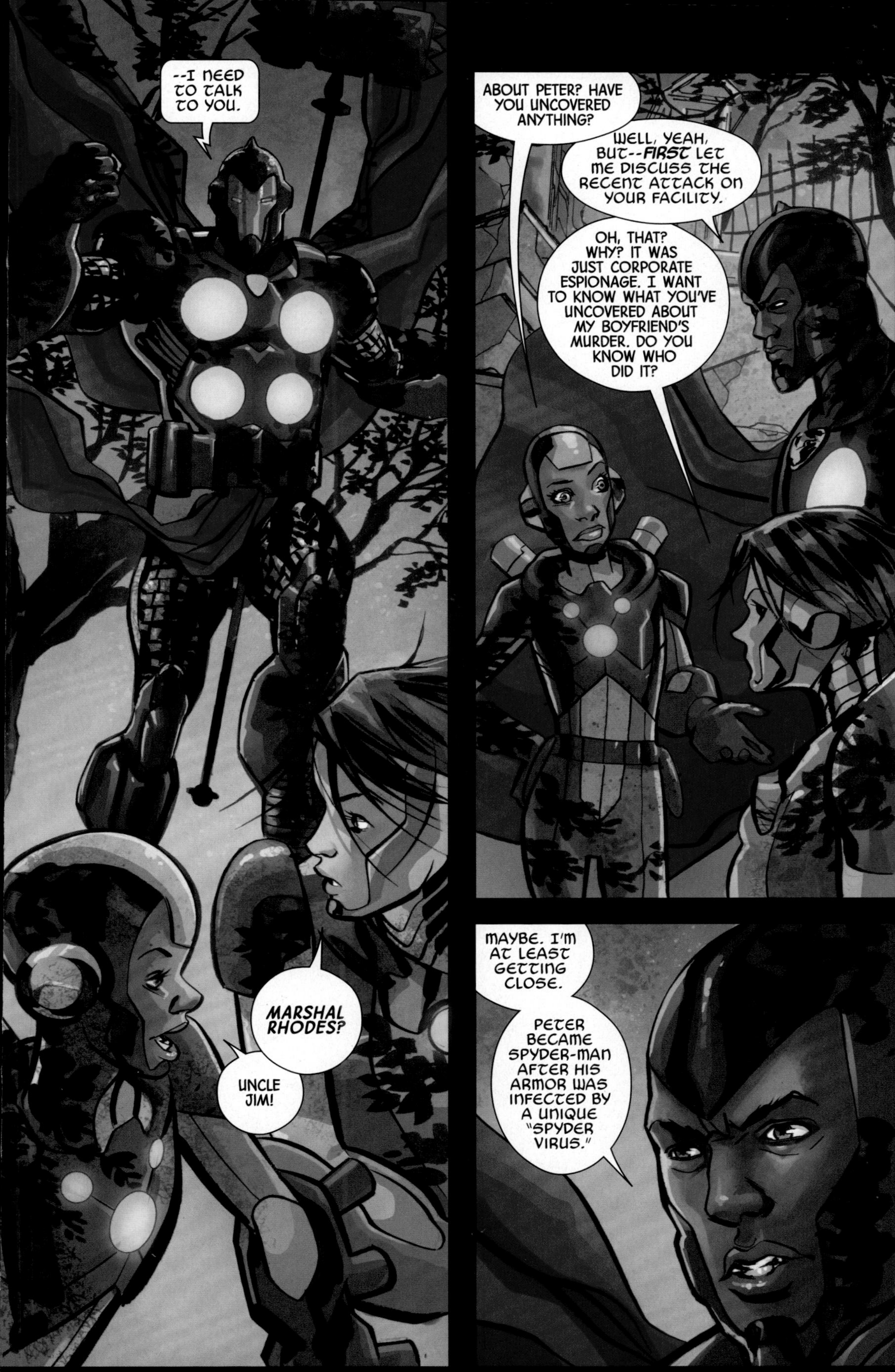
--I NEED TO TALK TO YOU.
MARSHAL RHODES?
UNCLE JIM!
ABOUT PETER? HAVE YOU UNCOVERED ANYTHING?
WELL, YEAH, BUT--FIRST LET ME DISCUSS THE RECENT ATTACK ON YOUR FACILITY.
OH, THAT? WHY? IT WAS JUST CORPORATE ESPIONAGE. I WANT TO KNOW WHAT YOU'VE UNCOVERED ABOUT MY BOYFRIEND'S MURDER. DO YOU KNOW WHO DID IT?
MAYBE. I'M AT LEAST GETTING CLOSE.
PETER BECAME SPYDER-MAN AFTER HIS ARMOR WAS INFECTED BY A UNIQUE "SPYDER VIRUS."

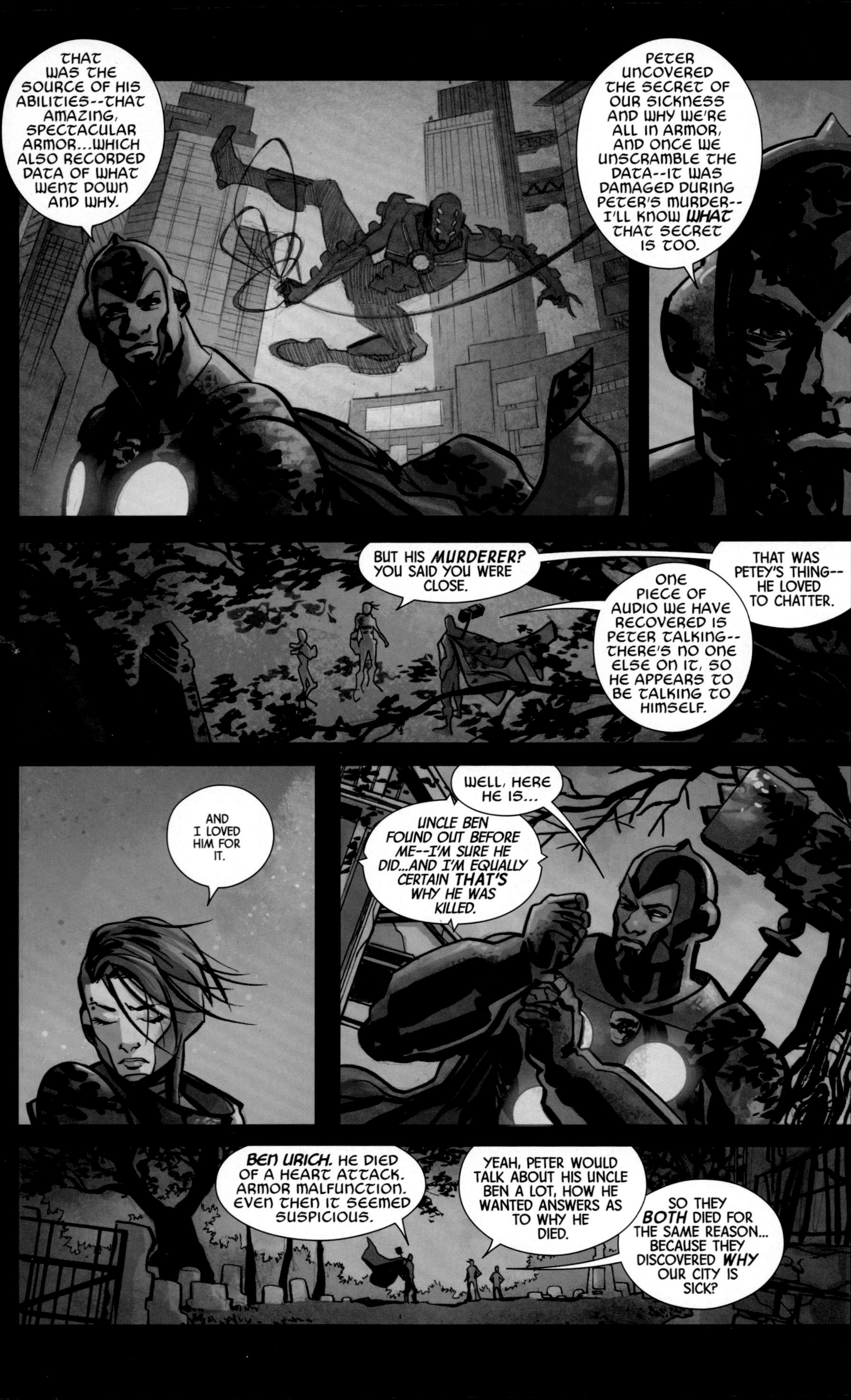
THAT WAS THE SOURCE OF HIS ABILITIES--THAT AMAZING, SPECTACULAR ARMOR...WHICH ALSO RECORDED DATA OF WHAT WENT DOWN AND WHY.
PETER UNCOVERED THE SECRET OF OUR SICKNESS AND WHY WE'RE ALL IN ARMOR, AND ONCE WE UNSCRAMBLE THE DATA--IT WAS DAMAGED DURING PETER'S MURDER--I'LL KNOW WHAT THAT SECRET IS TOO.
BUT HIS MURDERER? YOU SAID YOU WERE CLOSE.
ONE PIECE OF AUDIO WE HAVE RECOVERED IS PETER TALKING--THERE'S NO ONE ELSE ON IT, SO HE APPEARS TO BE TALKING TO HIMSELF.
THAT WAS PETEY'S THING--HE LOVED TO CHATTER.
AND I LOVED HIM FOR IT.
WELL, HERE HE IS...
UNCLE BEN FOUND OUT BEFORE ME--I'M SURE HE DID...AND I'M EQUALLY CERTAIN THAT'S WHY HE WAS KILLED.
BEN URICH. HE DIED OF A HEART ATTACK. ARMOR MALFUNCTION. EVEN THEN IT SEEMED SUSPICIOUS.
YEAH, PETER WOULD TALK ABOUT HIS UNCLE BEN A LOT, HOW HE WANTED ANSWERS AS TO WHY HE DIED.
SO THEY BOTH DIED FOR THE SAME REASON... BECAUSE THEY DISCOVERED WHY OUR CITY IS SICK?

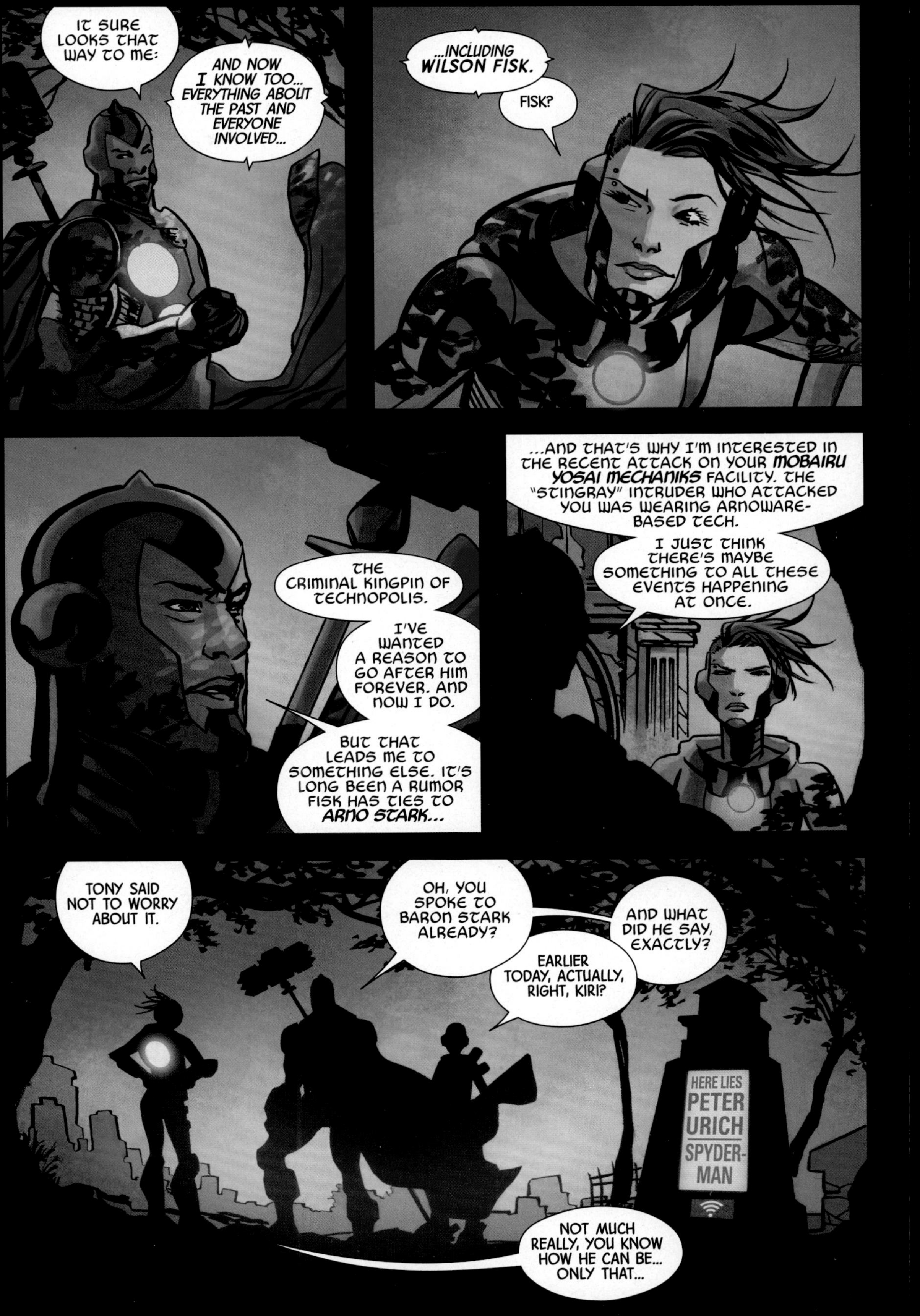
IT SURE LOOKS THAT WAY TO ME:
AND NOW I KNOW TOO... EVERYTHING ABOUT THE PAST AND EVERYONE INVOLVED...
...INCLUDING WILSON FISK.
FISK?
THE CRIMINAL KINGPIN OF TECHNOPOLIS.
I'VE WANTED A REASON TO GO AFTER HIM FOREVER. AND NOW I DO.
BUT THAT LEADS ME TO SOMETHING ELSE. IT'S LONG BEEN A RUMOR FISK HAS TIES TO ARNO STARK...
...AND THAT'S WHY I'M INTERESTED IN THE RECENT ATTACK ON YOUR MOBAIRU YOSAI MECHANIKS FACILITY. THE "STINGRAY" INTRUDER WHO ATTACKED YOU WAS WEARING ARNOWARE-BASED TECH.
I JUST THINK THERE'S MAYBE SOMETHING TO ALL THESE EVENTS HAPPENING AT ONCE.
TONY SAID NOT TO WORRY ABOUT IT.
OH, YOU SPOKE TO BARON STARK ALREADY?
AND WHAT DID HE SAY, EXACTLY?
EARLIER TODAY, ACTUALLY, RIGHT, KIRI?
HERE LIES PETER URICH SPYDER-MAN
NOT MUCH REALLY, YOU KNOW HOW HE CAN BE... ONLY THAT...

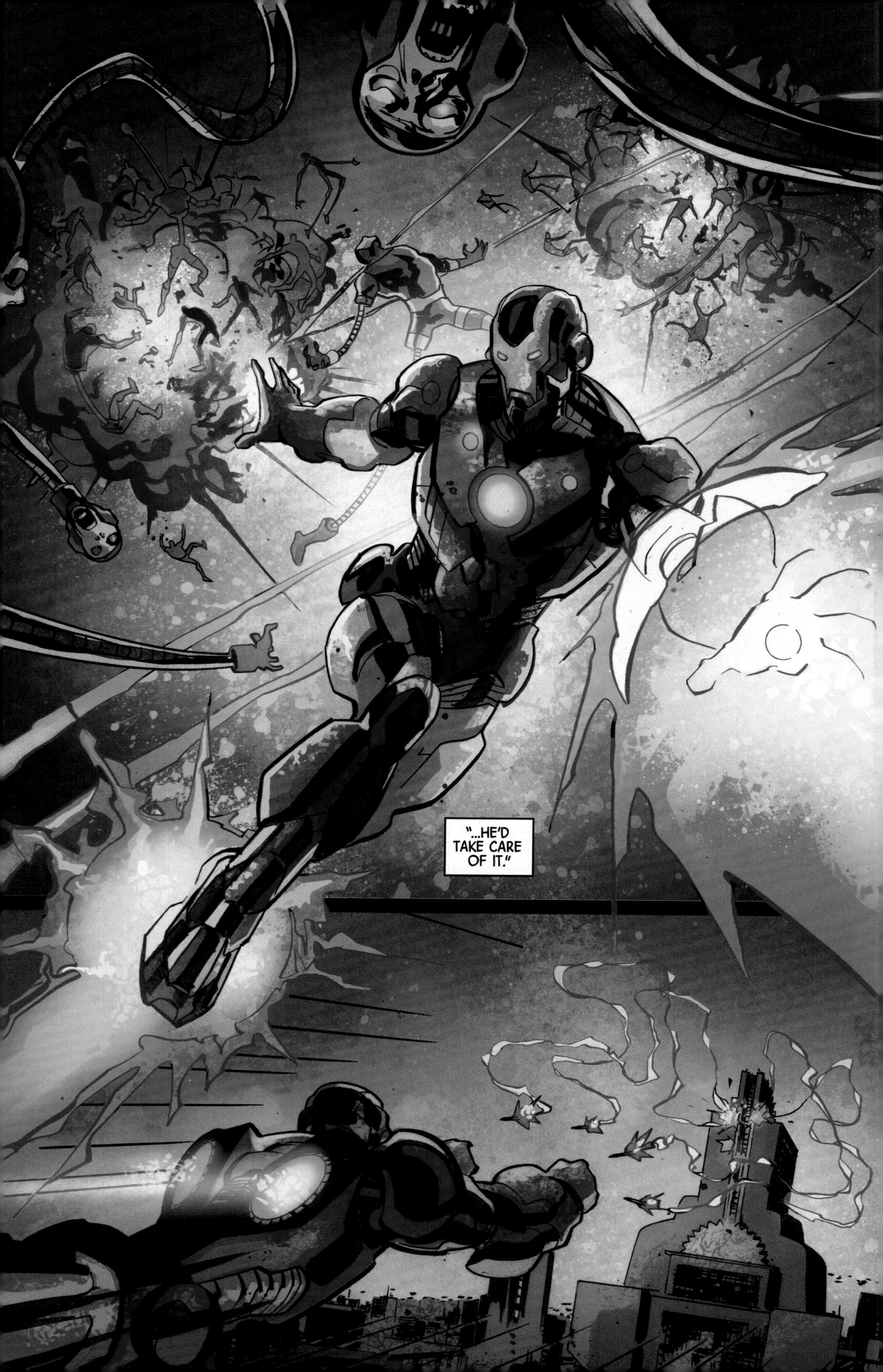
"...HE'D TAKE CARE OF IT."

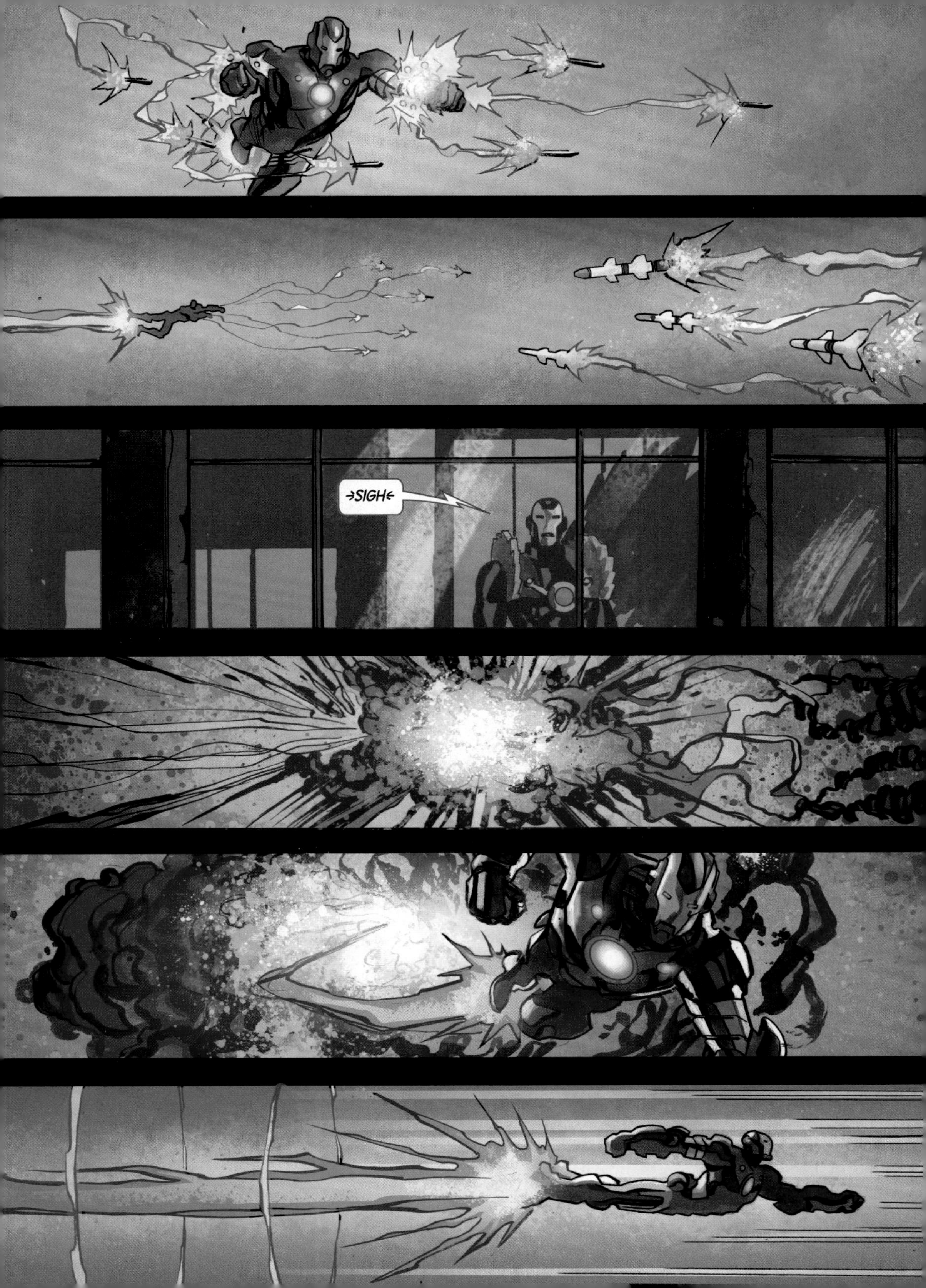

>SIGH<

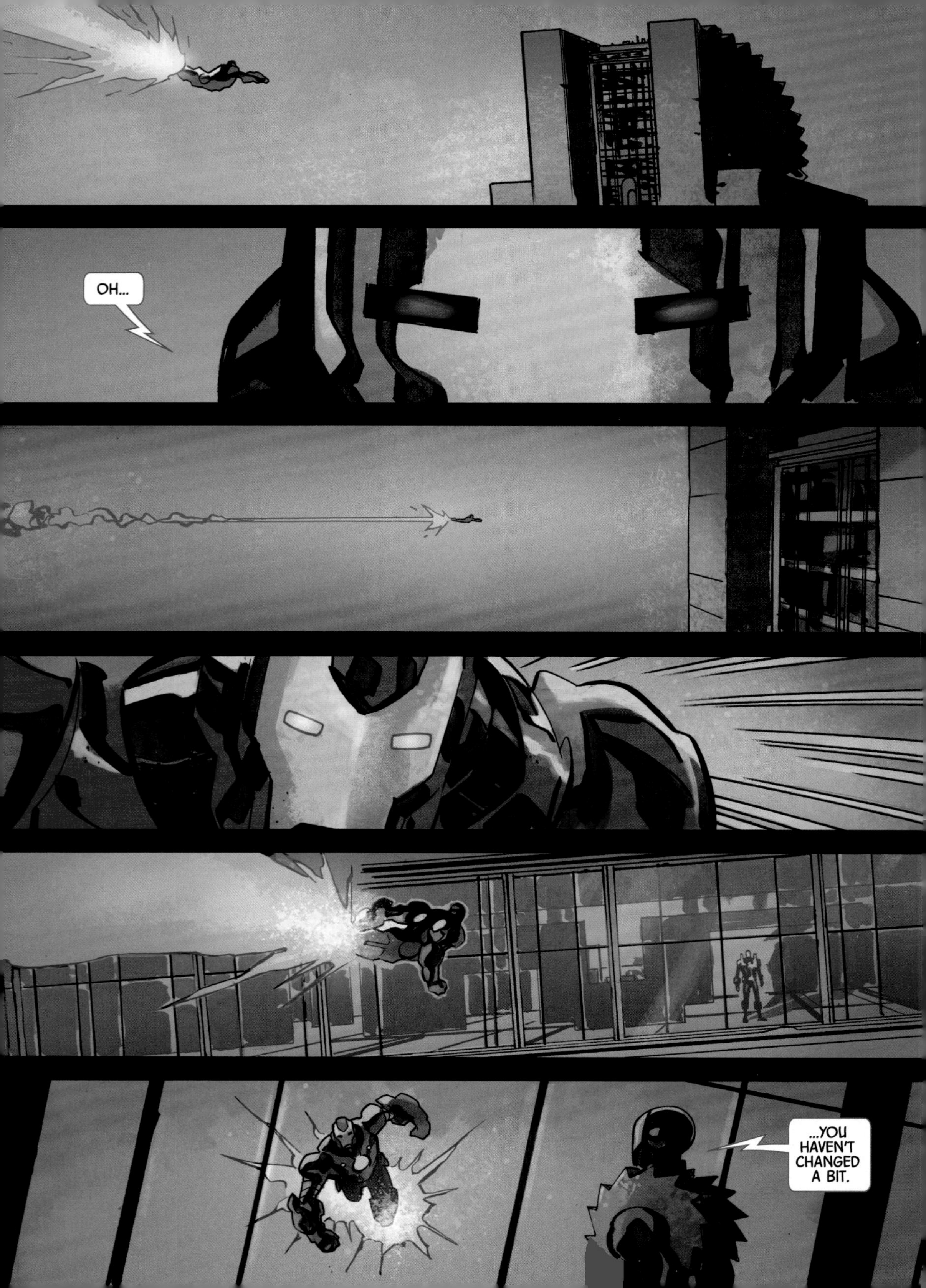
OH...
...YOU HAVEN'T CHANGED A BIT.

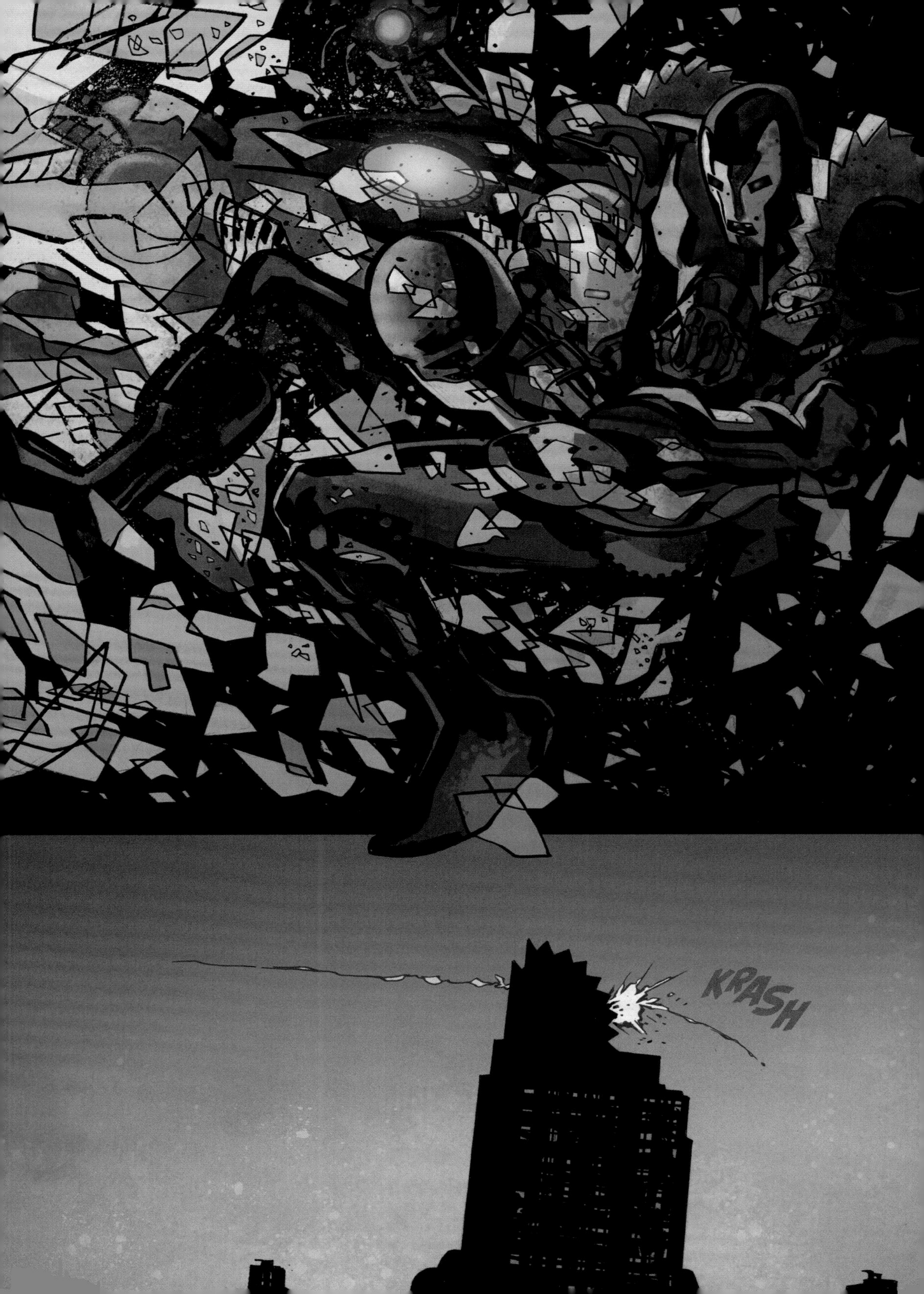
KRASH

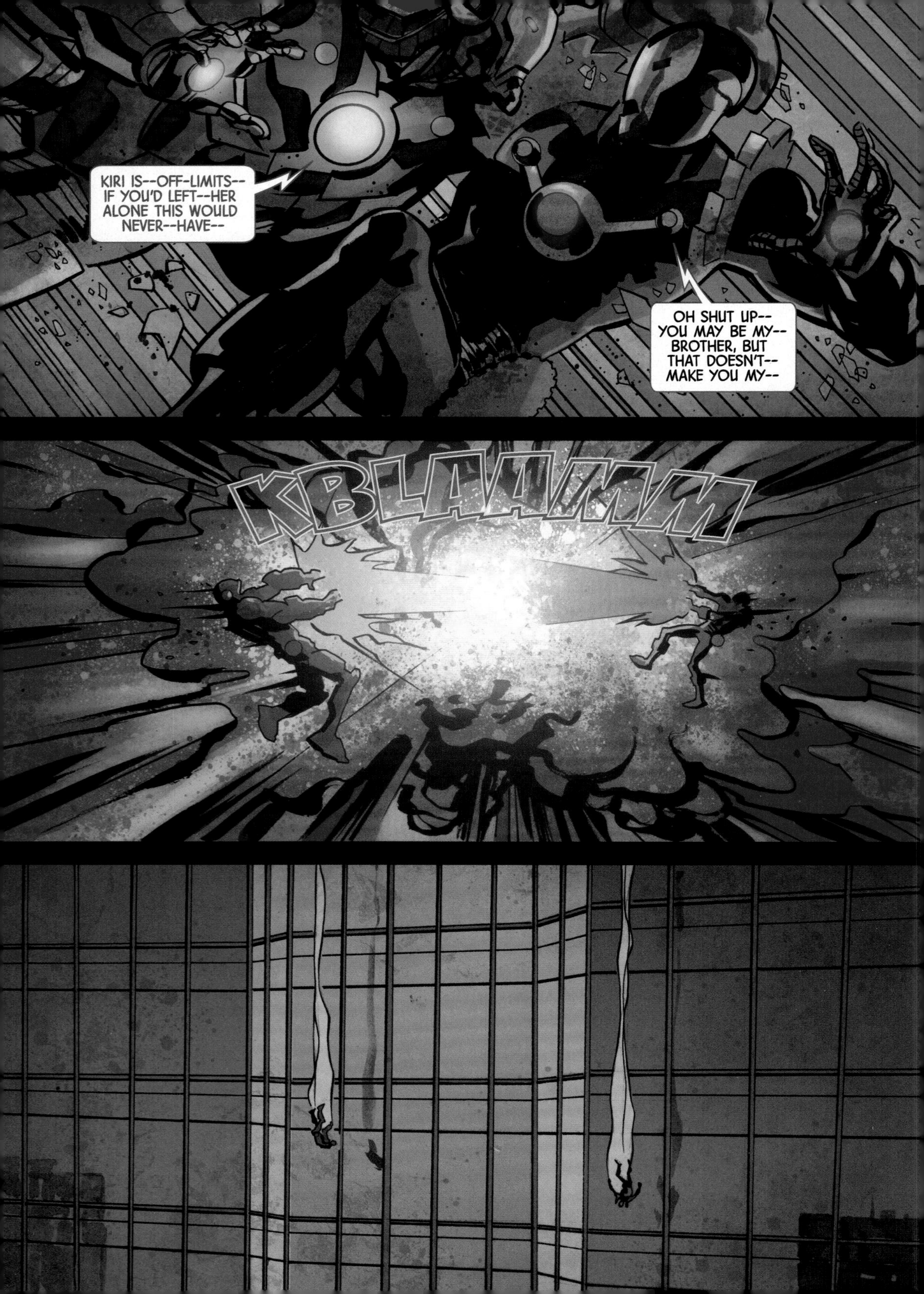
KIRI IS--OFF-LIMITS--IF YOU'D LEFT--HER ALONE THIS WOULD NEVER--HAVE--
OH SHUT UP--YOU MAY BE MY--BROTHER, BUT THAT DOESN'T--MAKE YOU MY--
KBLAAMM

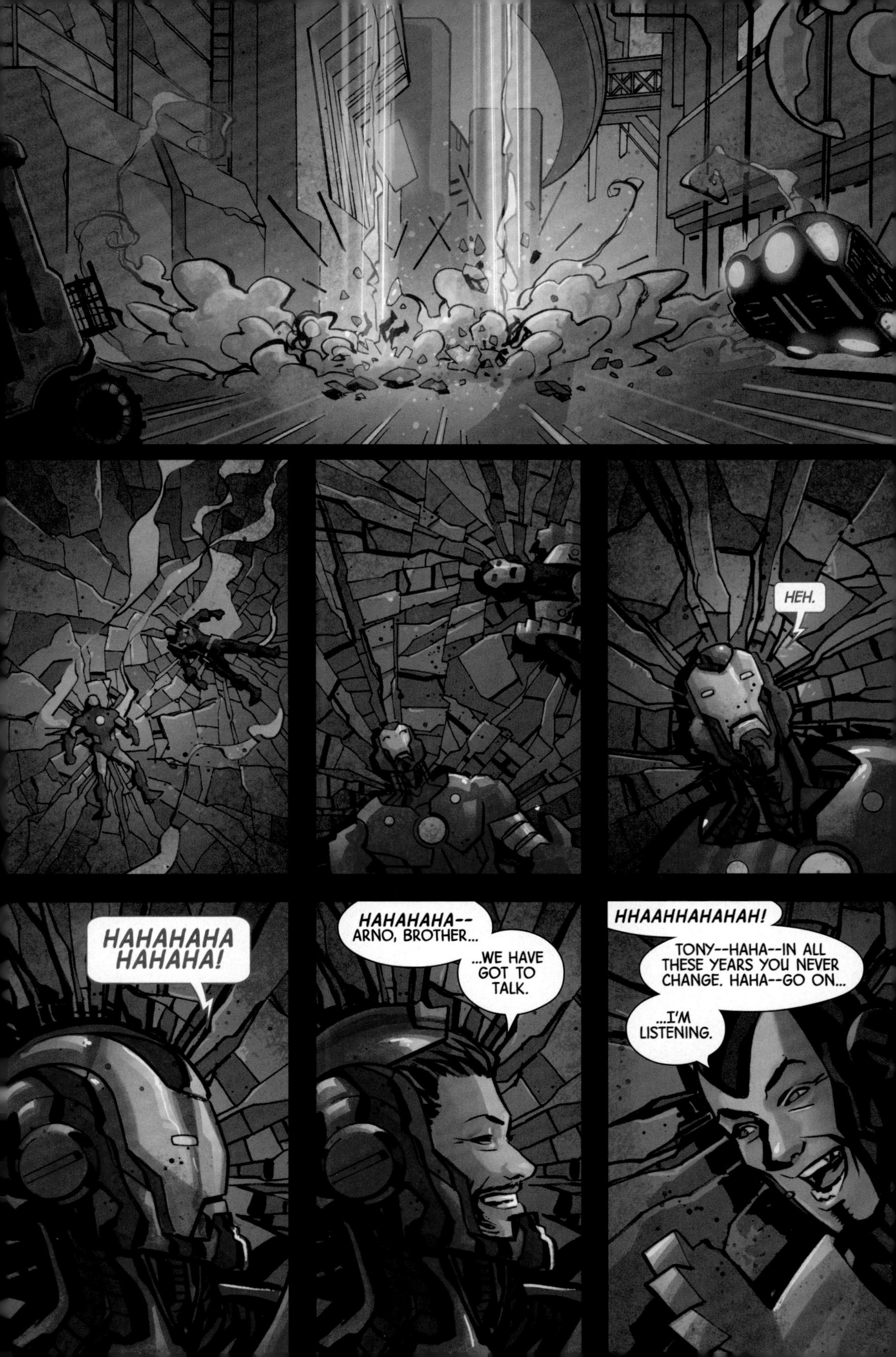
HEH.
HAHAHAHA HAHAHA!
HAHAHAHA-- ARNO, BROTHER...
...WE HAVE GOT TO TALK.
HHAAHHAHAHAH!
TONY--HAHA--IN ALL THESE YEARS YOU NEVER CHANGE. HAHA--GO ON...
...I'M LISTENING.

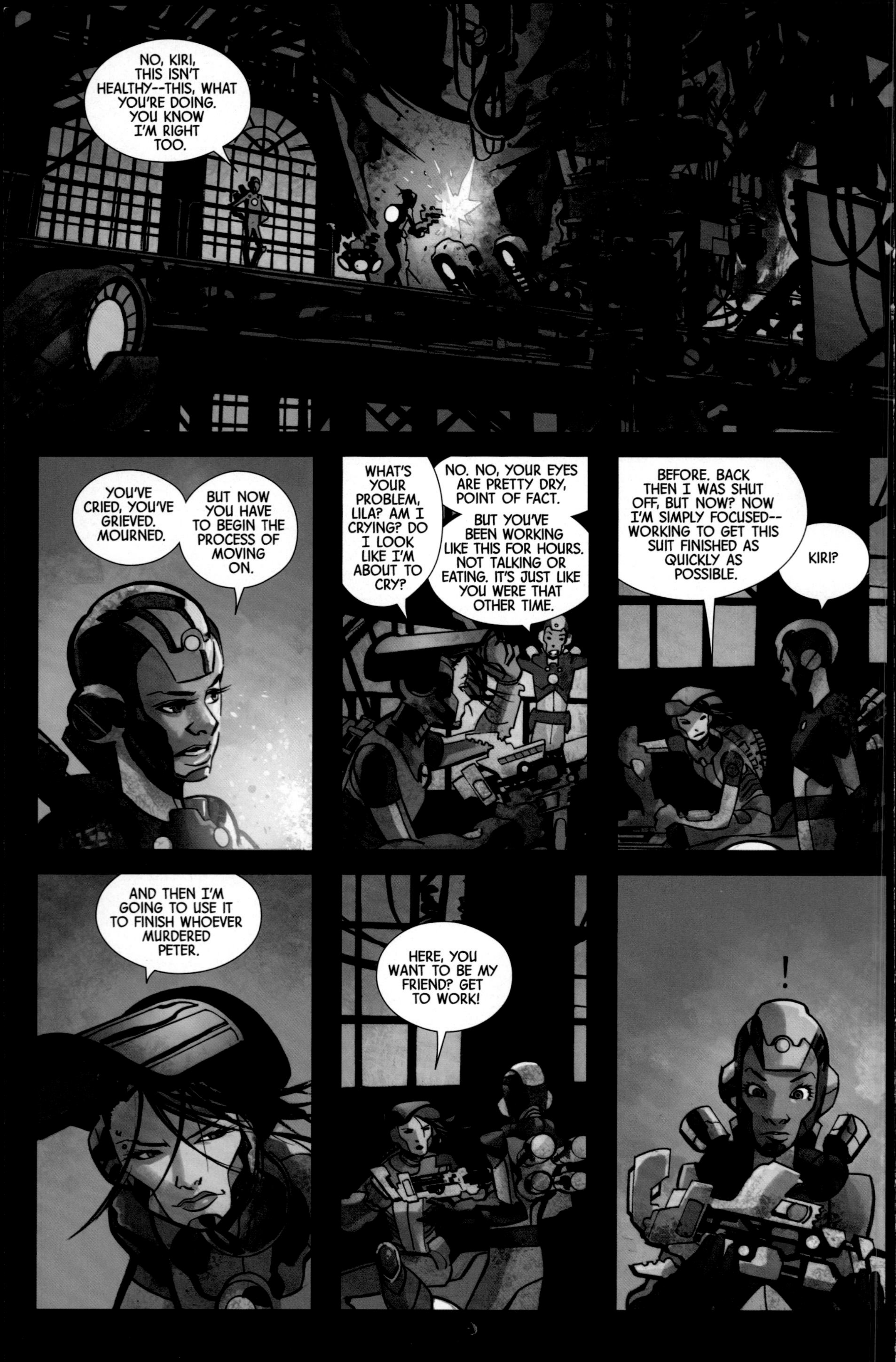
NO, KIRI, THIS ISN'T HEALTHY--THIS, WHAT YOU'RE DOING. YOU KNOW I'M RIGHT TOO.
YOU'VE CRIED, YOU'VE GRIEVED. MOURNED.
BUT NOW YOU HAVE TO BEGIN THE PROCESS OF MOVING ON.
WHAT'S YOUR PROBLEM, LILA? AM I CRYING? DO I LOOK LIKE I'M ABOUT TO CRY?
NO. NO, YOUR EYES ARE PRETTY DRY, POINT OF FACT.
BUT YOU'VE BEEN WORKING LIKE THIS FOR HOURS. NOT TALKING OR EATING. IT'S JUST LIKE YOU WERE THAT OTHER TIME.
BEFORE. BACK THEN I WAS SHUT OFF, BUT NOW? NOW I'M SIMPLY FOCUSED--WORKING TO GET THIS SUIT FINISHED AS QUICKLY AS POSSIBLE.
KIRI?
AND THEN I'M GOING TO USE IT TO FINISH WHOEVER MURDERED PETER.
HERE, YOU WANT TO BE MY FRIEND? GET TO WORK!
!

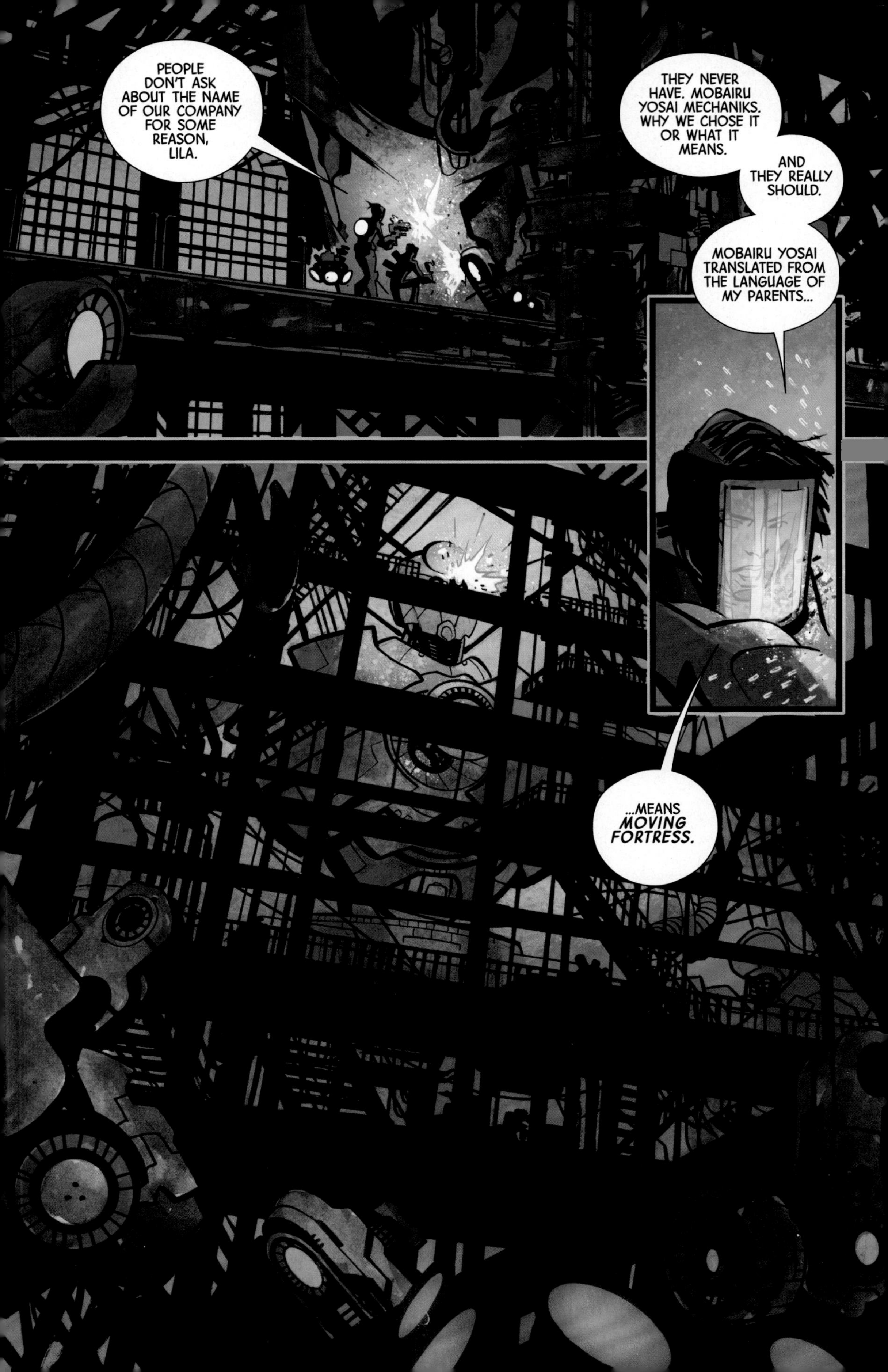
PEOPLE DON'T ASK ABOUT THE NAME OF OUR COMPANY FOR SOME REASON, LILA.
THEY NEVER HAVE. MOBAIRU YOSAI MECHANIKS. WHY WE CHOSE IT OR WHAT IT MEANS.
AND THEY REALLY SHOULD.
MOBAIRU YOSAI TRANSLATED FROM THE LANGUAGE OF MY PARENTS...
...MEANS *MOVING FORTRESS.*

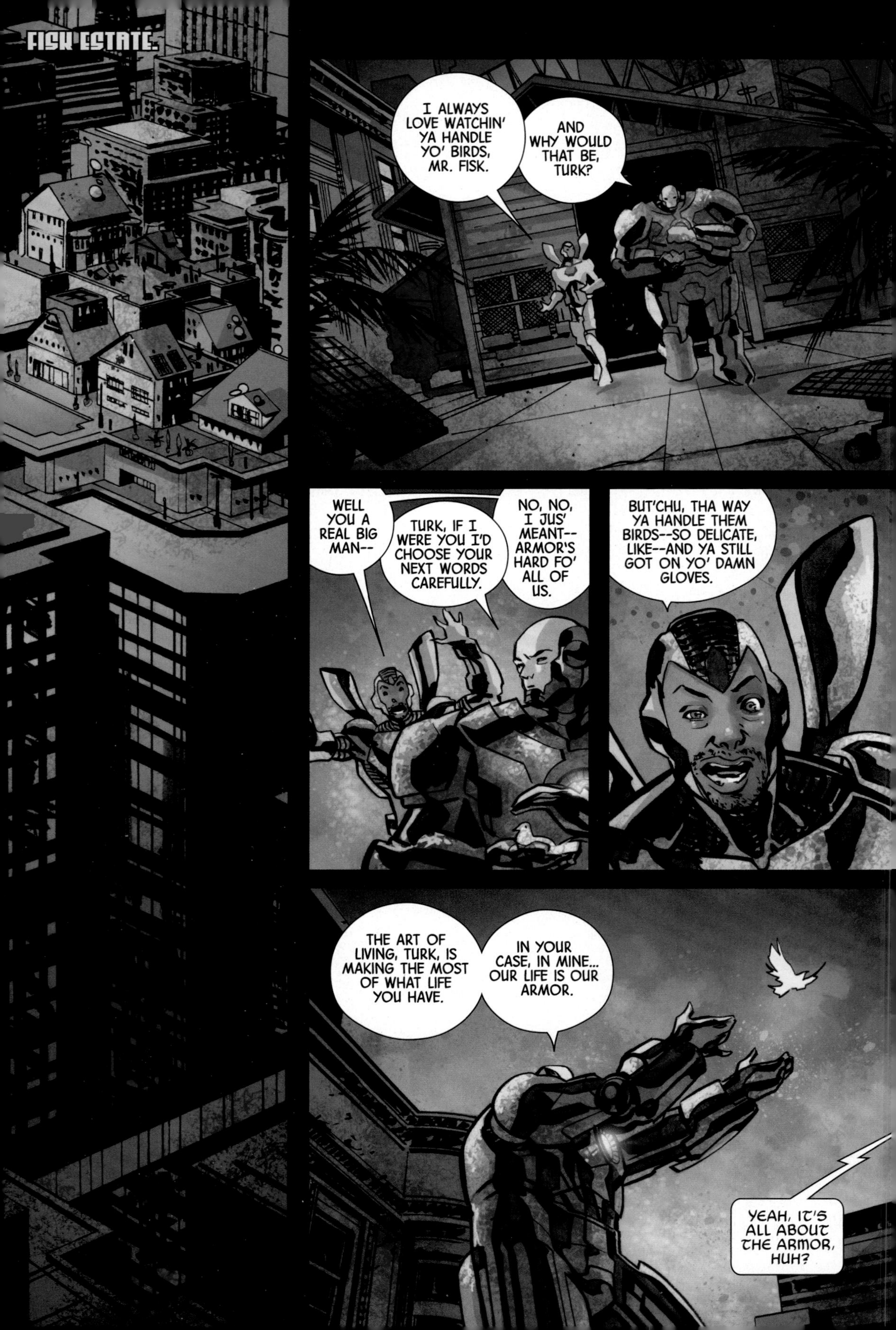
FISK ESTATE.
I ALWAYS LOVE WATCHIN' YA HANDLE YO' BIRDS, MR. FISK.
AND WHY WOULD THAT BE, TURK?
WELL YOU A REAL BIG MAN--
TURK, IF I WERE YOU I'D CHOOSE YOUR NEXT WORDS CAREFULLY.
NO, NO, I JUS' MEANT--ARMOR'S HARD FO' ALL OF US.
BUT'CHU, THA WAY YA HANDLE THEM BIRDS--SO DELICATE, LIKE--AND YA STILL GOT ON YO' DAMN GLOVES.
THE ART OF LIVING, TURK, IS MAKING THE MOST OF WHAT LIFE YOU HAVE.
IN YOUR CASE, IN MINE... OUR LIFE IS OUR ARMOR.
YEAH, IT'S ALL ABOUT THE ARMOR, HUH?

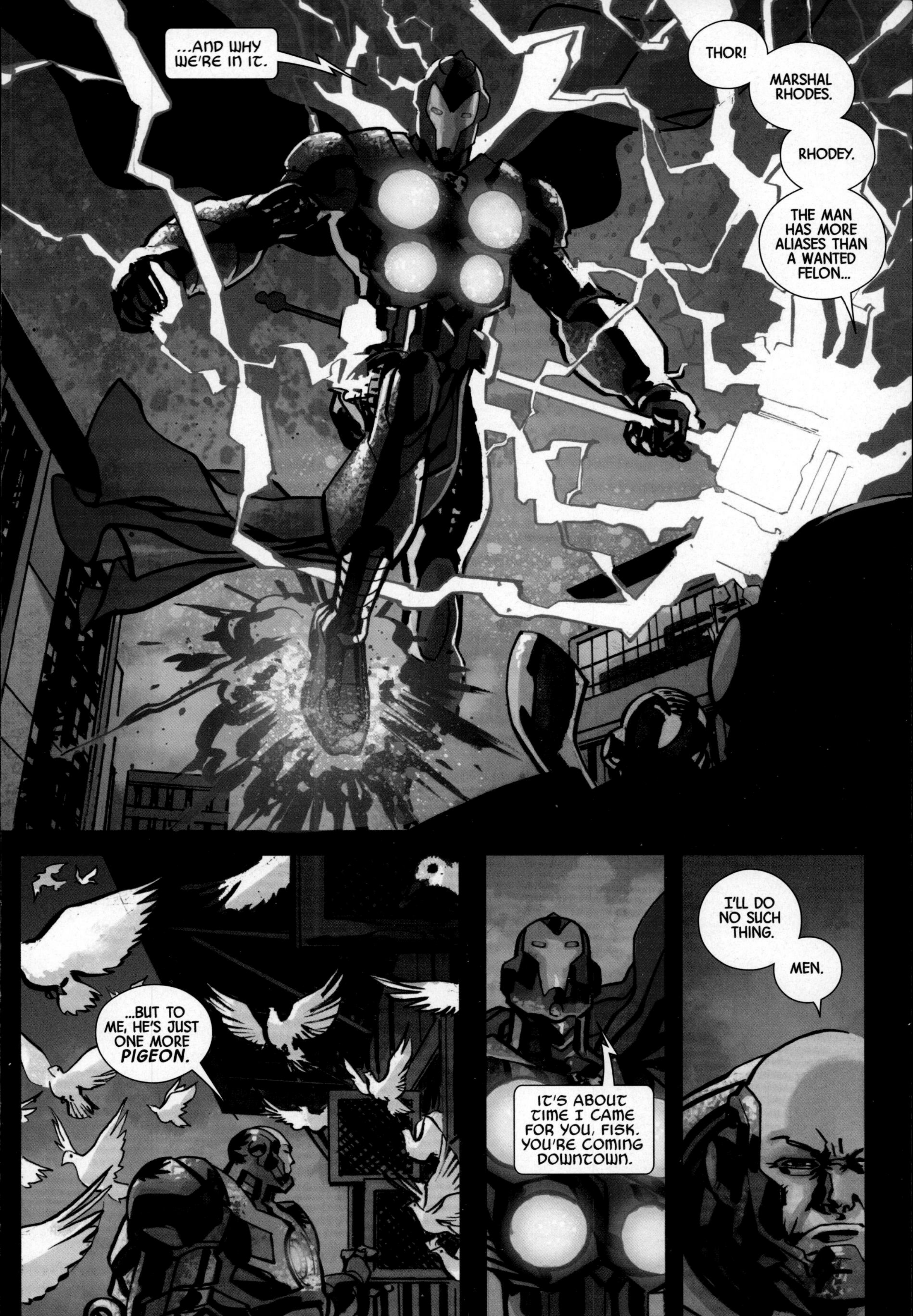

...AND WHY WE'RE IN IT.
THOR!
MARSHAL RHODES.
RHODEY.
THE MAN HAS MORE ALIASES THAN A WANTED FELON...
...BUT TO ME, HE'S JUST ONE MORE PIGEON.
IT'S ABOUT TIME I CAME FOR YOU, FISK. YOU'RE COMING DOWNTOWN.
I'LL DO NO SUCH THING.
MEN.

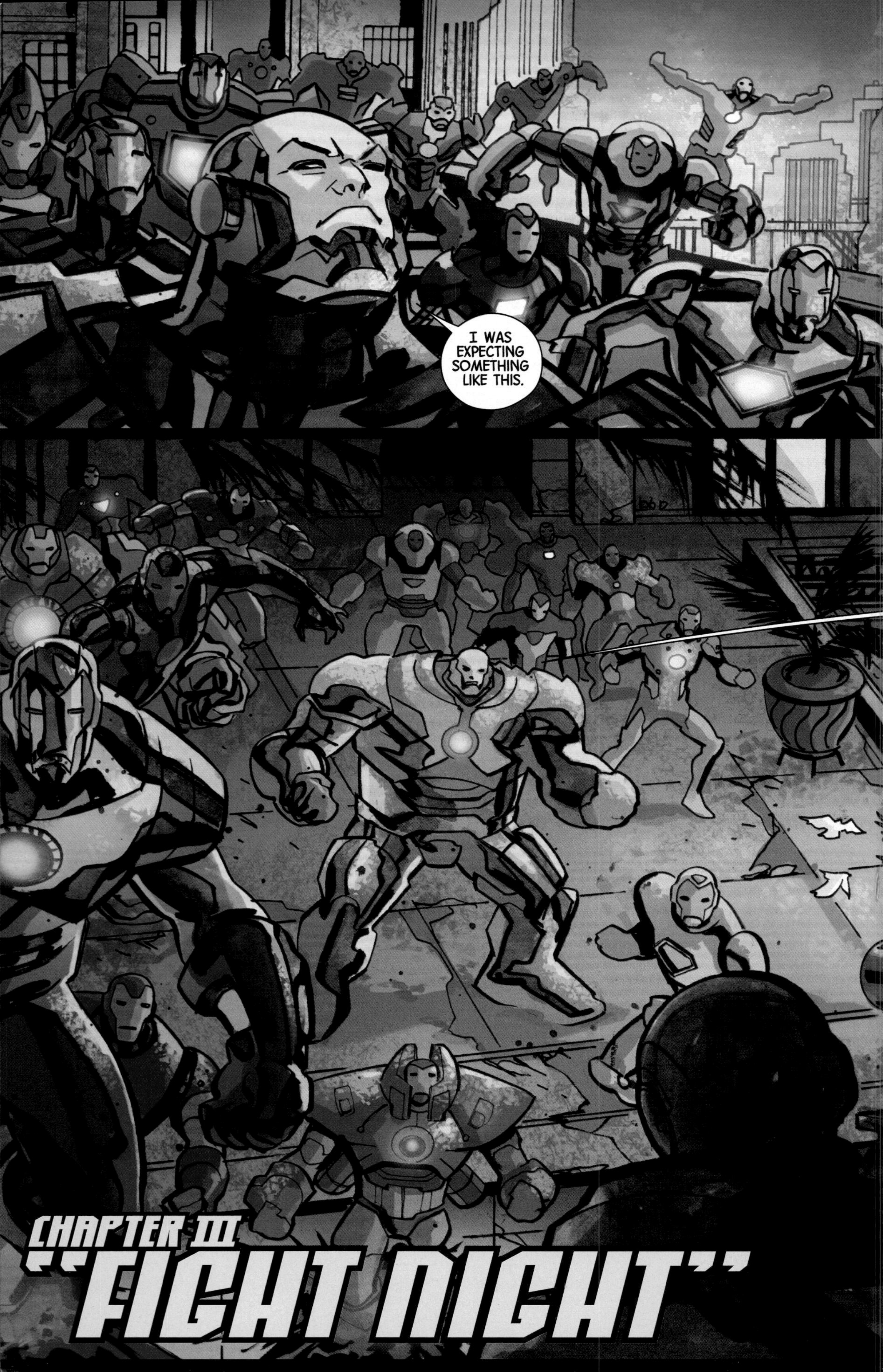
I WAS EXPECTING SOMETHING LIKE THIS.
CHAPTER III
"FIGHT NIGHT"

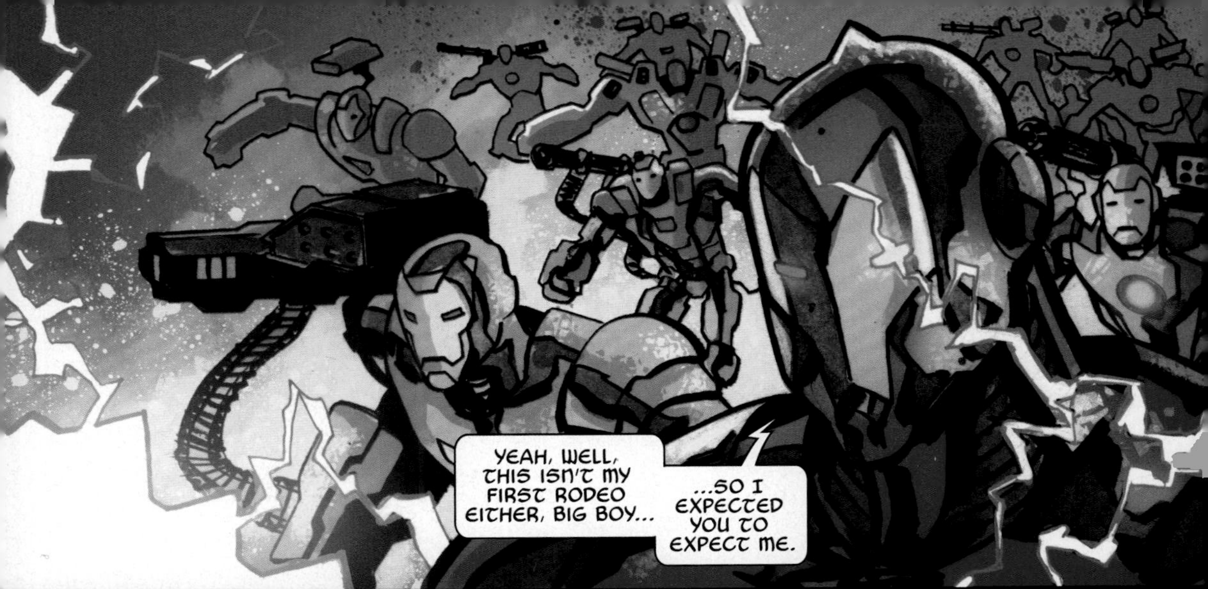
YEAH, WELL, THIS ISN'T MY FIRST RODEO EITHER, BIG BOY...
...SO I EXPECTED YOU TO EXPECT ME.

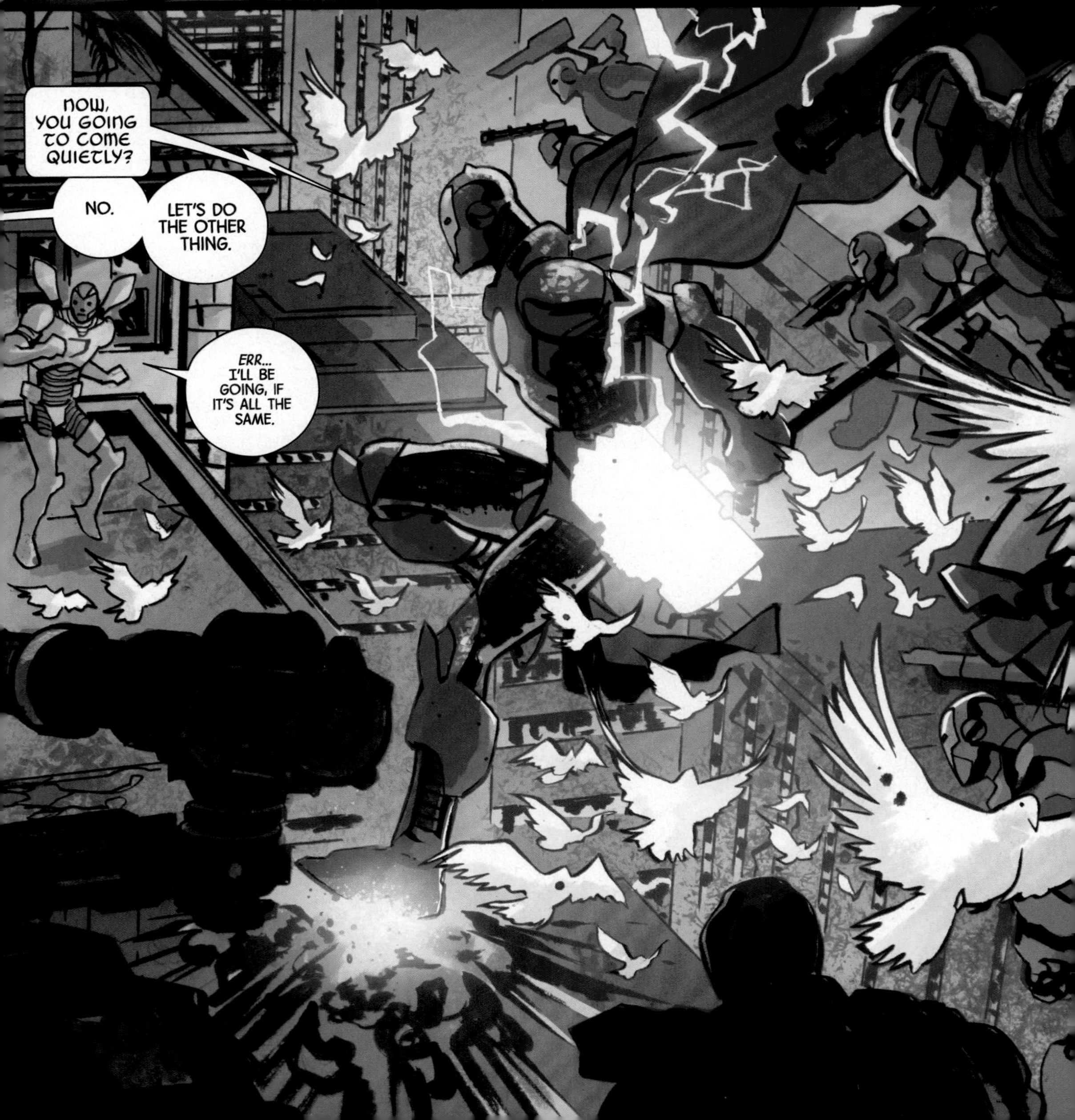
NOW, YOU GOING TO COME QUIETLY?
NO.
LET'S DO THE OTHER THING.
ERR... I'LL BE GOING, IF IT'S ALL THE SAME.

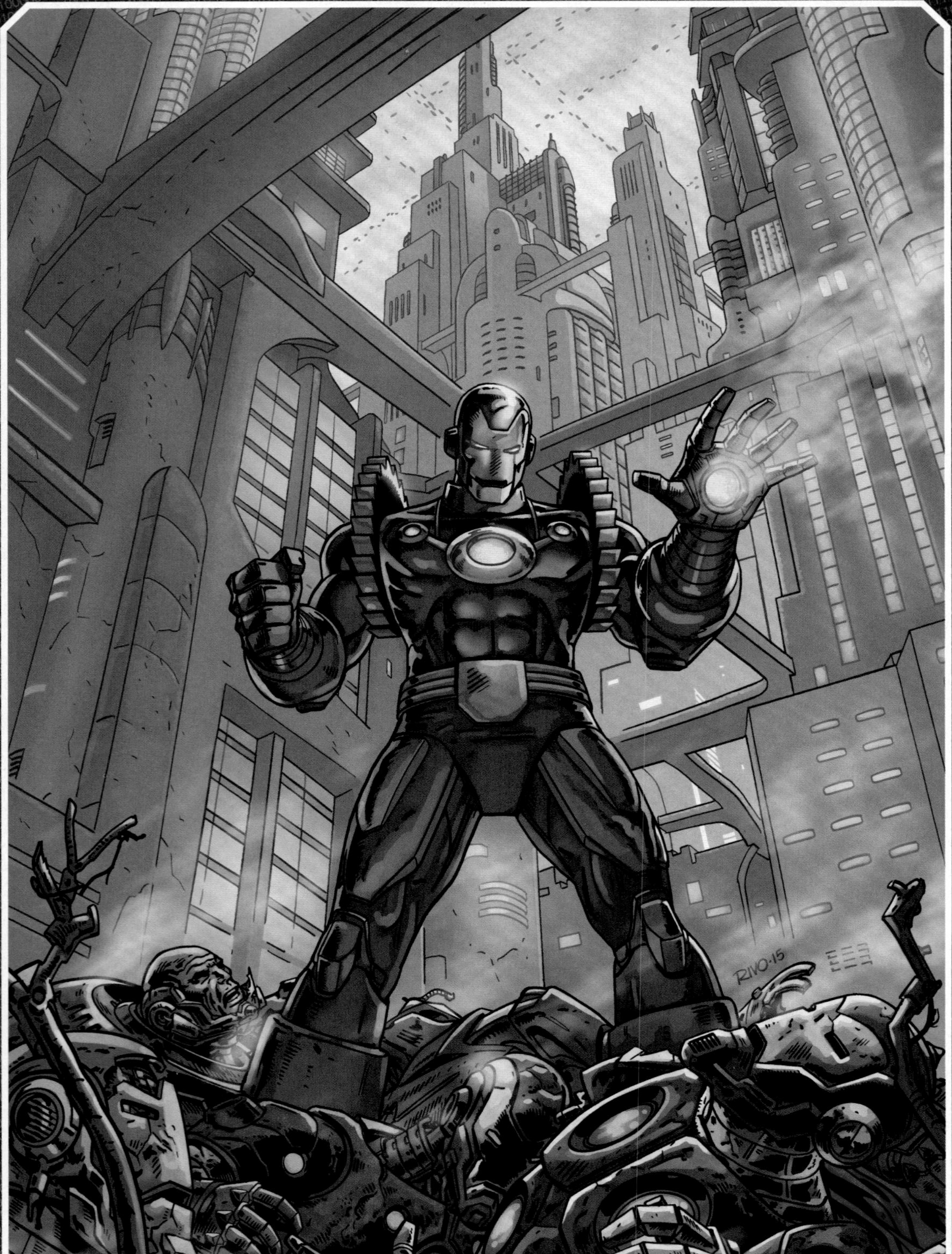
RIVO·15

4

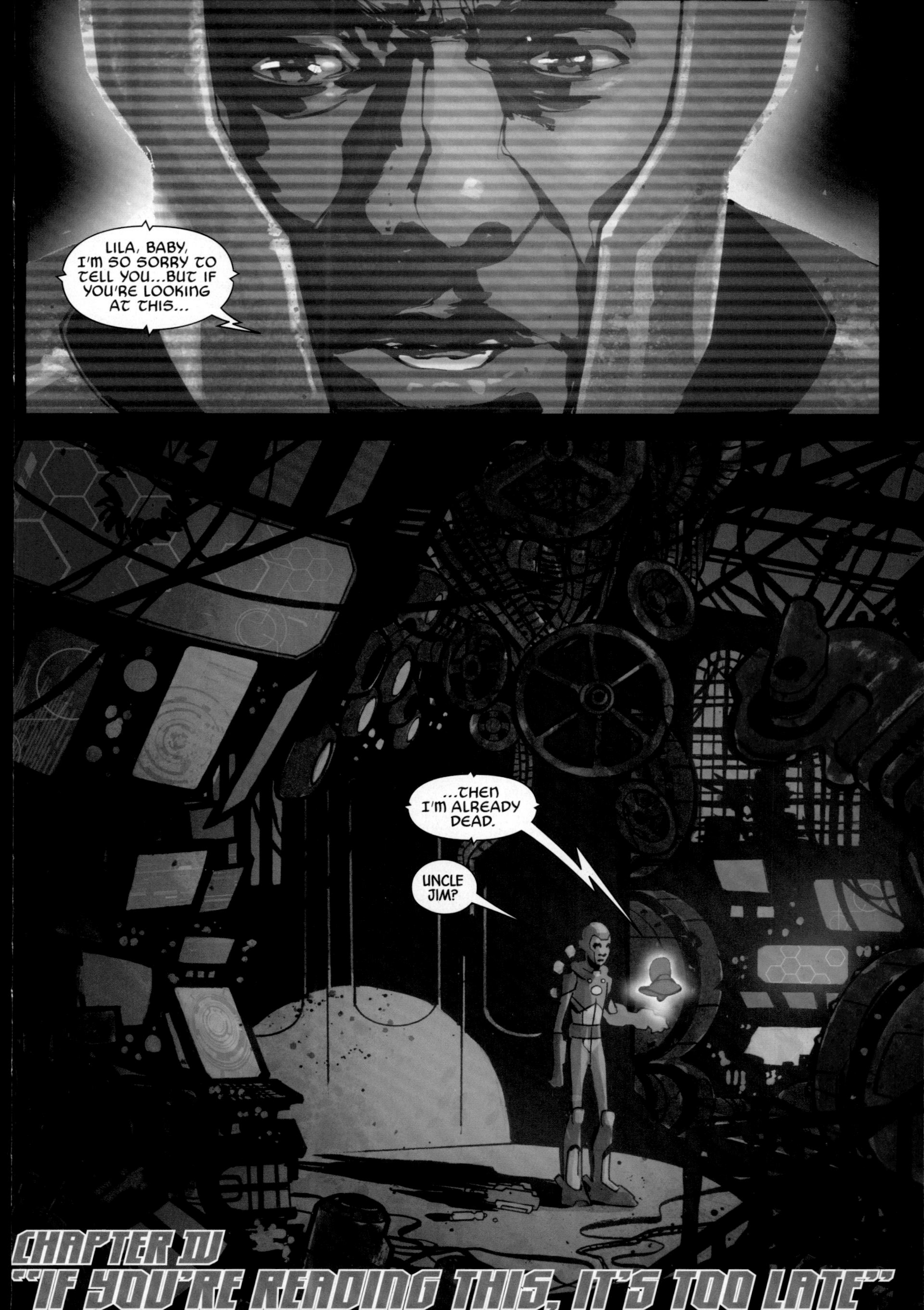
LILA, BABY, I'M SO SORRY TO TELL YOU...BUT IF YOU'RE LOOKING AT THIS...
...THEN I'M ALREADY DEAD.
UNCLE JIM?
CHAPTER IV
"IF YOU'RE READING THIS, IT'S TOO LATE"

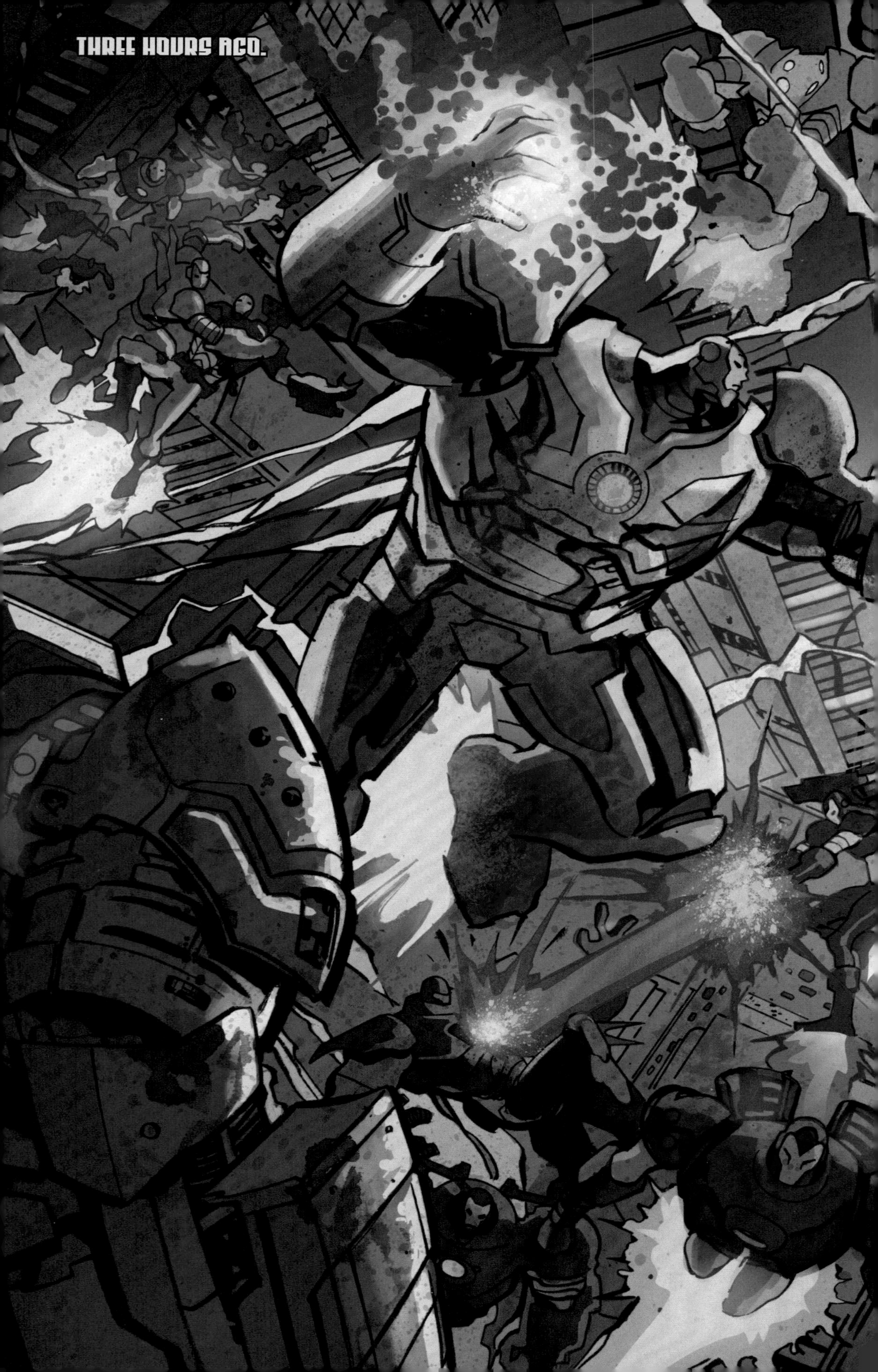
THREE HOURS AGO.

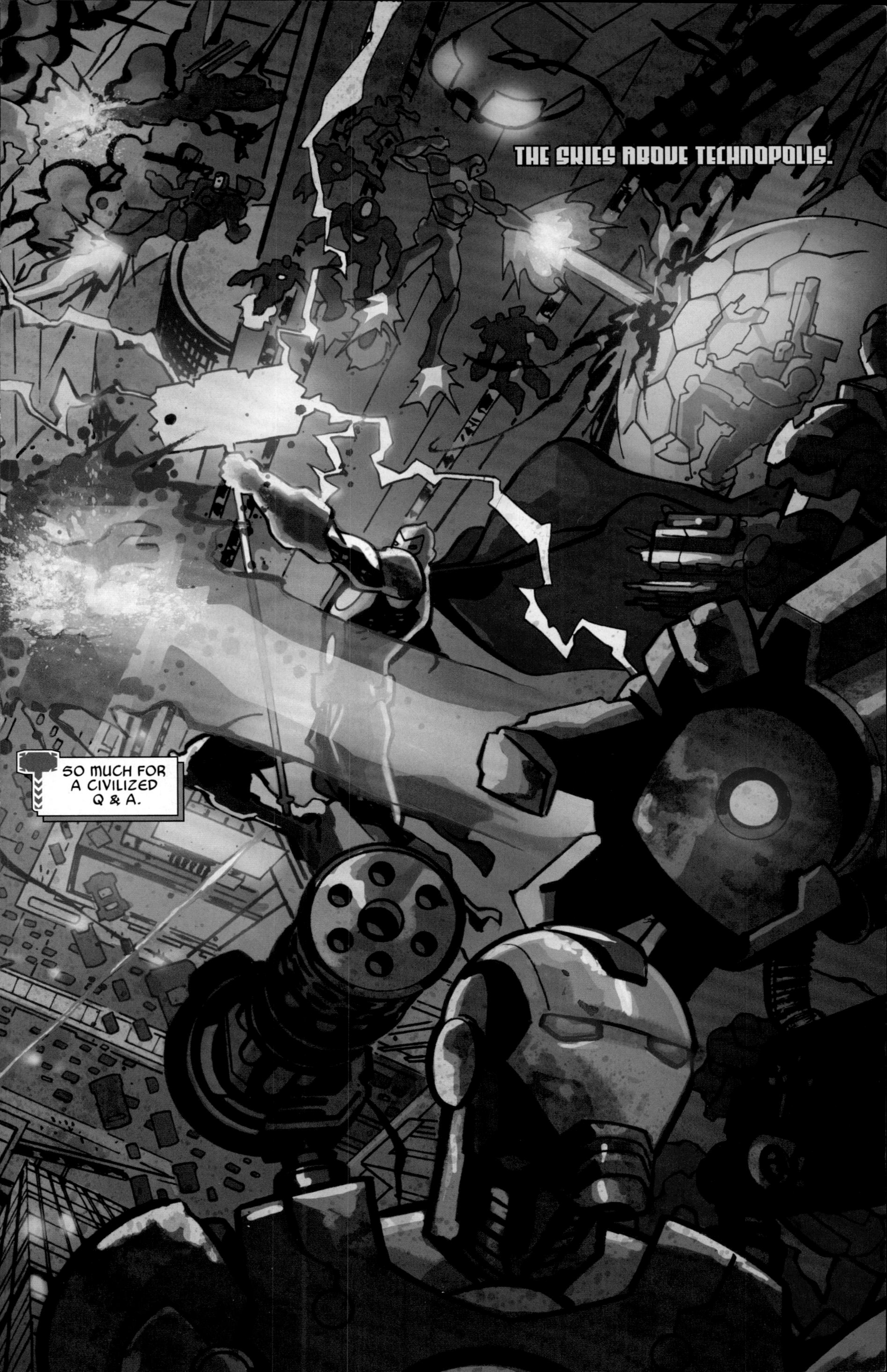
THE SKIES ABOVE TECHNOPOLIS.
SO MUCH FOR A CIVILIZED Q & A.

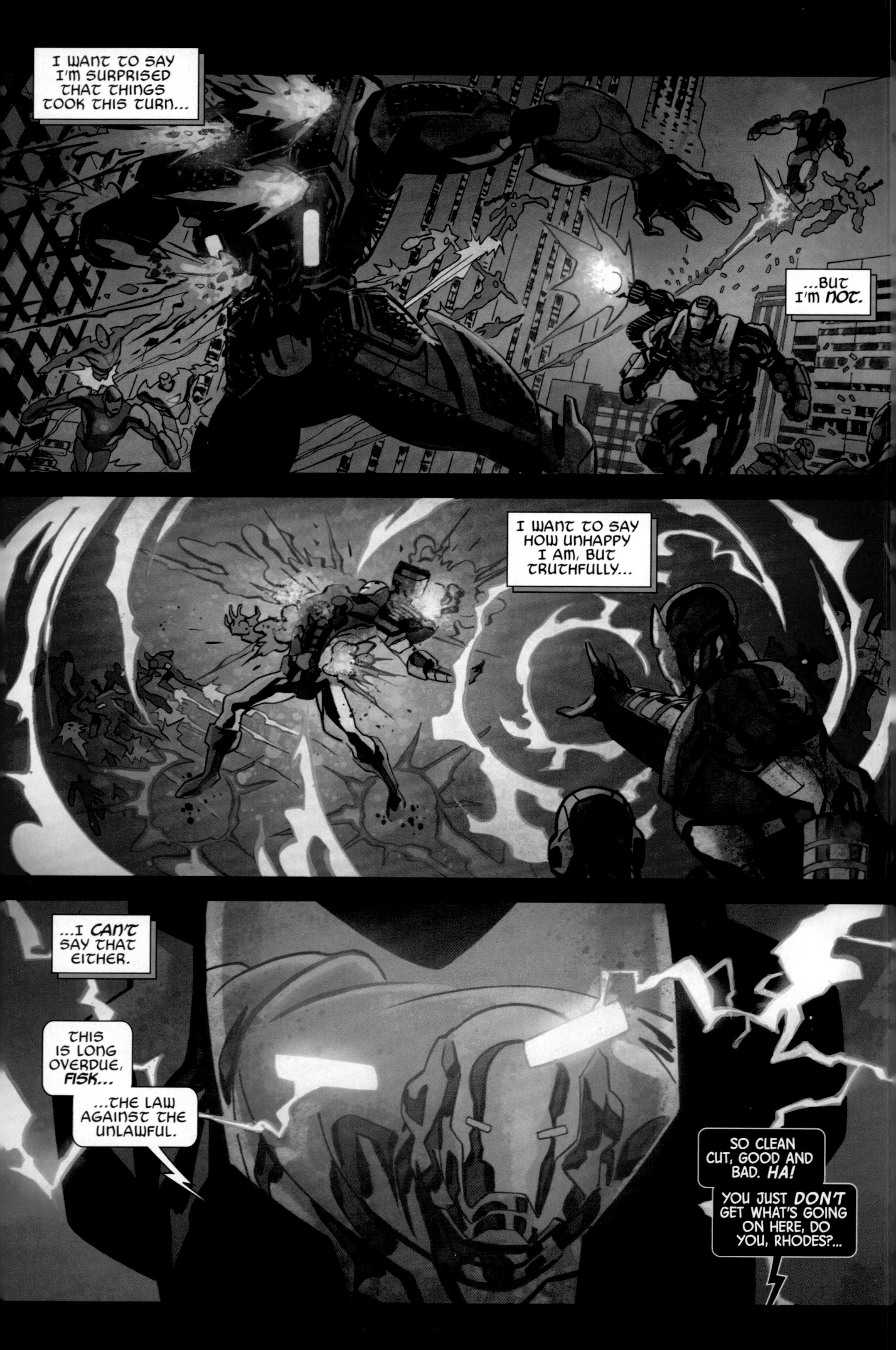
I WANT TO SAY I'M SURPRISED THAT THINGS TOOK THIS TURN...
...BUT I'M NOT.
I WANT TO SAY HOW UNHAPPY I AM, BUT TRUTHFULLY...
...I CAN'T SAY THAT EITHER.
THIS IS LONG OVERDUE, FISK...
...THE LAW AGAINST THE UNLAWFUL.
SO CLEAN CUT, GOOD AND BAD. HA!
YOU JUST DON'T GET WHAT'S GOING ON HERE, DO YOU, RHODES?...

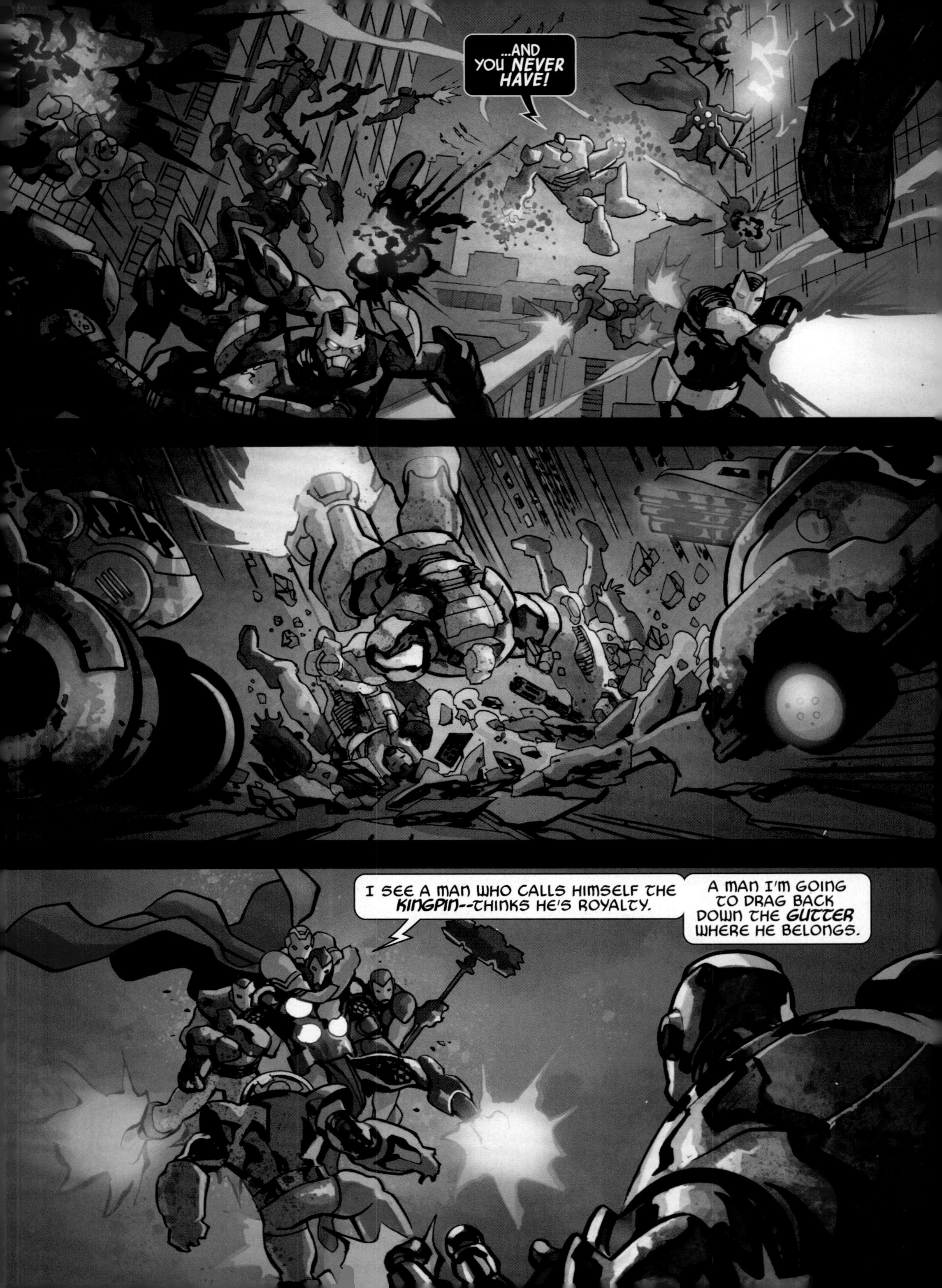
...AND YOU NEVER HAVE!
I SEE A MAN WHO CALLS HIMSELF THE KINGPIN--THINKS HE'S ROYALTY.
A MAN I'M GOING TO DRAG BACK DOWN THE GUTTER WHERE HE BELONGS.

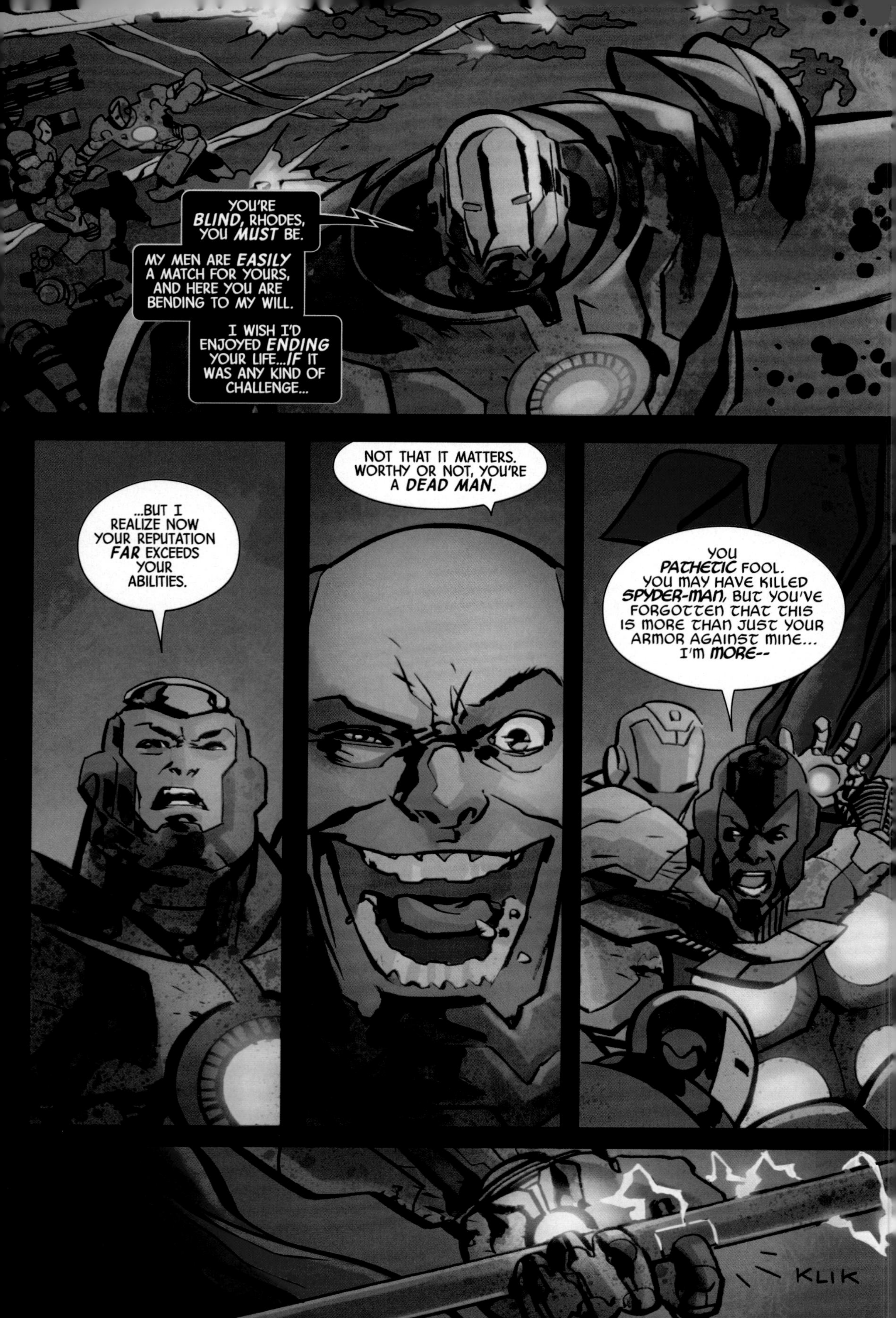
YOU'RE BLIND, RHODES, YOU MUST BE.
MY MEN ARE EASILY A MATCH FOR YOURS, AND HERE YOU ARE BENDING TO MY WILL.
I WISH I'D ENJOYED ENDING YOUR LIFE...IF IT WAS ANY KIND OF CHALLENGE...
...BUT I REALIZE NOW YOUR REPUTATION FAR EXCEEDS YOUR ABILITIES.
NOT THAT IT MATTERS. WORTHY OR NOT, YOU'RE A DEAD MAN.
YOU PATHETIC FOOL. YOU MAY HAVE KILLED SPYDER-MAN, BUT YOU'VE FORGOTTEN THAT THIS IS MORE THAN JUST YOUR ARMOR AGAINST MINE... I'M MORE--
KLIK

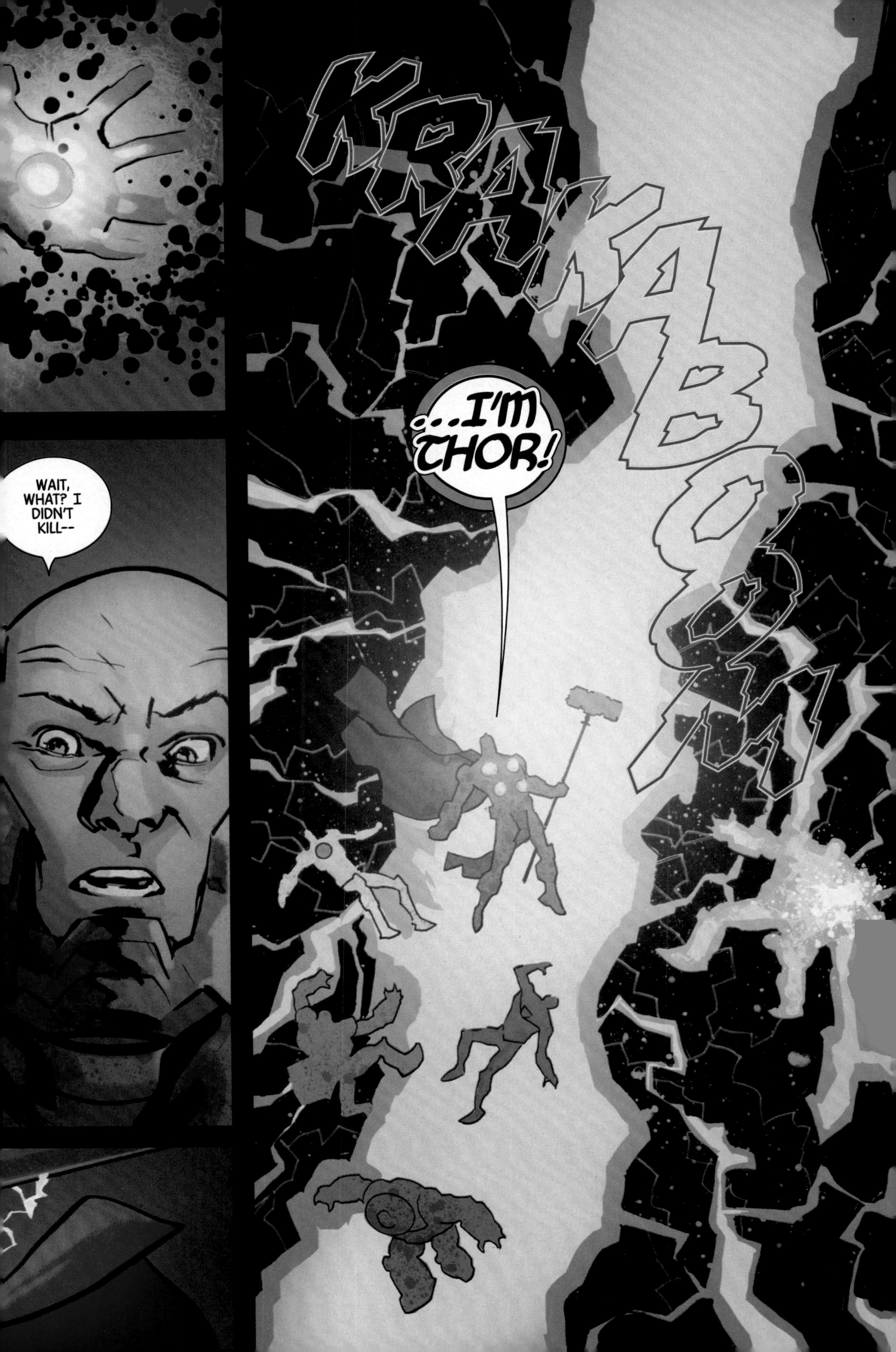
WAIT, WHAT? I DIDN'T KILL--
KRAKABOOM
...I'M THOR!

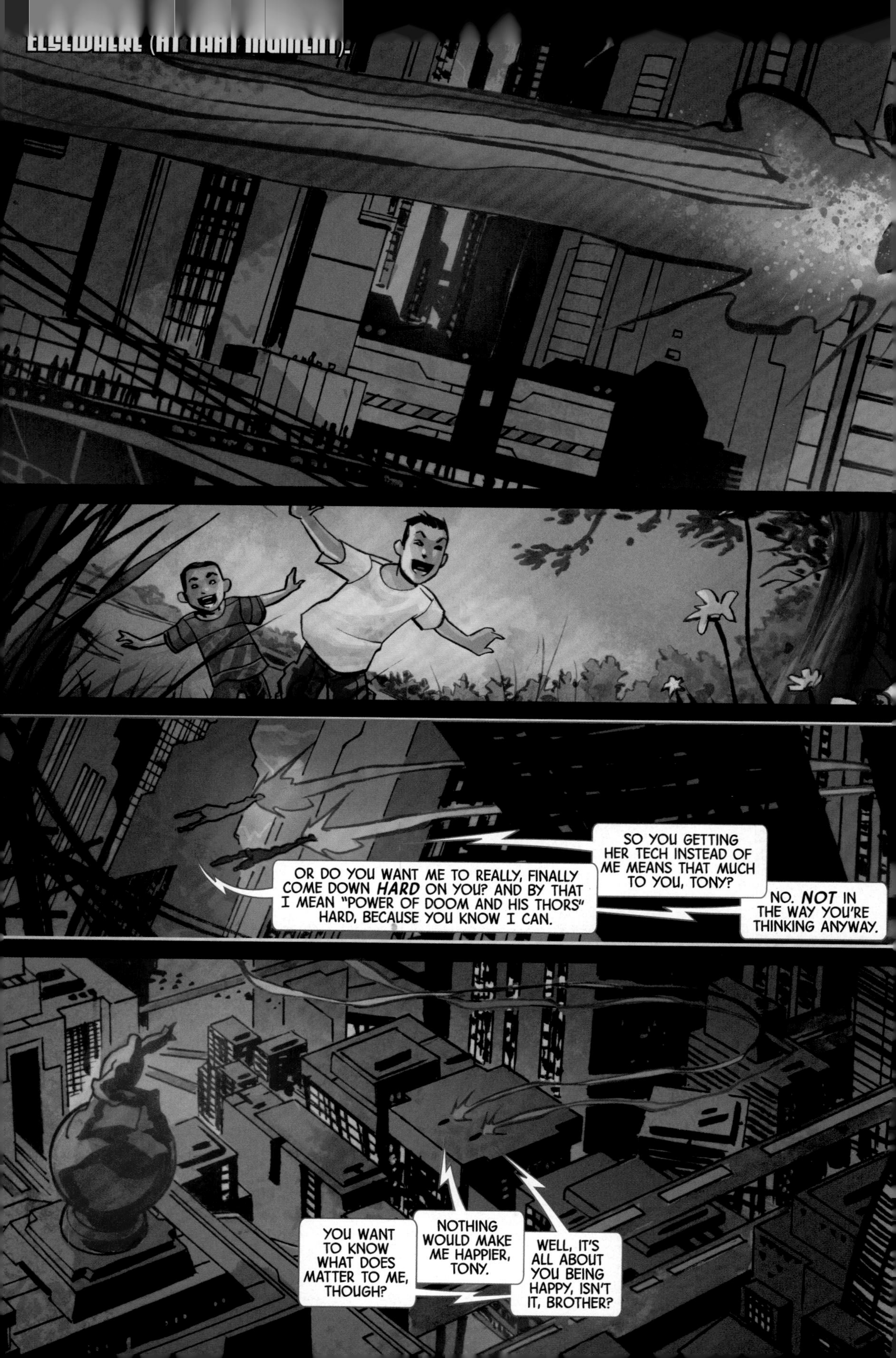
ELSEWHERE (AT THAT MOMENT).
SO YOU GETTING HER TECH INSTEAD OF ME MEANS THAT MUCH TO YOU, TONY?
NO. *NOT* IN THE WAY YOU'RE THINKING ANYWAY.
OR DO YOU WANT ME TO REALLY, FINALLY COME DOWN *HARD* ON YOU? AND BY THAT I MEAN "POWER OF DOOM AND HIS THORS" HARD, BECAUSE YOU KNOW I CAN.
YOU WANT TO KNOW WHAT DOES MATTER TO ME, THOUGH?
NOTHING WOULD MAKE ME HAPPIER, TONY.
WELL, IT'S ALL ABOUT YOU BEING HAPPY, ISN'T IT, BROTHER?

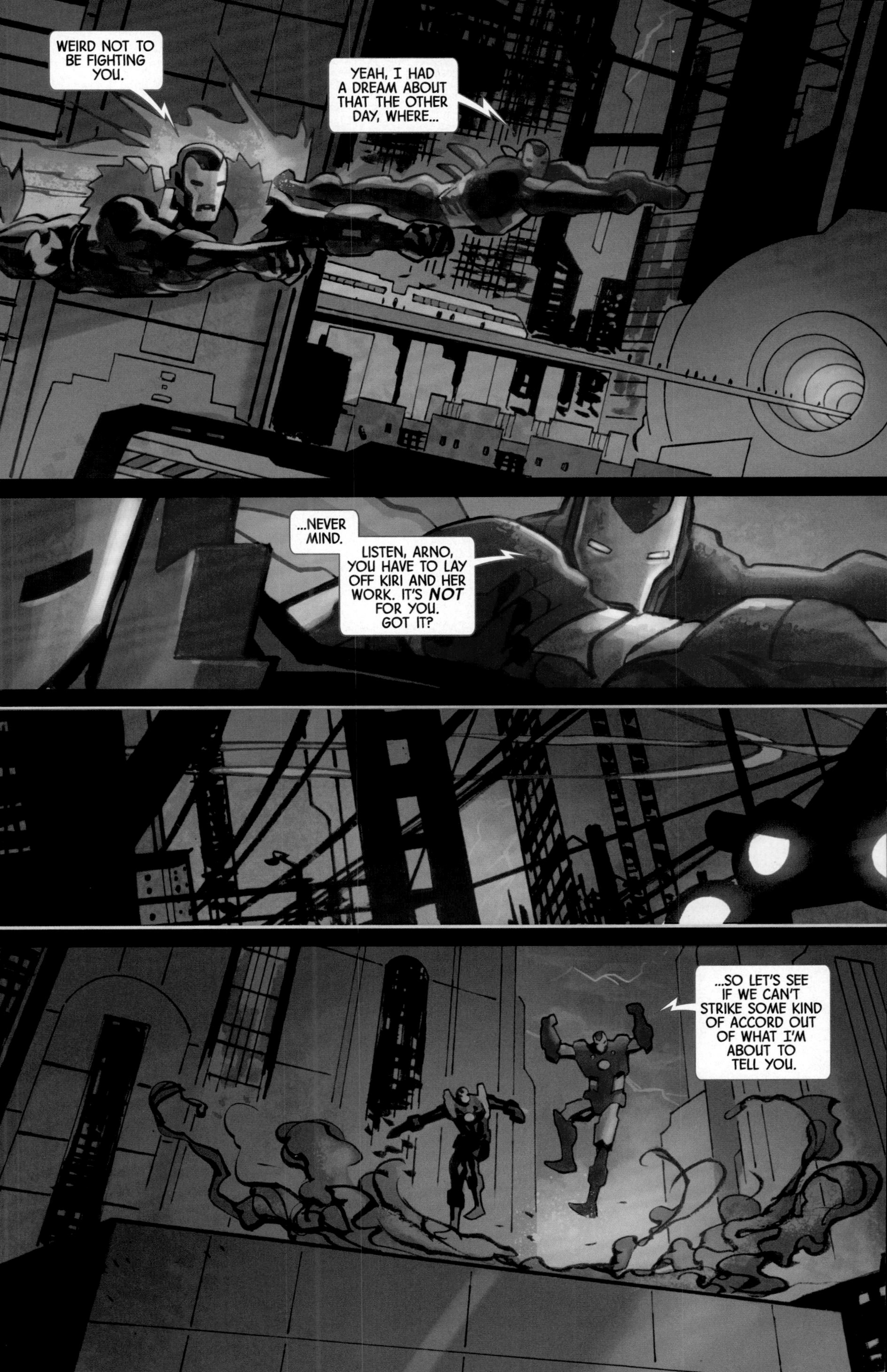
WEIRD NOT TO BE FIGHTING YOU.
YEAH, I HAD A DREAM ABOUT THAT THE OTHER DAY, WHERE...
...NEVER MIND.
LISTEN, ARNO, YOU HAVE TO LAY OFF KIRI AND HER WORK. IT'S *NOT* FOR YOU. GOT IT?
...SO LET'S SEE IF WE CAN'T STRIKE SOME KIND OF ACCORD OUT OF WHAT I'M ABOUT TO TELL YOU.

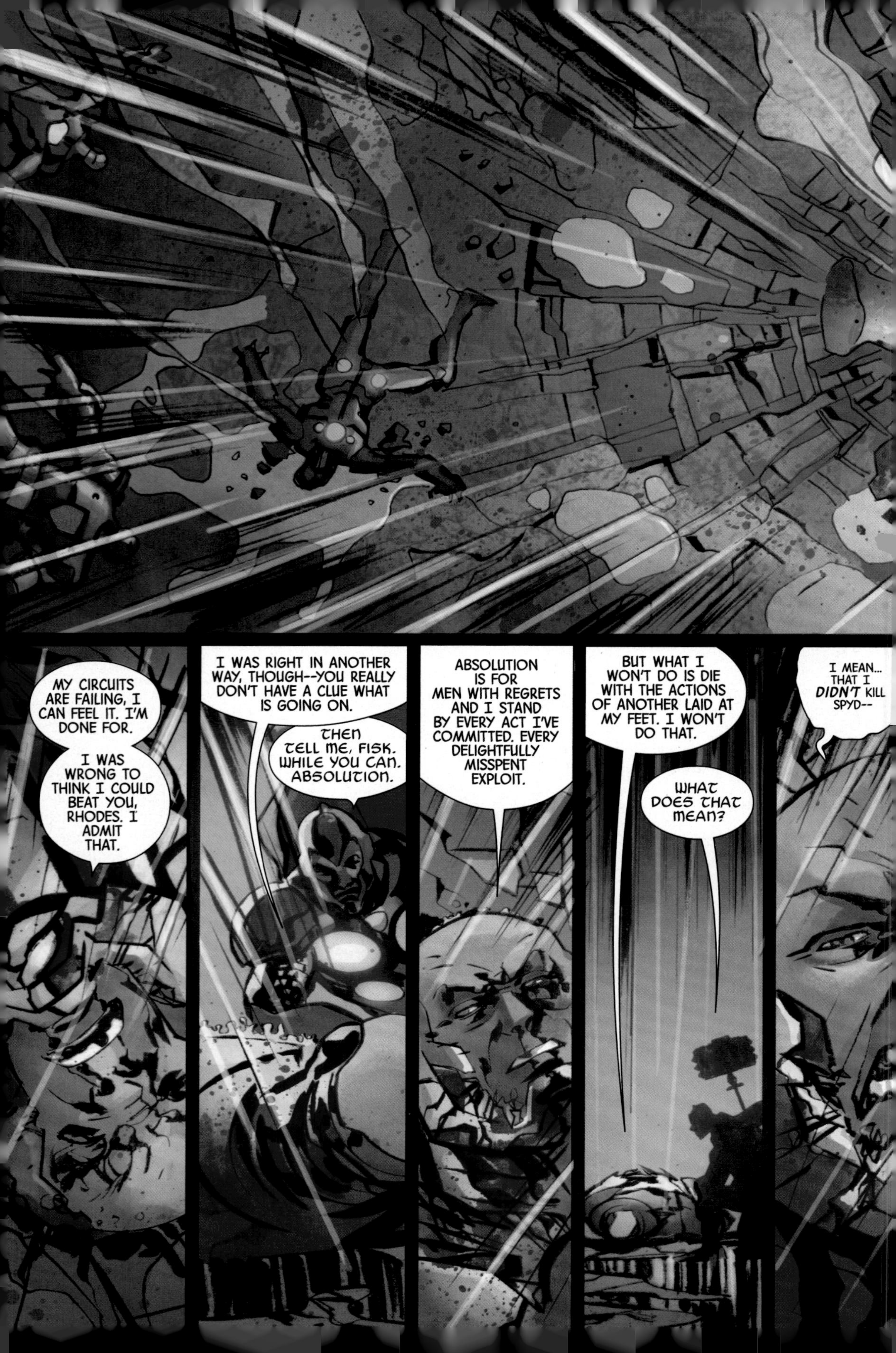
MY CIRCUITS ARE FAILING, I CAN FEEL IT. I'M DONE FOR.
I WAS WRONG TO THINK I COULD BEAT YOU, RHODES. I ADMIT THAT.
I WAS RIGHT IN ANOTHER WAY, THOUGH--YOU REALLY DON'T HAVE A CLUE WHAT IS GOING ON.
THEN TELL ME, FISK. WHILE YOU CAN. ABSOLUTION.
ABSOLUTION IS FOR MEN WITH REGRETS AND I STAND BY EVERY ACT I'VE COMMITTED. EVERY DELIGHTFULLY MISSPENT EXPLOIT.
BUT WHAT I WON'T DO IS DIE WITH THE ACTIONS OF ANOTHER LAID AT MY FEET. I WON'T DO THAT.
WHAT DOES THAT MEAN?
I MEAN... THAT I *DIDN'T* KILL SPYD--

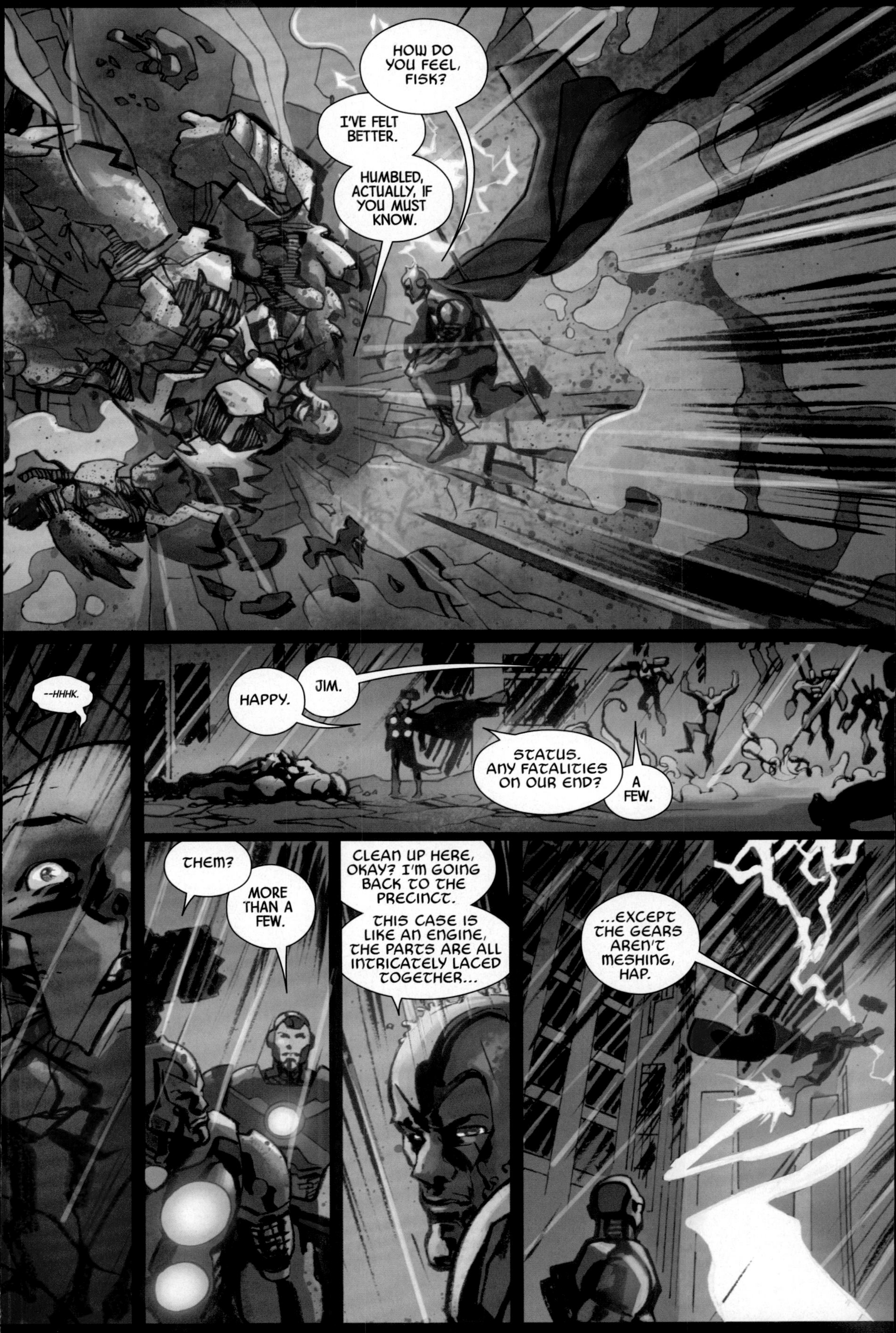
HOW DO YOU FEEL, FISK?
I'VE FELT BETTER.
HUMBLED, ACTUALLY, IF YOU MUST KNOW.
--HHHK.
JIM.
HAPPY.
STATUS. ANY FATALITIES ON OUR END?
A FEW.
THEM?
MORE THAN A FEW.
CLEAN UP HERE, OKAY? I'M GOING BACK TO THE PRECINCT.
THIS CASE IS LIKE AN ENGINE, THE PARTS ARE ALL INTRICATELY LACED TOGETHER...
...EXCEPT THE GEARS AREN'T MESHING, HAP.

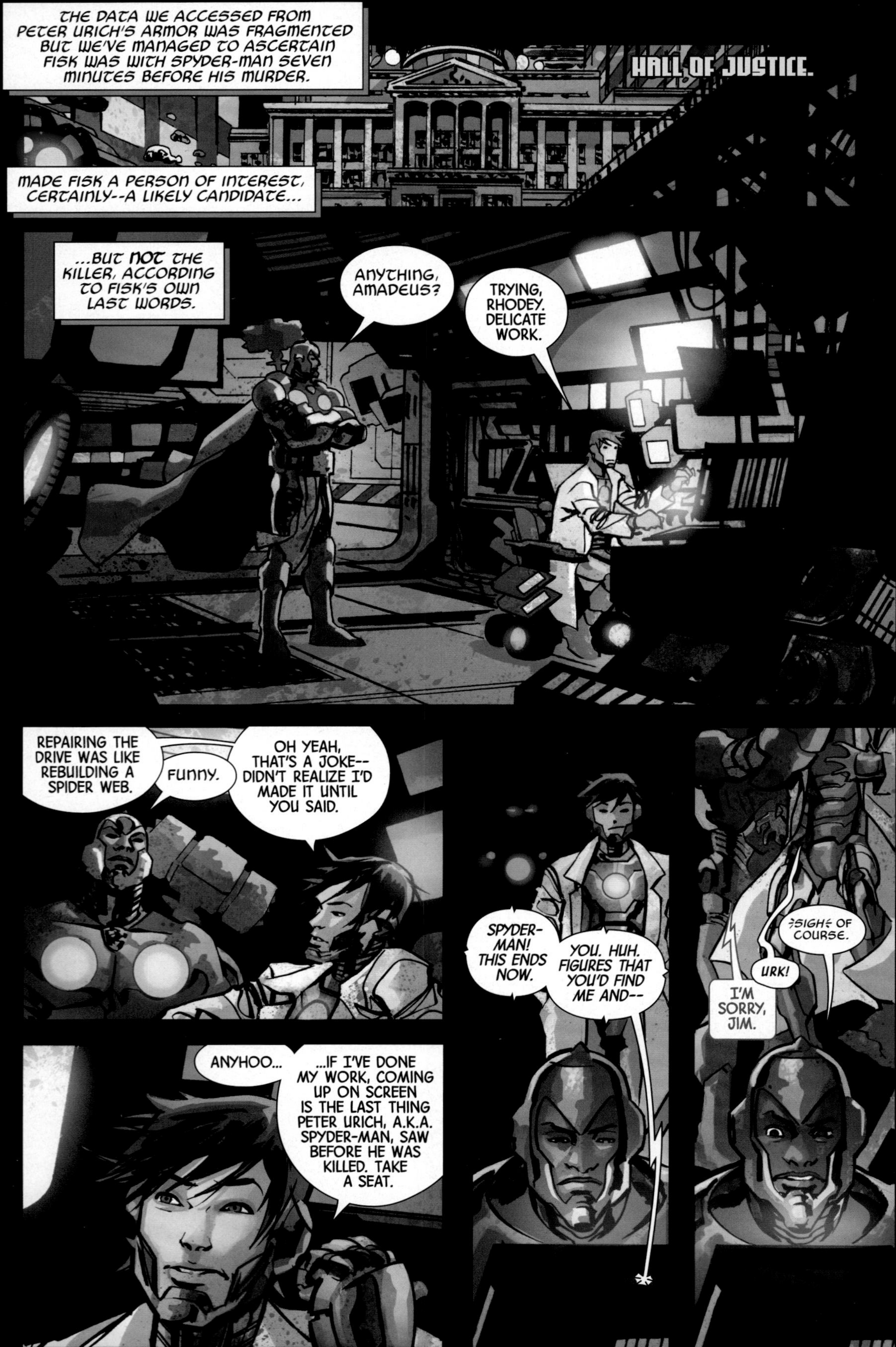
THE DATA WE ACCESSED FROM PETER URICH'S ARMOR WAS FRAGMENTED BUT WE'VE MANAGED TO ASCERTAIN FISK WAS WITH SPYDER-MAN SEVEN MINUTES BEFORE HIS MURDER.
HALL OF JUSTICE.
MADE FISK A PERSON OF INTEREST, CERTAINLY--A LIKELY CANDIDATE...
...BUT NOT THE KILLER, ACCORDING TO FISK'S OWN LAST WORDS.
ANYTHING, AMADEUS?
TRYING, RHODEY. DELICATE WORK.
REPAIRING THE DRIVE WAS LIKE REBUILDING A SPIDER WEB.
FUNNY.
OH YEAH, THAT'S A JOKE--DIDN'T REALIZE I'D MADE IT UNTIL YOU SAID.
ANYHOO...
...IF I'VE DONE MY WORK, COMING UP ON SCREEN IS THE LAST THING PETER URICH, A.K.A. SPYDER-MAN, SAW BEFORE HE WAS KILLED. TAKE A SEAT.
SPYDER-MAN! THIS ENDS NOW.
YOU. HUH. FIGURES THAT YOU'D FIND ME AND--
URK!
I'M SORRY, JIM.
=SIGH= OF COURSE.

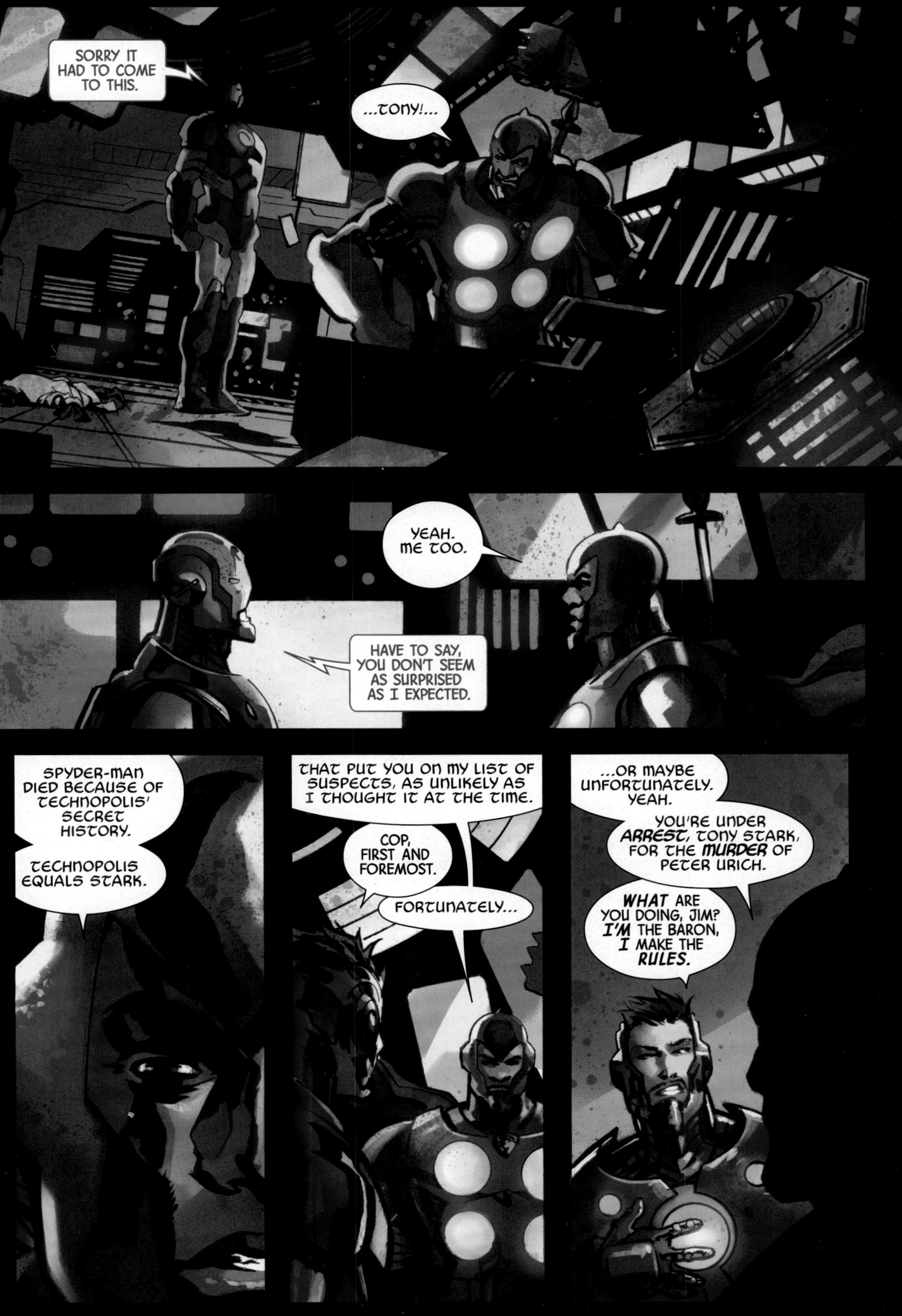
SORRY IT HAD TO COME TO THIS.
...TONY!...
YEAH. ME TOO.
HAVE TO SAY, YOU DON'T SEEM AS SURPRISED AS I EXPECTED.
SPYDER-MAN DIED BECAUSE OF TECHNOPOLIS' SECRET HISTORY.
TECHNOPOLIS EQUALS STARK.
THAT PUT YOU ON MY LIST OF SUSPECTS, AS UNLIKELY AS I THOUGHT IT AT THE TIME.
COP, FIRST AND FOREMOST.
FORTUNATELY...
...OR MAYBE UNFORTUNATELY. YEAH.
YOU'RE UNDER ARREST, TONY STARK, FOR THE MURDER OF PETER URICH.
WHAT ARE YOU DOING, JIM? I'M THE BARON, I MAKE THE RULES.

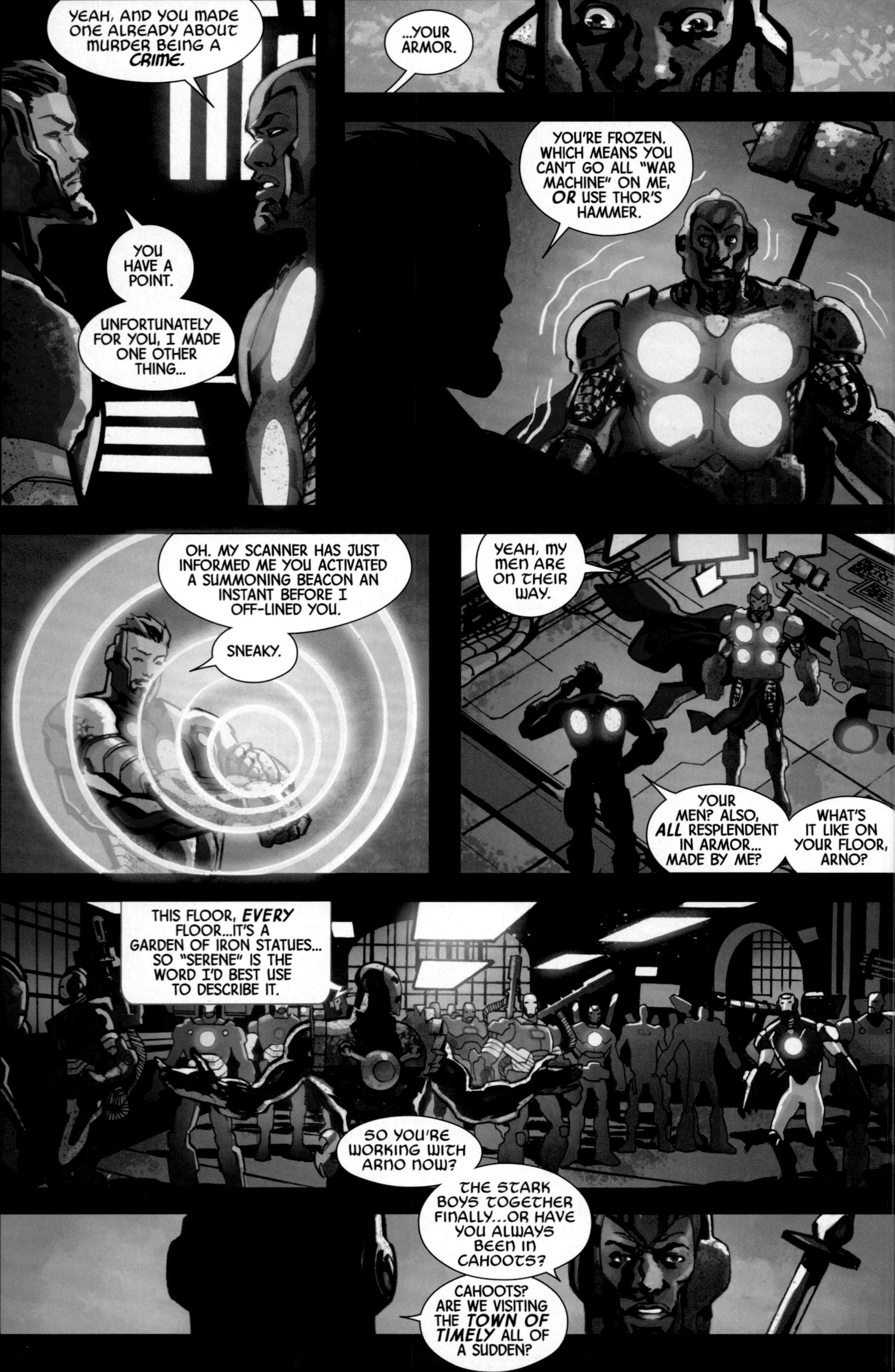
YEAH, AND YOU MADE ONE ALREADY ABOUT MURDER BEING A CRIME.
YOU HAVE A POINT.
UNFORTUNATELY FOR YOU, I MADE ONE OTHER THING...
...YOUR ARMOR.
YOU'RE FROZEN. WHICH MEANS YOU CAN'T GO ALL "WAR MACHINE" ON ME, OR USE THOR'S HAMMER.
OH. MY SCANNER HAS JUST INFORMED ME YOU ACTIVATED A SUMMONING BEACON AN INSTANT BEFORE I OFF-LINED YOU.
SNEAKY.
YEAH, MY MEN ARE ON THEIR WAY.
YOUR MEN? ALSO, ALL RESPLENDENT IN ARMOR... MADE BY ME?
WHAT'S IT LIKE ON YOUR FLOOR, ARNO?
THIS FLOOR, EVERY FLOOR...IT'S A GARDEN OF IRON STATUES... SO "SERENE" IS THE WORD I'D BEST USE TO DESCRIBE IT.
SO YOU'RE WORKING WITH ARNO NOW?
THE STARK BOYS TOGETHER FINALLY...OR HAVE YOU ALWAYS BEEN IN CAHOOTS?
CAHOOTS? ARE WE VISITING THE TOWN OF TIMELY ALL OF A SUDDEN?

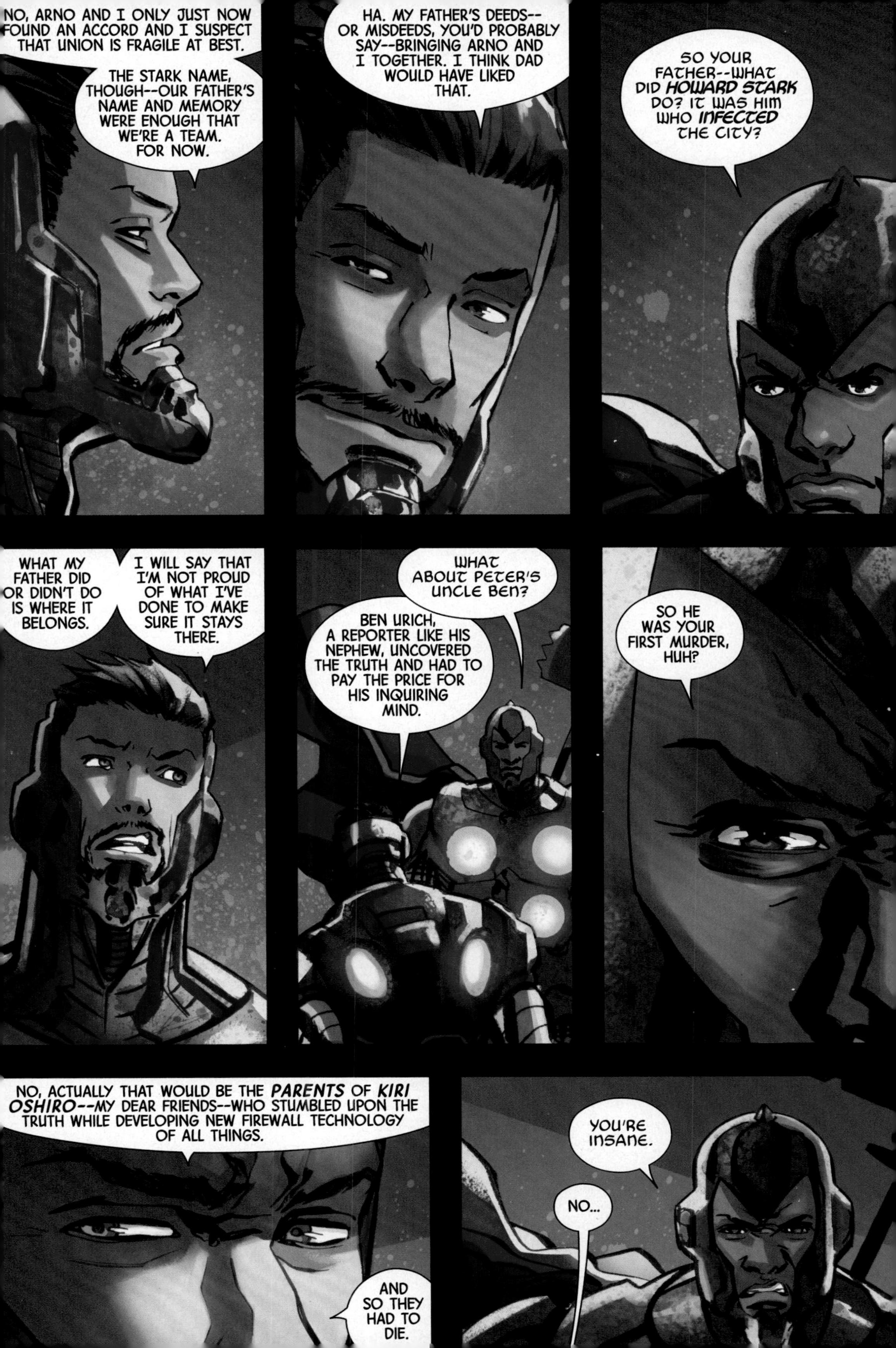
NO, ARNO AND I ONLY JUST NOW FOUND AN ACCORD AND I SUSPECT THAT UNION IS FRAGILE AT BEST.
THE STARK NAME, THOUGH--OUR FATHER'S NAME AND MEMORY WERE ENOUGH THAT WE'RE A TEAM. FOR NOW.
HA. MY FATHER'S DEEDS-- OR MISDEEDS, YOU'D PROBABLY SAY--BRINGING ARNO AND I TOGETHER. I THINK DAD WOULD HAVE LIKED THAT.
SO YOUR FATHER--WHAT DID HOWARD STARK DO? IT WAS HIM WHO INFECTED THE CITY?
WHAT MY FATHER DID OR DIDN'T DO IS WHERE IT BELONGS.
I WILL SAY THAT I'M NOT PROUD OF WHAT I'VE DONE TO MAKE SURE IT STAYS THERE.
WHAT ABOUT PETER'S UNCLE BEN?
BEN URICH, A REPORTER LIKE HIS NEPHEW, UNCOVERED THE TRUTH AND HAD TO PAY THE PRICE FOR HIS INQUIRING MIND.
SO HE WAS YOUR FIRST MURDER, HUH?
NO, ACTUALLY THAT WOULD BE THE PARENTS OF KIRI OSHIRO--MY DEAR FRIENDS--WHO STUMBLED UPON THE TRUTH WHILE DEVELOPING NEW FIREWALL TECHNOLOGY OF ALL THINGS.
AND SO THEY HAD TO DIE.
YOU'RE INSANE.
NO...

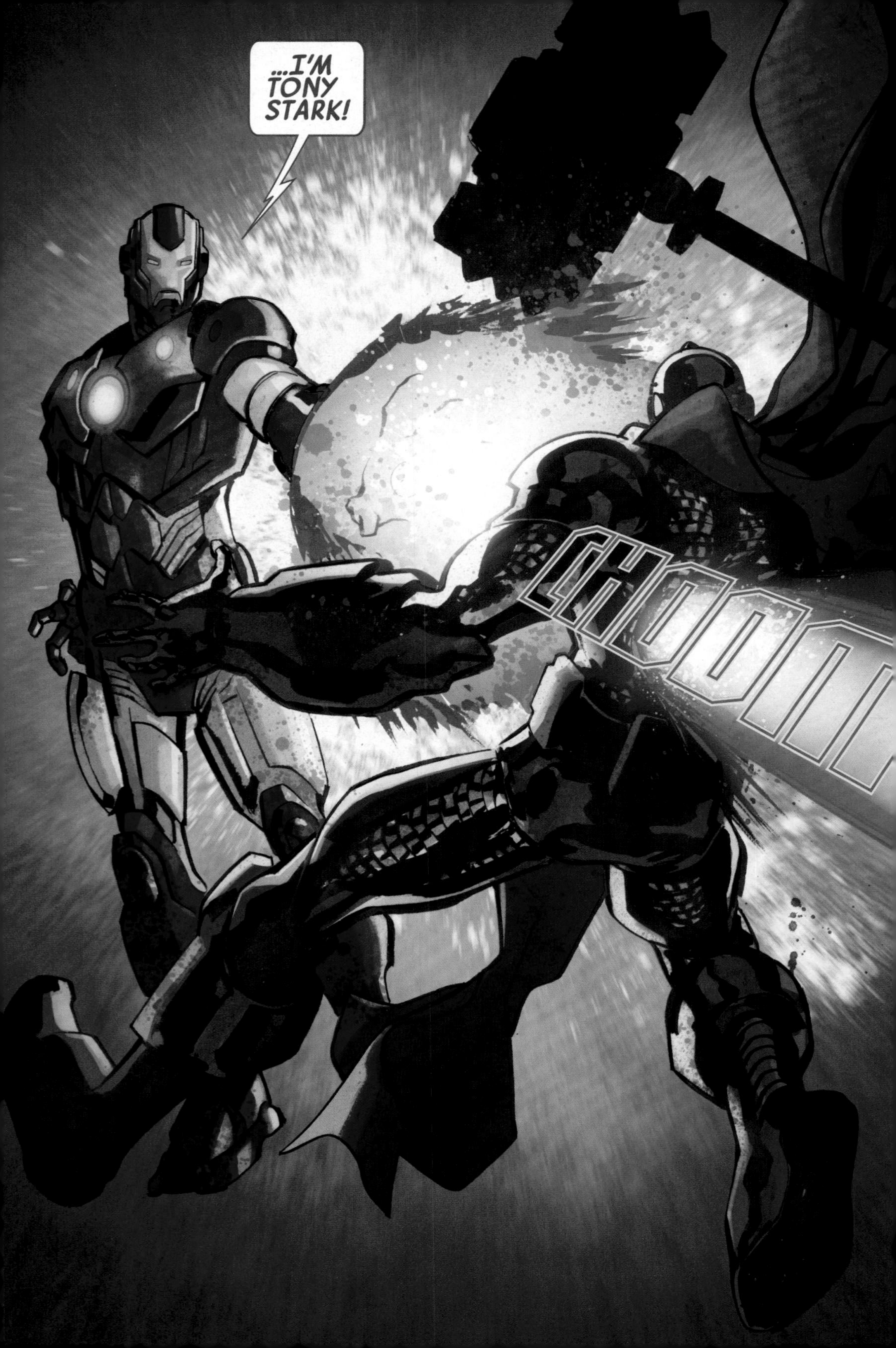
...I'M TONY STARK!
CHOO

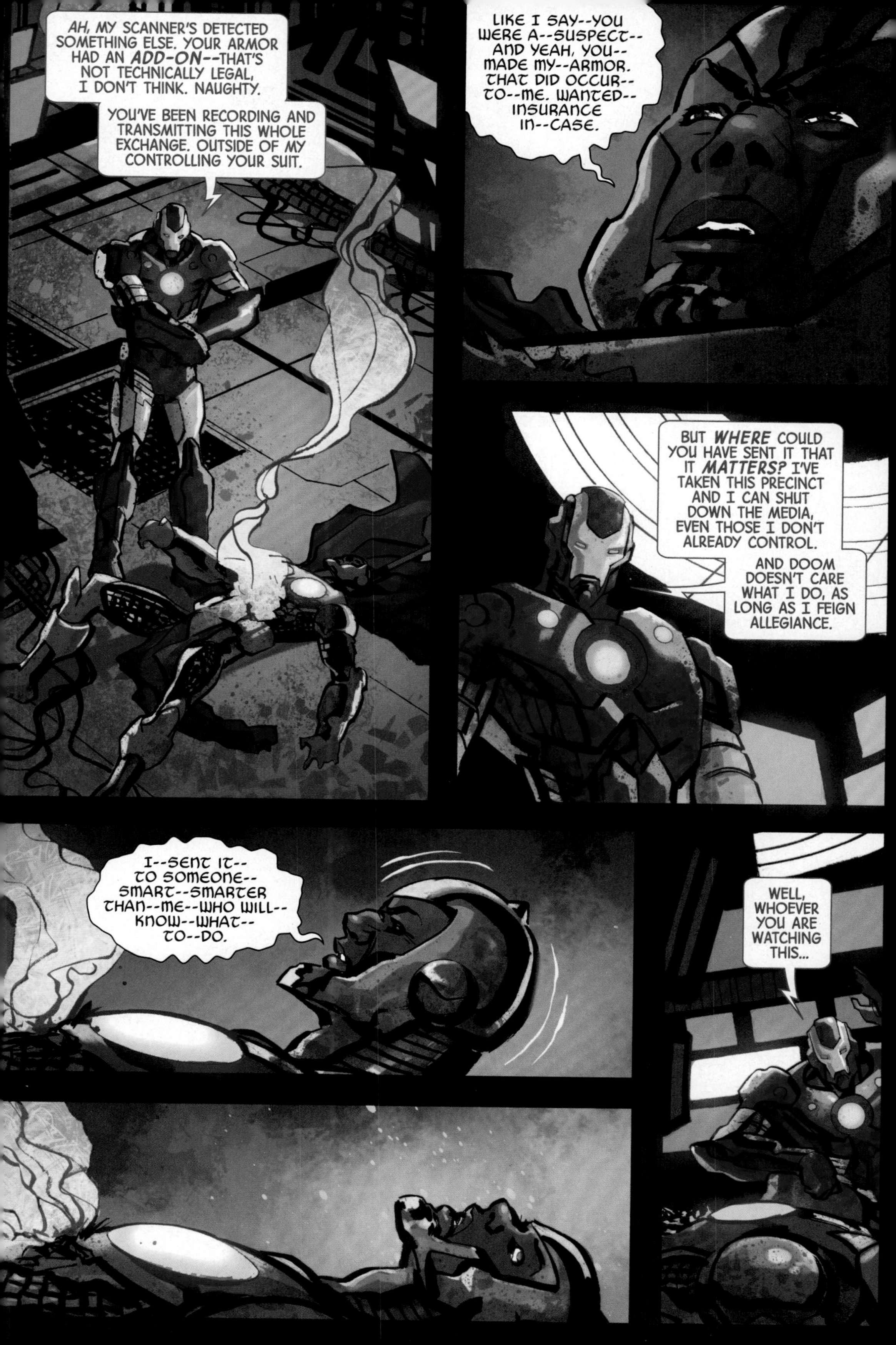
AH, MY SCANNER'S DETECTED SOMETHING ELSE. YOUR ARMOR HAD AN ADD-ON--THAT'S NOT TECHNICALLY LEGAL, I DON'T THINK. NAUGHTY.
YOU'VE BEEN RECORDING AND TRANSMITTING THIS WHOLE EXCHANGE. OUTSIDE OF MY CONTROLLING YOUR SUIT.
LIKE I SAY--YOU WERE A--SUSPECT--AND YEAH, YOU--MADE MY--ARMOR. THAT DID OCCUR--TO--ME. WANTED--INSURANCE IN--CASE.
BUT WHERE COULD YOU HAVE SENT IT THAT IT MATTERS? I'VE TAKEN THIS PRECINCT AND I CAN SHUT DOWN THE MEDIA, EVEN THOSE I DON'T ALREADY CONTROL.
AND DOOM DOESN'T CARE WHAT I DO, AS LONG AS I FEIGN ALLEGIANCE.
I--SENT IT--TO SOMEONE--SMART--SMARTER THAN--ME--WHO WILL--KNOW--WHAT--TO--DO.
WELL, WHOEVER YOU ARE WATCHING THIS...

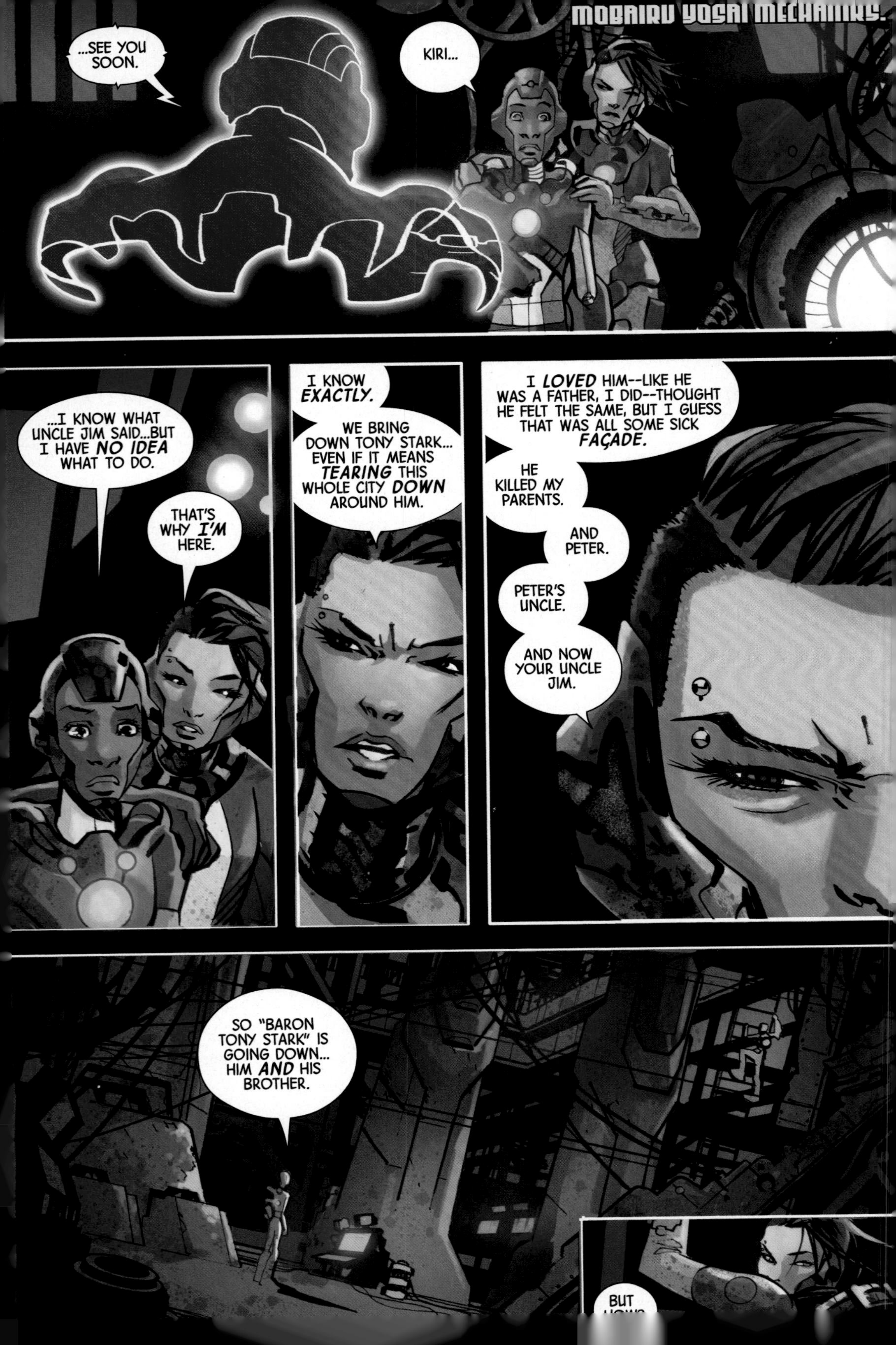
MOBAIRU YOSAI MECHANIKS.
...SEE YOU SOON.
KIRI...
...I KNOW WHAT UNCLE JIM SAID...BUT I HAVE NO IDEA WHAT TO DO.
THAT'S WHY I'M HERE.
I KNOW EXACTLY.
WE BRING DOWN TONY STARK... EVEN IF IT MEANS TEARING THIS WHOLE CITY DOWN AROUND HIM.
I LOVED HIM--LIKE HE WAS A FATHER, I DID--THOUGHT HE FELT THE SAME, BUT I GUESS THAT WAS ALL SOME SICK FAÇADE.
HE KILLED MY PARENTS.
AND PETER.
PETER'S UNCLE.
AND NOW YOUR UNCLE JIM.
SO "BARON TONY STARK" IS GOING DOWN... HIM AND HIS BROTHER.
BUT

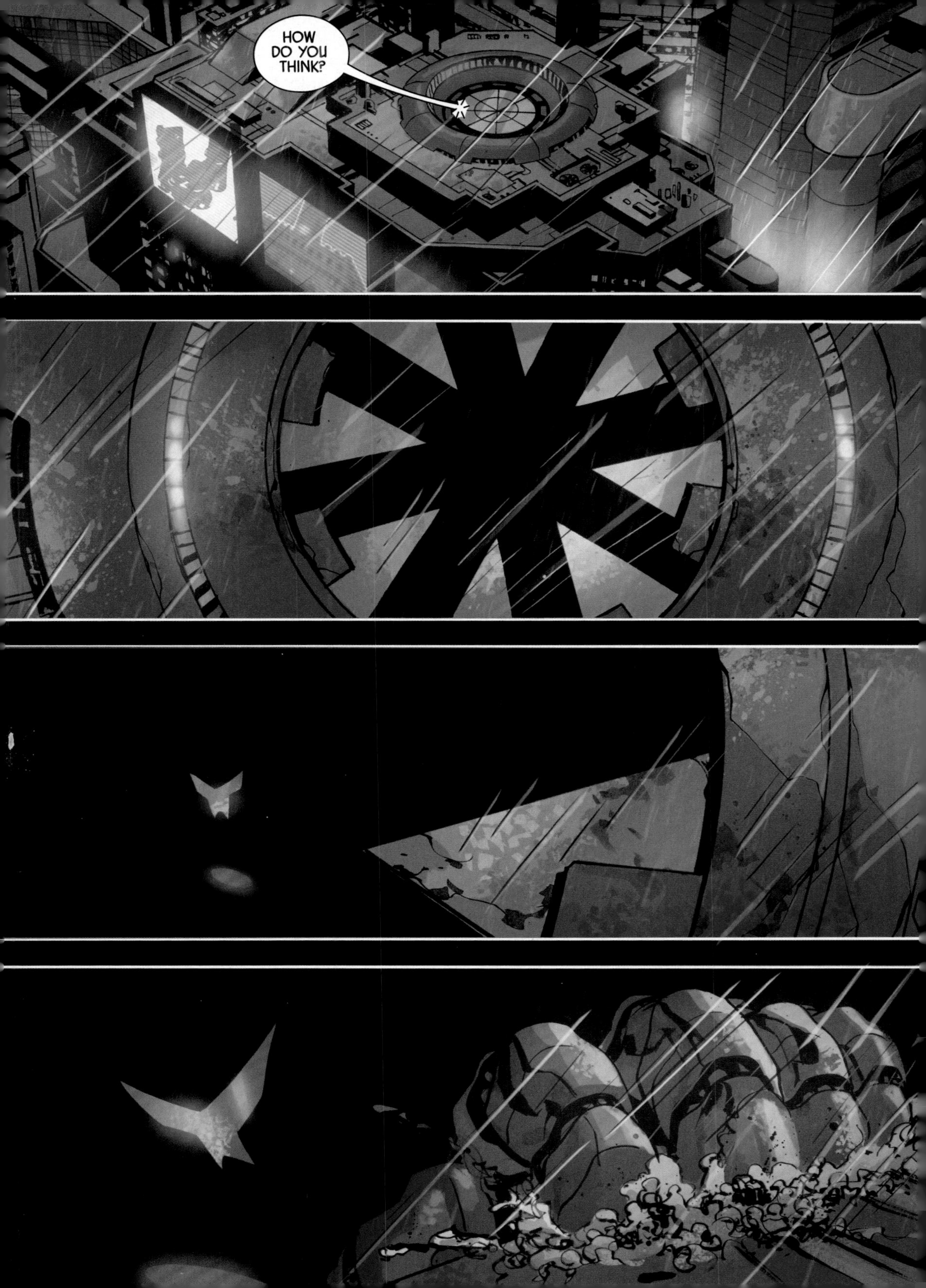
HOW DO YOU THINK?

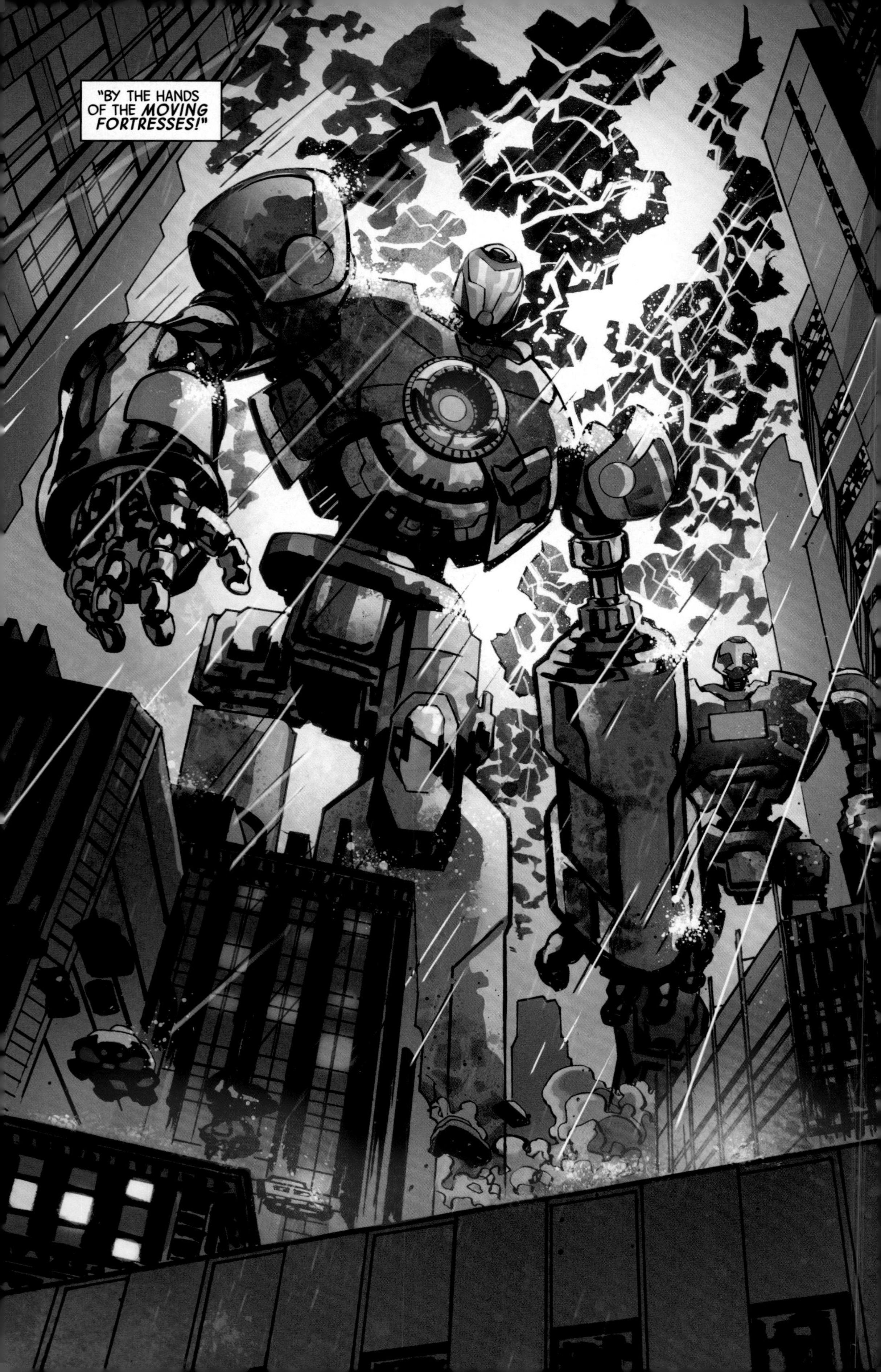
"BY THE HANDS OF THE *MOVING FORTRESSES!*"

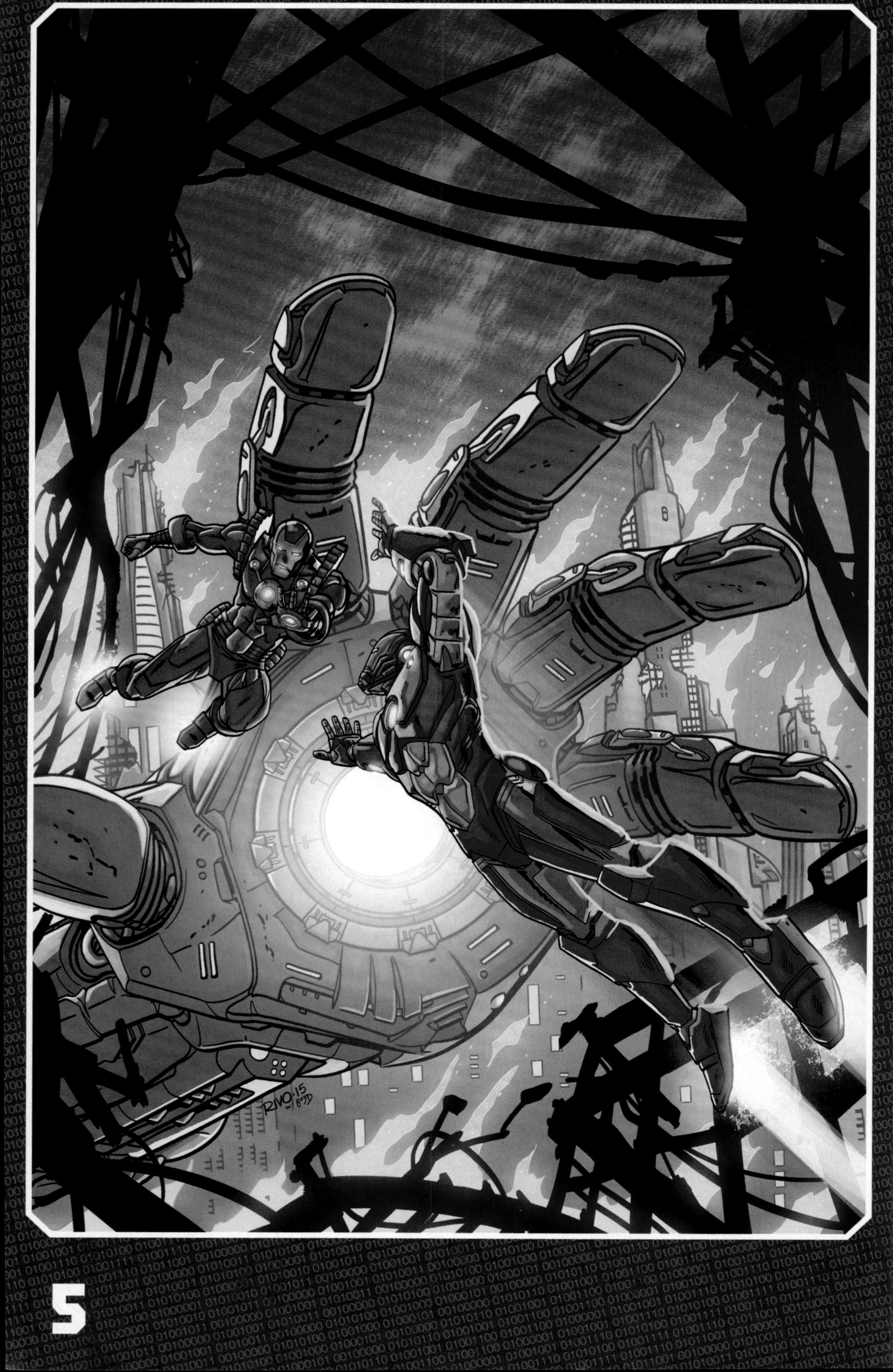

5

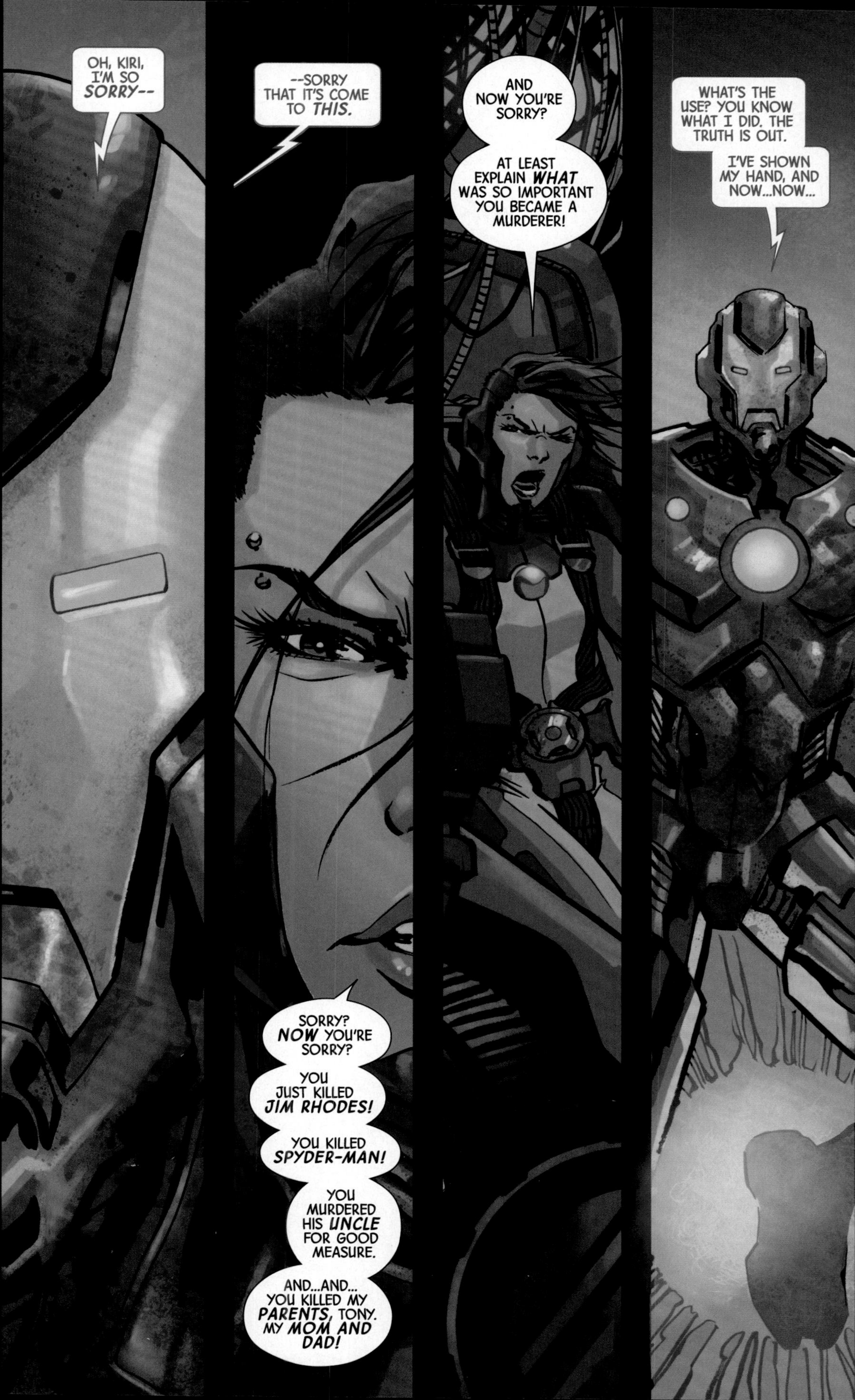
OH, KIRI, I'M SO SORRY--
--SORRY THAT IT'S COME TO THIS.
SORRY? NOW YOU'RE SORRY?
YOU JUST KILLED JIM RHODES!
YOU KILLED SPYDER-MAN!
YOU MURDERED HIS UNCLE FOR GOOD MEASURE.
AND...AND... YOU KILLED MY PARENTS, TONY. MY MOM AND DAD!
AND NOW YOU'RE SORRY?
AT LEAST EXPLAIN WHAT WAS SO IMPORTANT YOU BECAME A MURDERER!
WHAT'S THE USE? YOU KNOW WHAT I DID. THE TRUTH IS OUT.
I'VE SHOWN MY HAND, AND NOW...NOW...

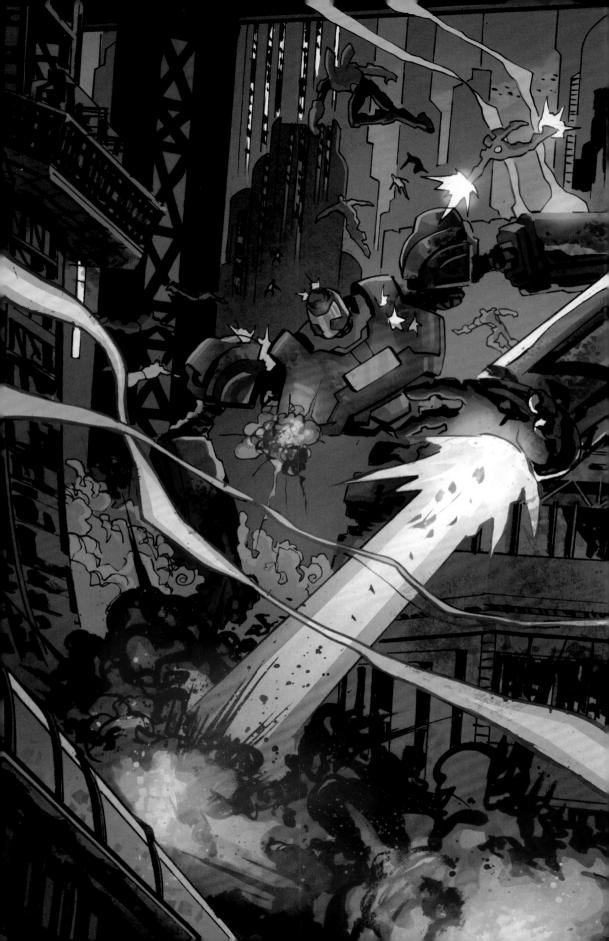

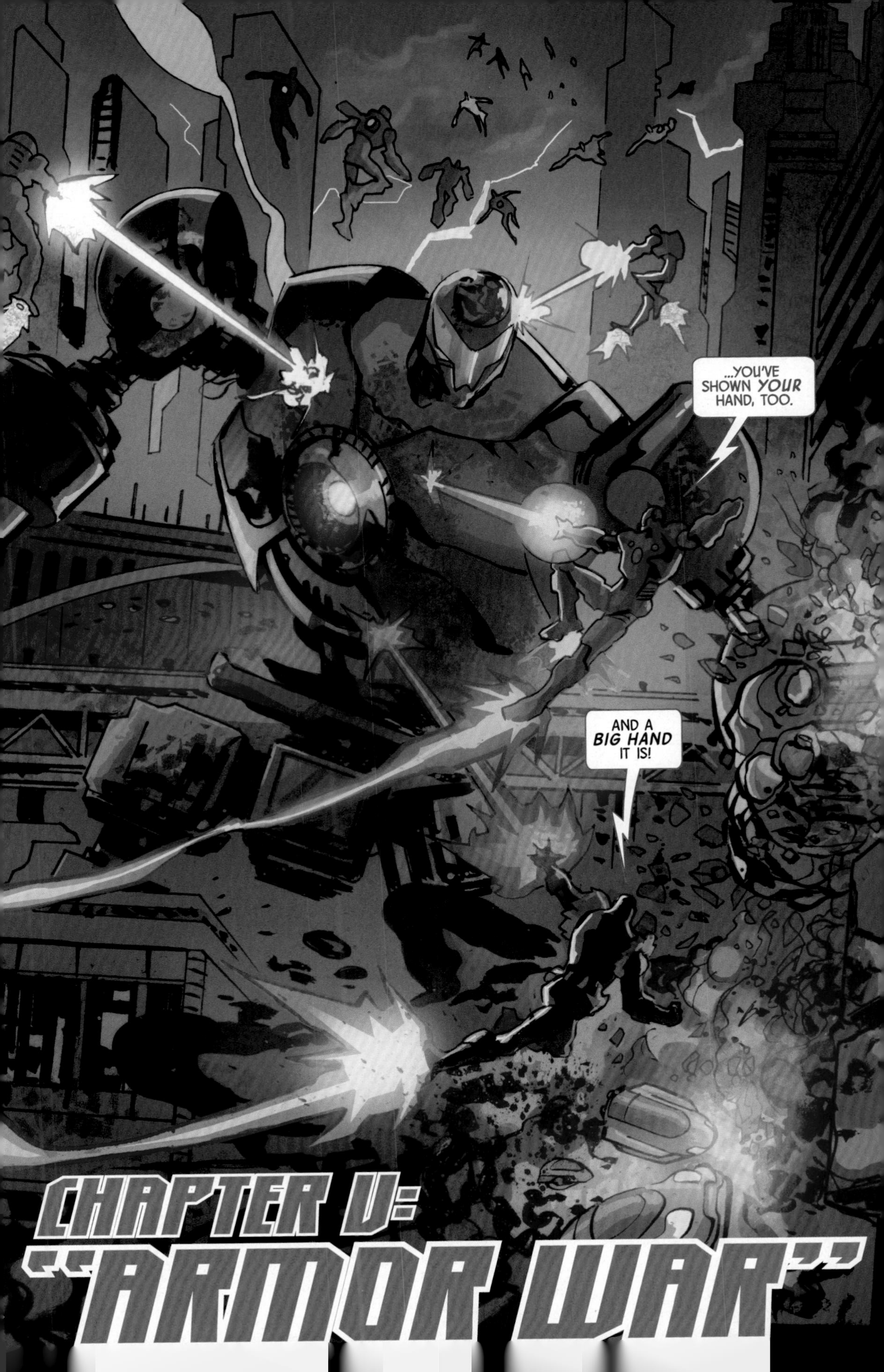
...YOU'VE SHOWN YOUR HAND, TOO.
AND A BIG HAND IT IS!
CHAPTER V: "ARMOR WAR"

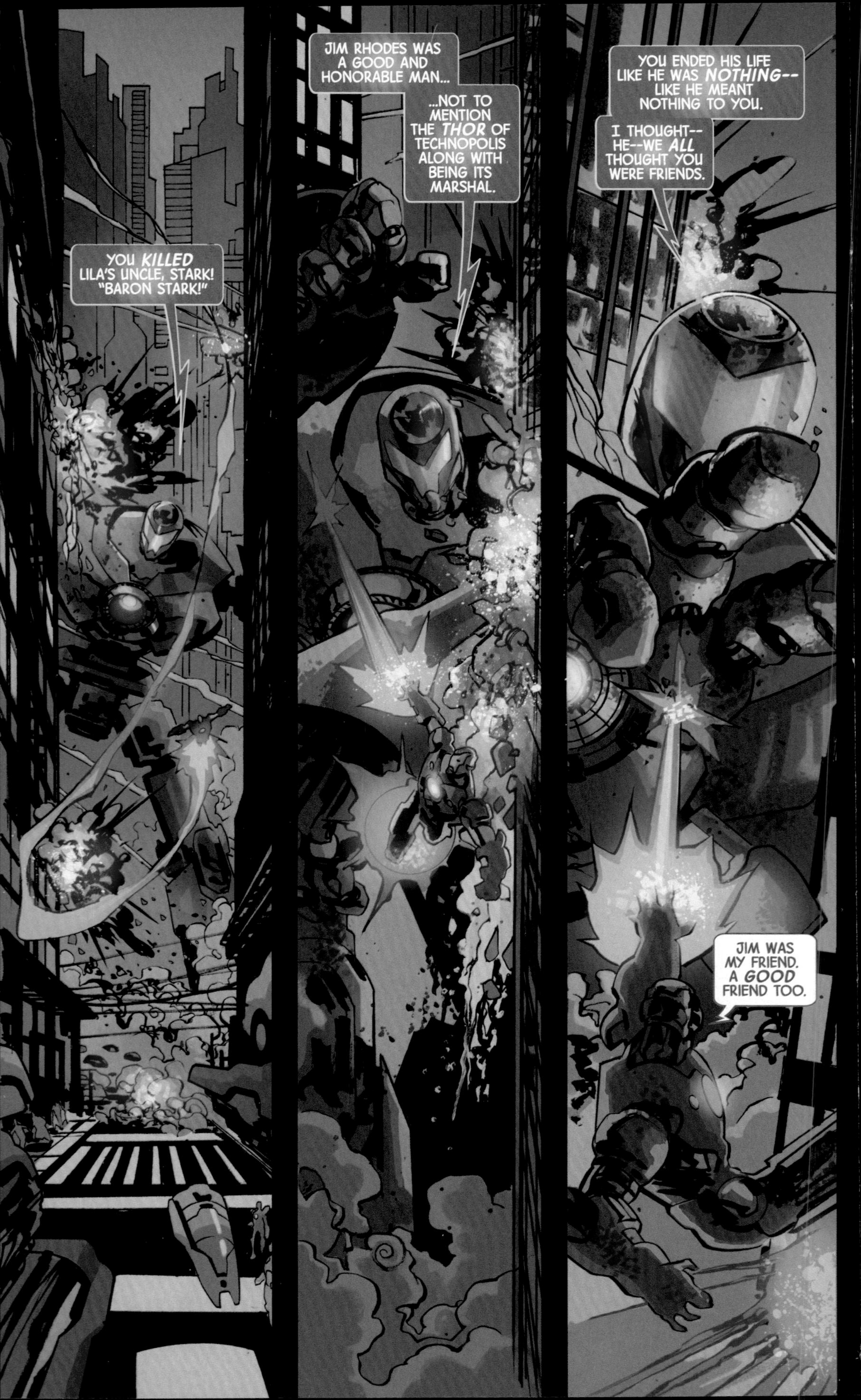

YOU KILLED LILA'S UNCLE, STARK! "BARON STARK!"
JIM RHODES WAS A GOOD AND HONORABLE MAN...
...NOT TO MENTION THE THOR OF TECHNOPOLIS ALONG WITH BEING ITS MARSHAL.
YOU ENDED HIS LIFE LIKE HE WAS NOTHING-- LIKE HE MEANT NOTHING TO YOU.
I THOUGHT-- HE--WE ALL THOUGHT YOU WERE FRIENDS.
JIM WAS MY FRIEND. A GOOD FRIEND TOO.

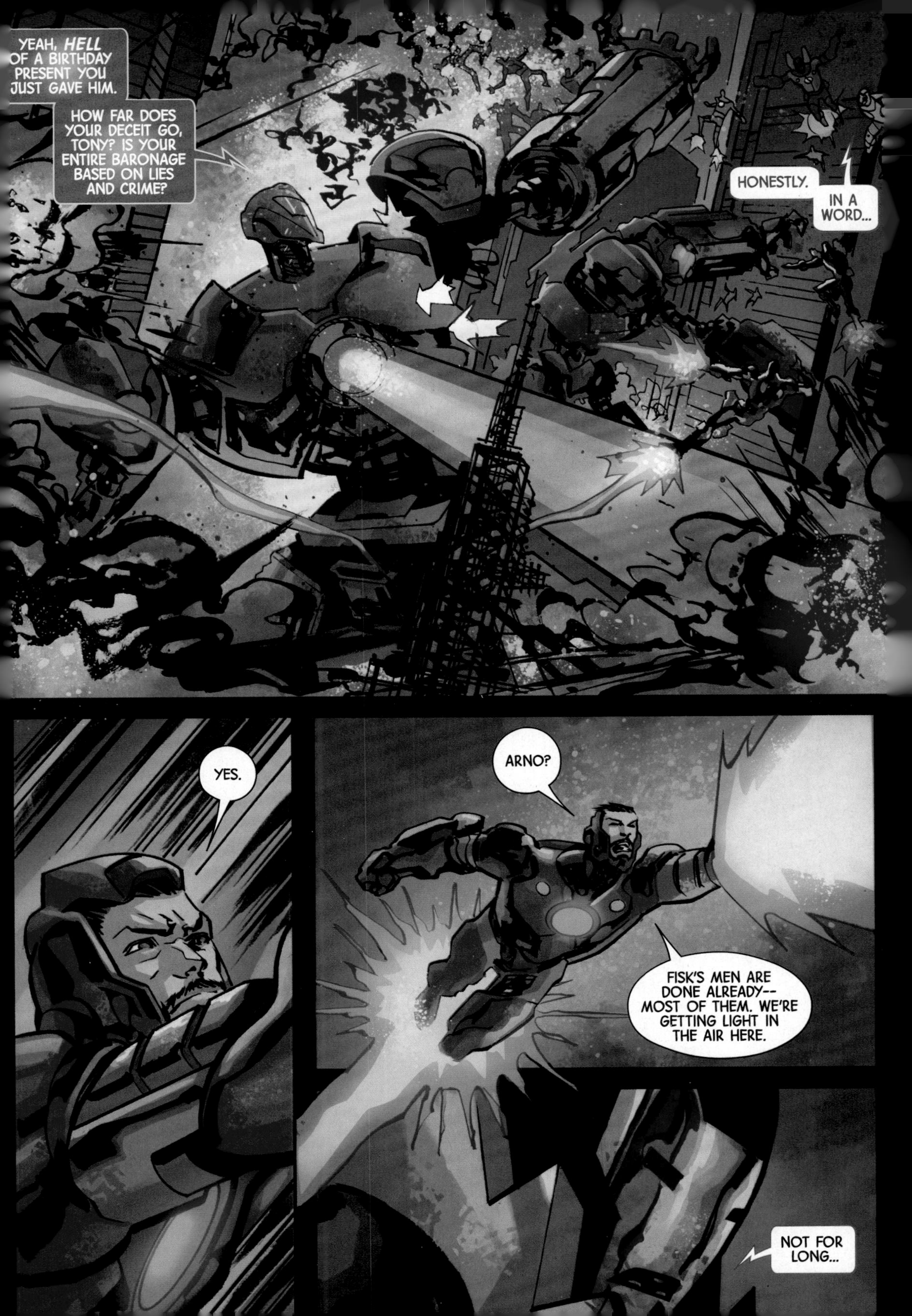
YEAH, HELL OF A BIRTHDAY PRESENT YOU JUST GAVE HIM.
HOW FAR DOES YOUR DECEIT GO, TONY? IS YOUR ENTIRE BARONAGE BASED ON LIES AND CRIME?
HONESTLY.
IN A WORD...
YES.
ARNO?
FISK'S MEN ARE DONE ALREADY-- MOST OF THEM. WE'RE GETTING LIGHT IN THE AIR HERE.
NOT FOR LONG...

"...I HAVE SALVOS OF MACHINE MEN INCOMING."

TWO LITTLE GIRLS--

HA.

HELL OF A THING.

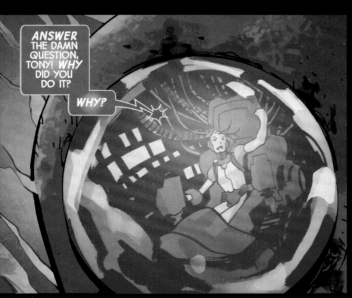

ANSWER THE DAMN QUESTION, TONY! *WHY* DID YOU DO IT?

WHY?

AGAIN. IN A WORD... ONE WORD...

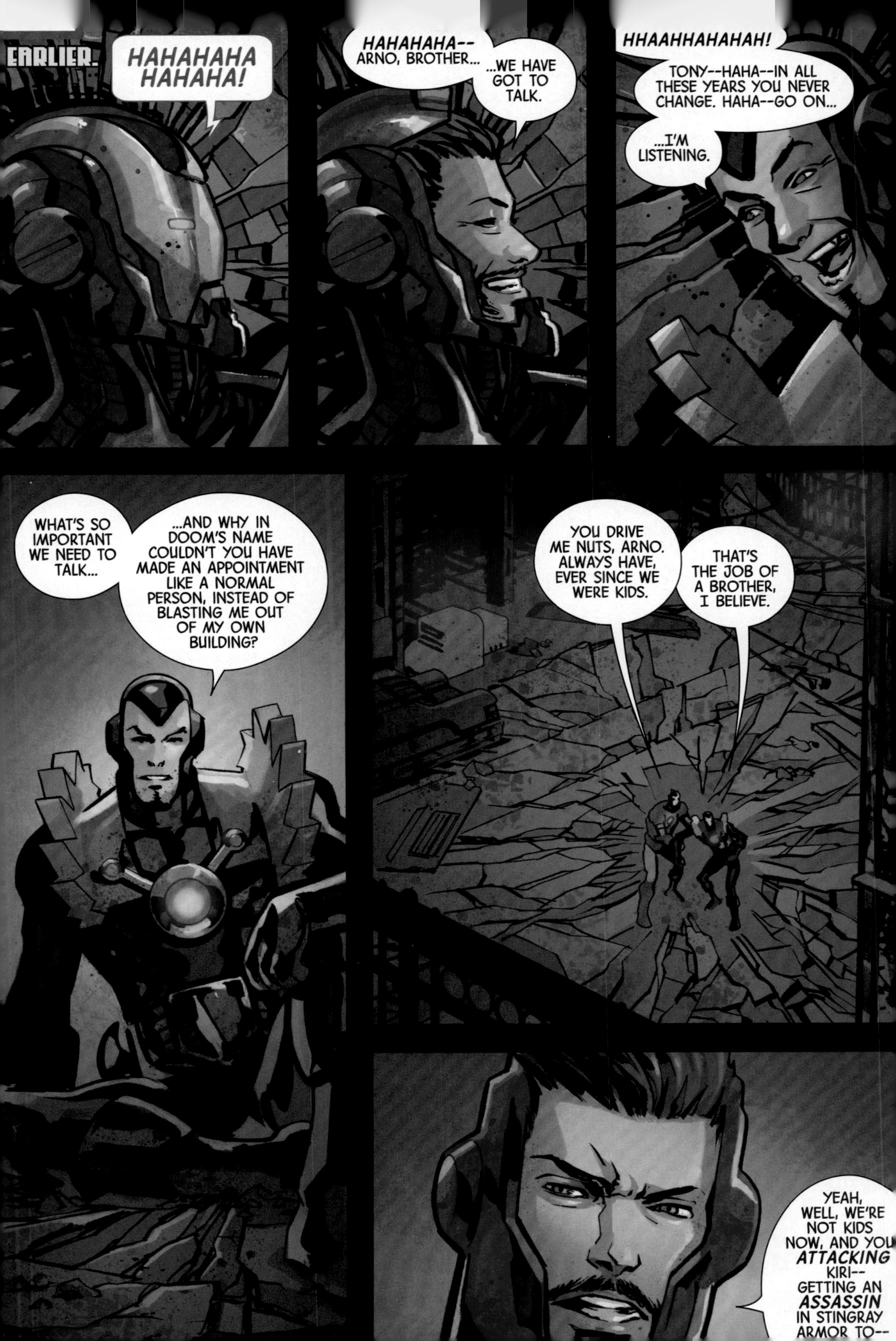

EARLIER.
HAHAHAHA HAHAHA!
HAHAHAHA-- ARNO, BROTHER...
...WE HAVE GOT TO TALK.
HHAAHHAHAHAH!
TONY--HAHA--IN ALL THESE YEARS YOU NEVER CHANGE. HAHA--GO ON...
...I'M LISTENING.
WHAT'S SO IMPORTANT WE NEED TO TALK...
...AND WHY IN DOOM'S NAME COULDN'T YOU HAVE MADE AN APPOINTMENT LIKE A NORMAL PERSON, INSTEAD OF BLASTING ME OUT OF MY OWN BUILDING?
YOU DRIVE ME NUTS, ARNO. ALWAYS HAVE, EVER SINCE WE WERE KIDS.
THAT'S THE JOB OF A BROTHER, I BELIEVE.
YEAH, WELL, WE'RE NOT KIDS NOW, AND YOU ATTACKING KIRI-- GETTING AN ASSASSIN IN STINGRAY ARMOR TO--

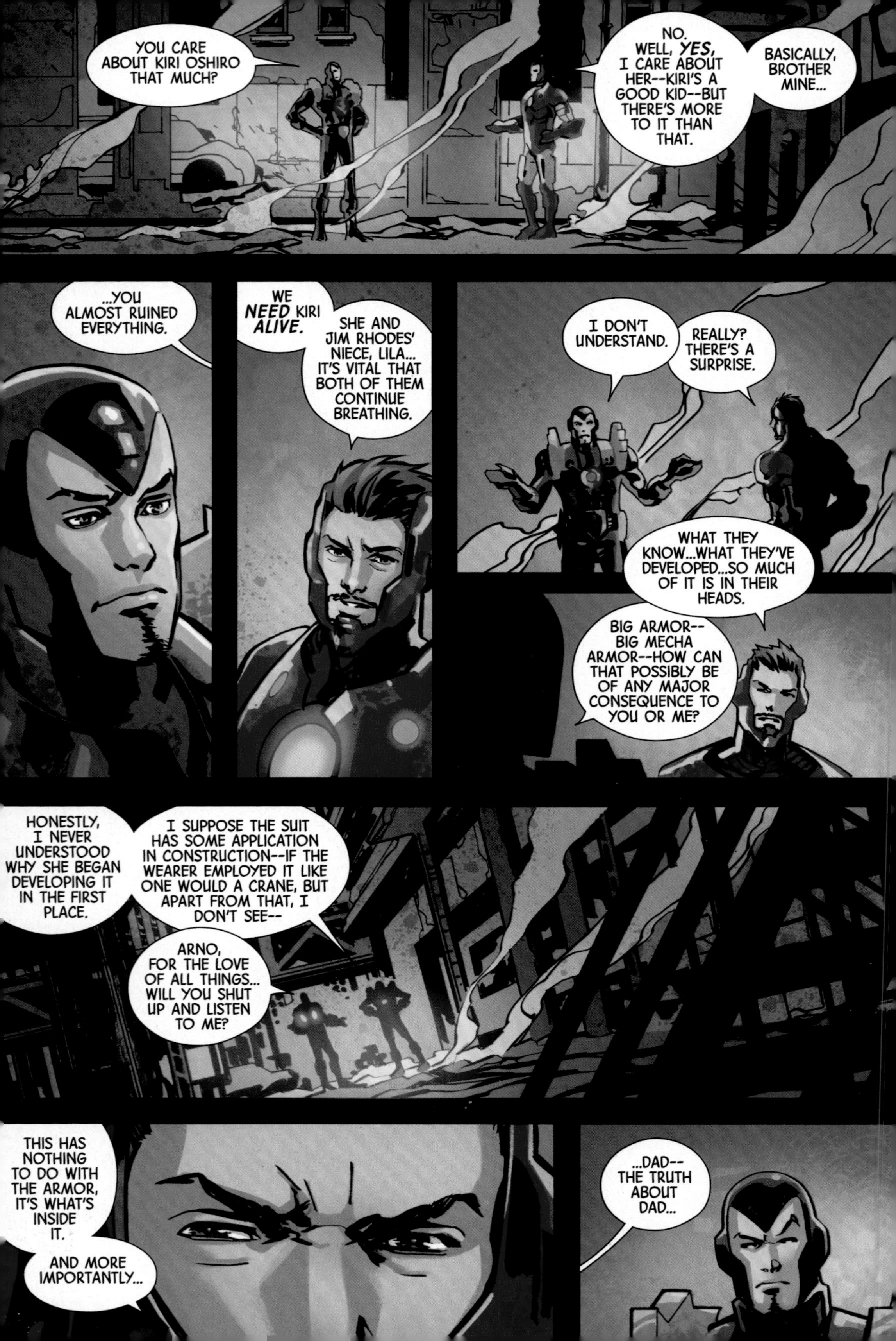
YOU CARE ABOUT KIRI OSHIRO THAT MUCH?
NO. WELL, YES, I CARE ABOUT HER--KIRI'S A GOOD KID--BUT THERE'S MORE TO IT THAN THAT.
BASICALLY, BROTHER MINE...
...YOU ALMOST RUINED EVERYTHING.
WE NEED KIRI ALIVE.
SHE AND JIM RHODES' NIECE, LILA... IT'S VITAL THAT BOTH OF THEM CONTINUE BREATHING.
I DON'T UNDERSTAND.
REALLY? THERE'S A SURPRISE.
WHAT THEY KNOW...WHAT THEY'VE DEVELOPED...SO MUCH OF IT IS IN THEIR HEADS.
BIG ARMOR--BIG MECHA ARMOR--HOW CAN THAT POSSIBLY BE OF ANY MAJOR CONSEQUENCE TO YOU OR ME?
HONESTLY, I NEVER UNDERSTOOD WHY SHE BEGAN DEVELOPING IT IN THE FIRST PLACE.
I SUPPOSE THE SUIT HAS SOME APPLICATION IN CONSTRUCTION--IF THE WEARER EMPLOYED IT LIKE ONE WOULD A CRANE, BUT APART FROM THAT, I DON'T SEE--
ARNO, FOR THE LOVE OF ALL THINGS... WILL YOU SHUT UP AND LISTEN TO ME?
THIS HAS NOTHING TO DO WITH THE ARMOR, IT'S WHAT'S INSIDE IT.
AND MORE IMPORTANTLY...
...DAD--THE TRUTH ABOUT DAD...

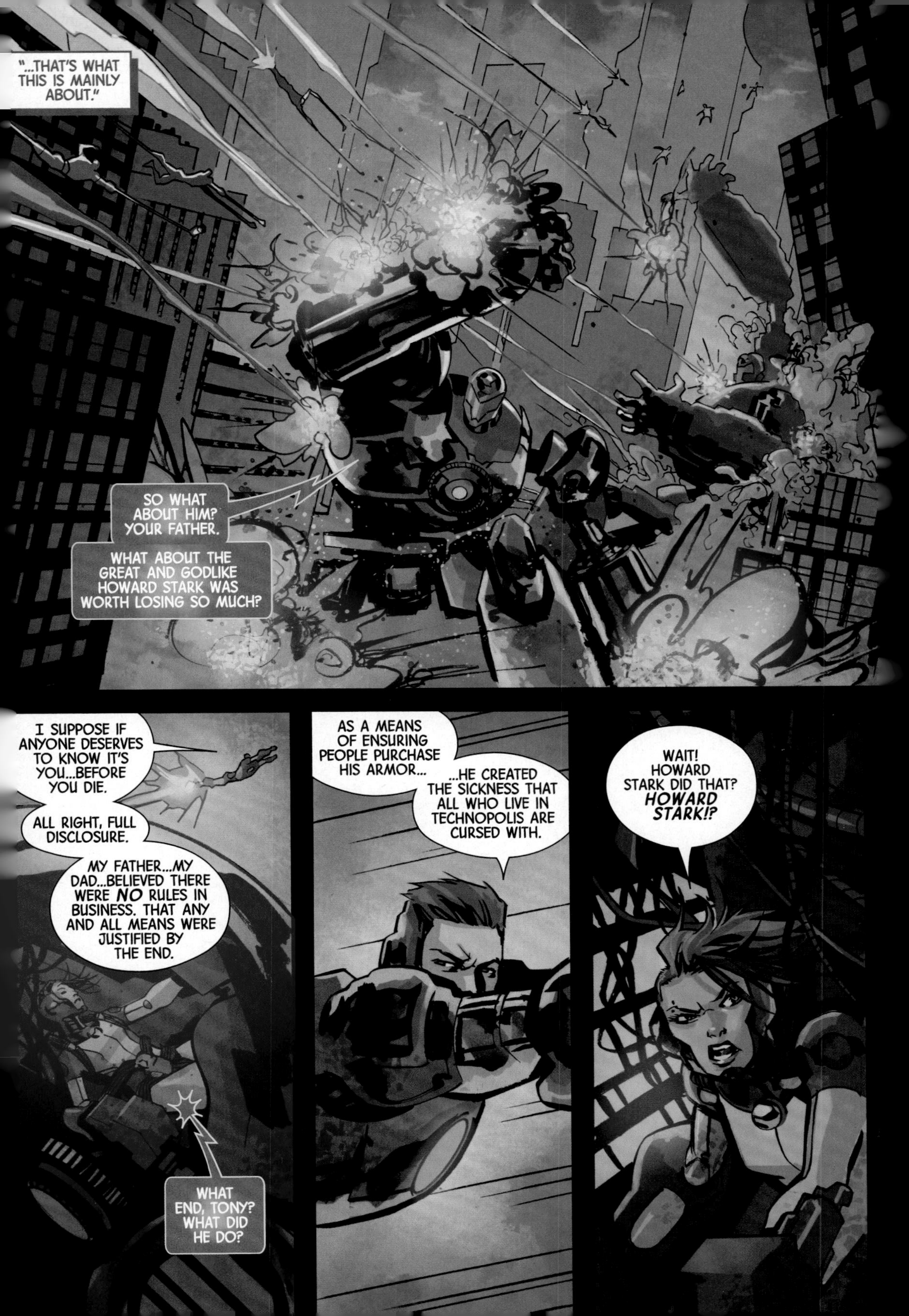
"...THAT'S WHAT THIS IS MAINLY ABOUT."
SO WHAT ABOUT HIM? YOUR FATHER.
WHAT ABOUT THE GREAT AND GODLIKE HOWARD STARK WAS WORTH LOSING SO MUCH?
I SUPPOSE IF ANYONE DESERVES TO KNOW IT'S YOU...BEFORE YOU DIE.
ALL RIGHT, FULL DISCLOSURE.
MY FATHER...MY DAD...BELIEVED THERE WERE NO RULES IN BUSINESS. THAT ANY AND ALL MEANS WERE JUSTIFIED BY THE END.
WHAT END, TONY? WHAT DID HE DO?
AS A MEANS OF ENSURING PEOPLE PURCHASE HIS ARMOR...
...HE CREATED THE SICKNESS THAT ALL WHO LIVE IN TECHNOPOLIS ARE CURSED WITH.
WAIT! HOWARD STARK DID THAT? HOWARD STARK!?

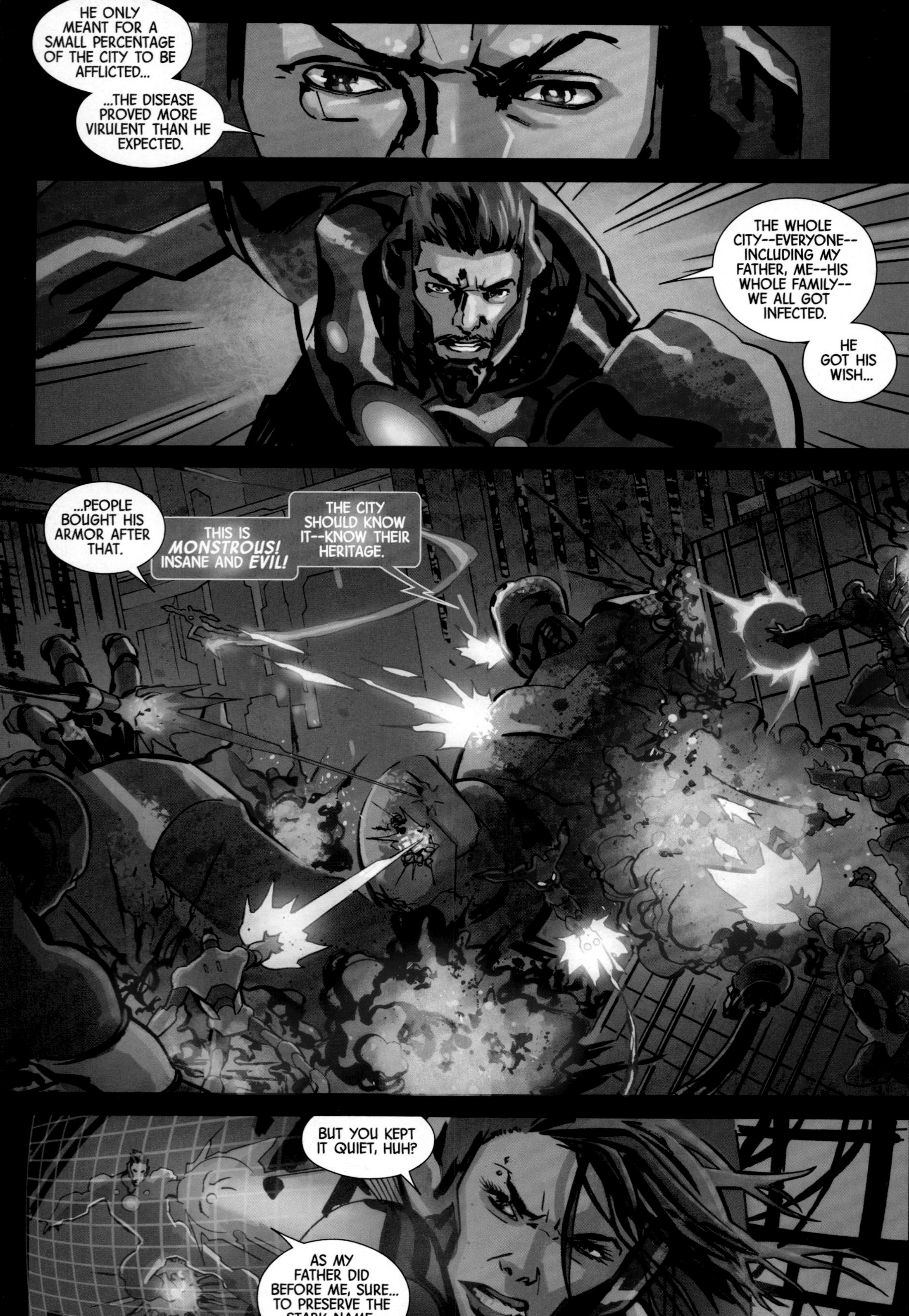
HE ONLY MEANT FOR A SMALL PERCENTAGE OF THE CITY TO BE AFFLICTED...
...THE DISEASE PROVED MORE VIRULENT THAN HE EXPECTED.
THE WHOLE CITY--EVERYONE--INCLUDING MY FATHER, ME--HIS WHOLE FAMILY--WE ALL GOT INFECTED.
HE GOT HIS WISH...
...PEOPLE BOUGHT HIS ARMOR AFTER THAT.
THIS IS *MONSTROUS!* INSANE AND *EVIL!*
THE CITY SHOULD KNOW IT--KNOW THEIR HERITAGE.
BUT YOU KEPT IT QUIET, HUH?
AS MY FATHER DID BEFORE ME, SURE... TO PRESERVE THE

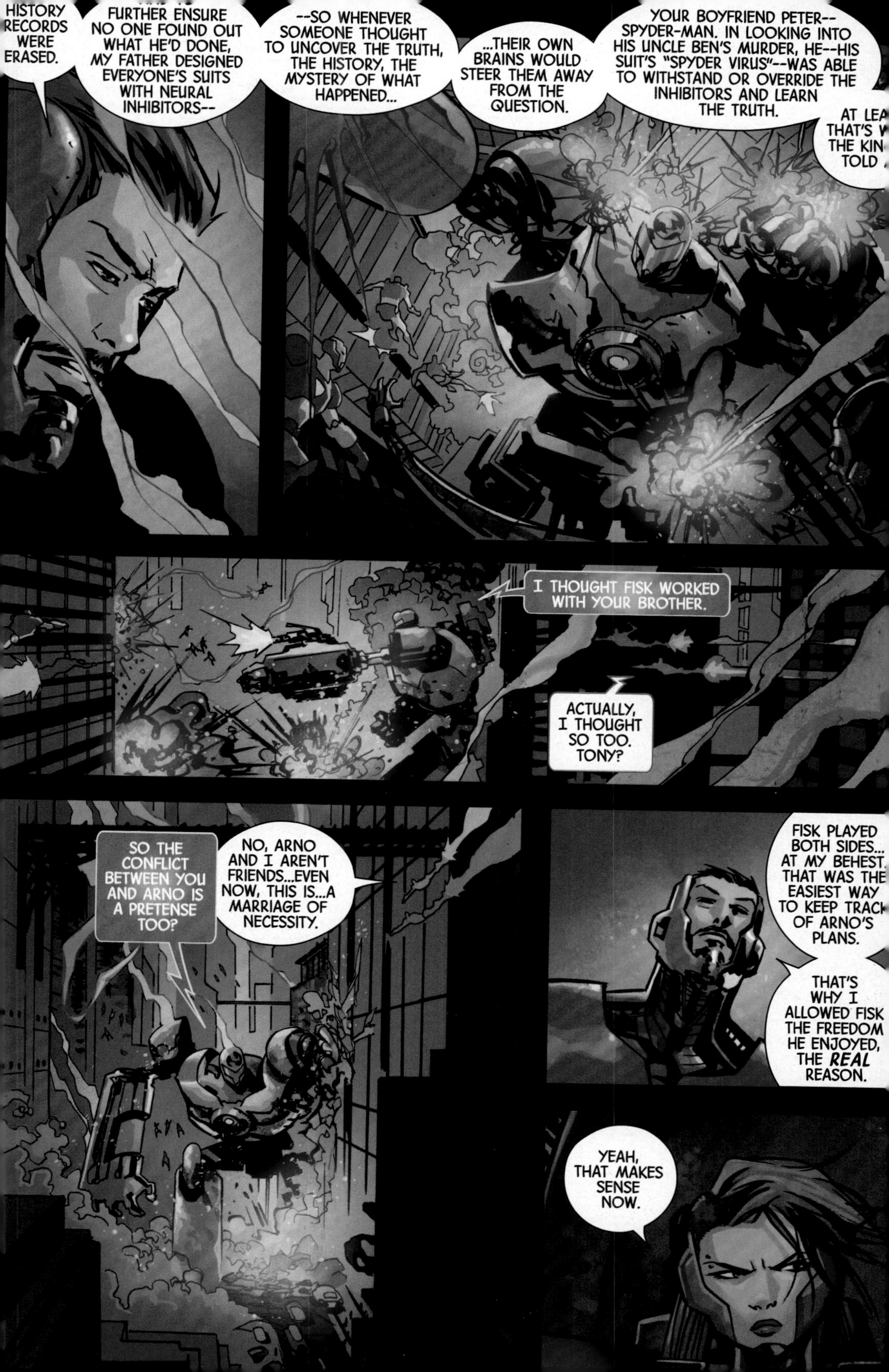
HISTORY RECORDS WERE ERASED.
FURTHER ENSURE NO ONE FOUND OUT WHAT HE'D DONE, MY FATHER DESIGNED EVERYONE'S SUITS WITH NEURAL INHIBITORS--
--SO WHENEVER SOMEONE THOUGHT TO UNCOVER THE TRUTH, THE HISTORY, THE MYSTERY OF WHAT HAPPENED...
...THEIR OWN BRAINS WOULD STEER THEM AWAY FROM THE QUESTION.
YOUR BOYFRIEND PETER--SPYDER-MAN. IN LOOKING INTO HIS UNCLE BEN'S MURDER, HE--HIS SUIT'S "SPYDER VIRUS"--WAS ABLE TO WITHSTAND OR OVERRIDE THE INHIBITORS AND LEARN THE TRUTH.
I THOUGHT FISK WORKED WITH YOUR BROTHER.
ACTUALLY, I THOUGHT SO TOO. TONY?
SO THE CONFLICT BETWEEN YOU AND ARNO IS A PRETENSE TOO?
NO, ARNO AND I AREN'T FRIENDS...EVEN NOW, THIS IS...A MARRIAGE OF NECESSITY.
FISK PLAYED BOTH SIDES... AT MY BEHEST. THAT WAS THE EASIEST WAY TO KEEP TRACK OF ARNO'S PLANS.
THAT'S WHY I ALLOWED FISK THE FREEDOM HE ENJOYED, THE *REAL* REASON.
YEAH, THAT MAKES SENSE NOW.

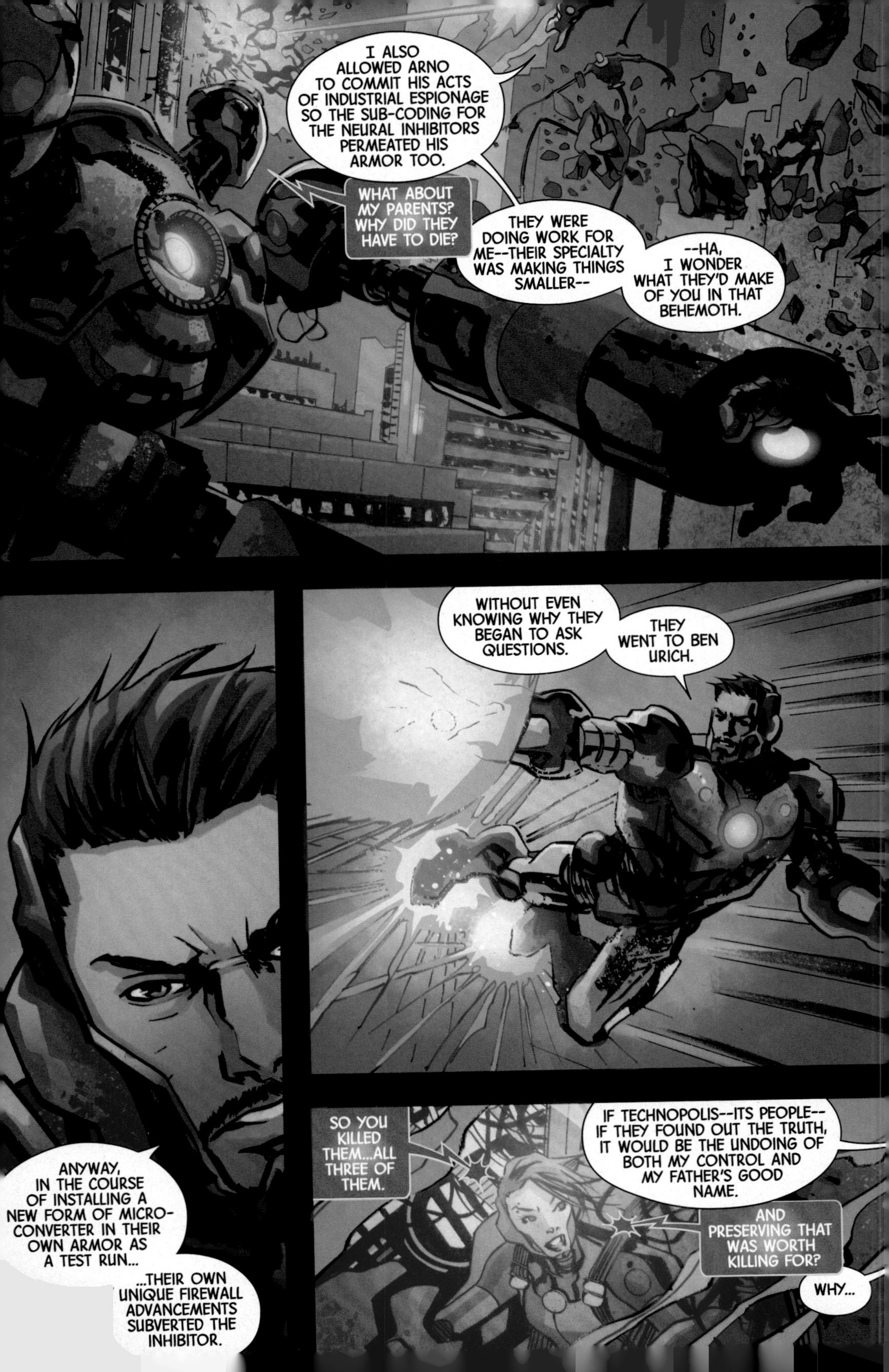
I ALSO ALLOWED ARNO TO COMMIT HIS ACTS OF INDUSTRIAL ESPIONAGE SO THE SUB-CODING FOR THE NEURAL INHIBITORS PERMEATED HIS ARMOR TOO.
WHAT ABOUT MY PARENTS? WHY DID THEY HAVE TO DIE?
THEY WERE DOING WORK FOR ME--THEIR SPECIALTY WAS MAKING THINGS SMALLER--
--HA, I WONDER WHAT THEY'D MAKE OF YOU IN THAT BEHEMOTH.
WITHOUT EVEN KNOWING WHY THEY BEGAN TO ASK QUESTIONS.
THEY WENT TO BEN URICH.
ANYWAY, IN THE COURSE OF INSTALLING A NEW FORM OF MICRO-CONVERTER IN THEIR OWN ARMOR AS A TEST RUN...
...THEIR OWN UNIQUE FIREWALL ADVANCEMENTS SUBVERTED THE INHIBITOR.
SO YOU KILLED THEM...ALL THREE OF THEM.
IF TECHNOPOLIS--ITS PEOPLE--IF THEY FOUND OUT THE TRUTH, IT WOULD BE THE UNDOING OF BOTH MY CONTROL AND MY FATHER'S GOOD NAME.
AND PRESERVING THAT WAS WORTH KILLING FOR?
WHY...

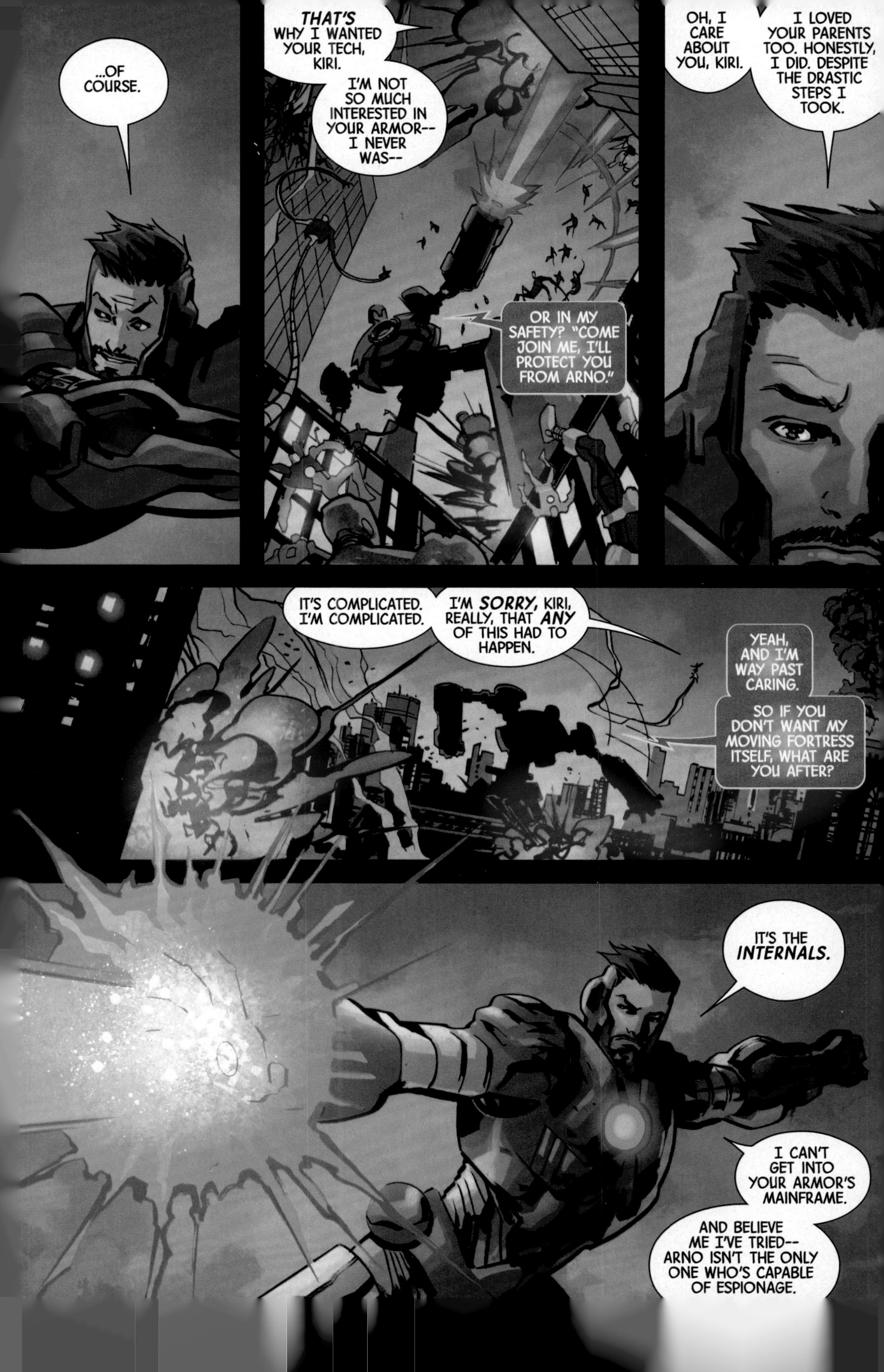
...OF COURSE.
THAT'S WHY I WANTED YOUR TECH, KIRI.
I'M NOT SO MUCH INTERESTED IN YOUR ARMOR-- I NEVER WAS--
OR IN MY SAFETY? "COME JOIN ME, I'LL PROTECT YOU FROM ARNO."
OH, I CARE ABOUT YOU, KIRI.
I LOVED YOUR PARENTS TOO. HONESTLY, I DID. DESPITE THE DRASTIC STEPS I TOOK.
IT'S COMPLICATED. I'M COMPLICATED.
I'M SORRY, KIRI, REALLY, THAT ANY OF THIS HAD TO HAPPEN.
YEAH, AND I'M WAY PAST CARING.
SO IF YOU DON'T WANT MY MOVING FORTRESS ITSELF, WHAT ARE YOU AFTER?
IT'S THE INTERNALS.
I CAN'T GET INTO YOUR ARMOR'S MAINFRAME.
AND BELIEVE ME I'VE TRIED-- ARNO ISN'T THE ONLY ONE WHO'S CAPABLE OF ESPIONAGE.

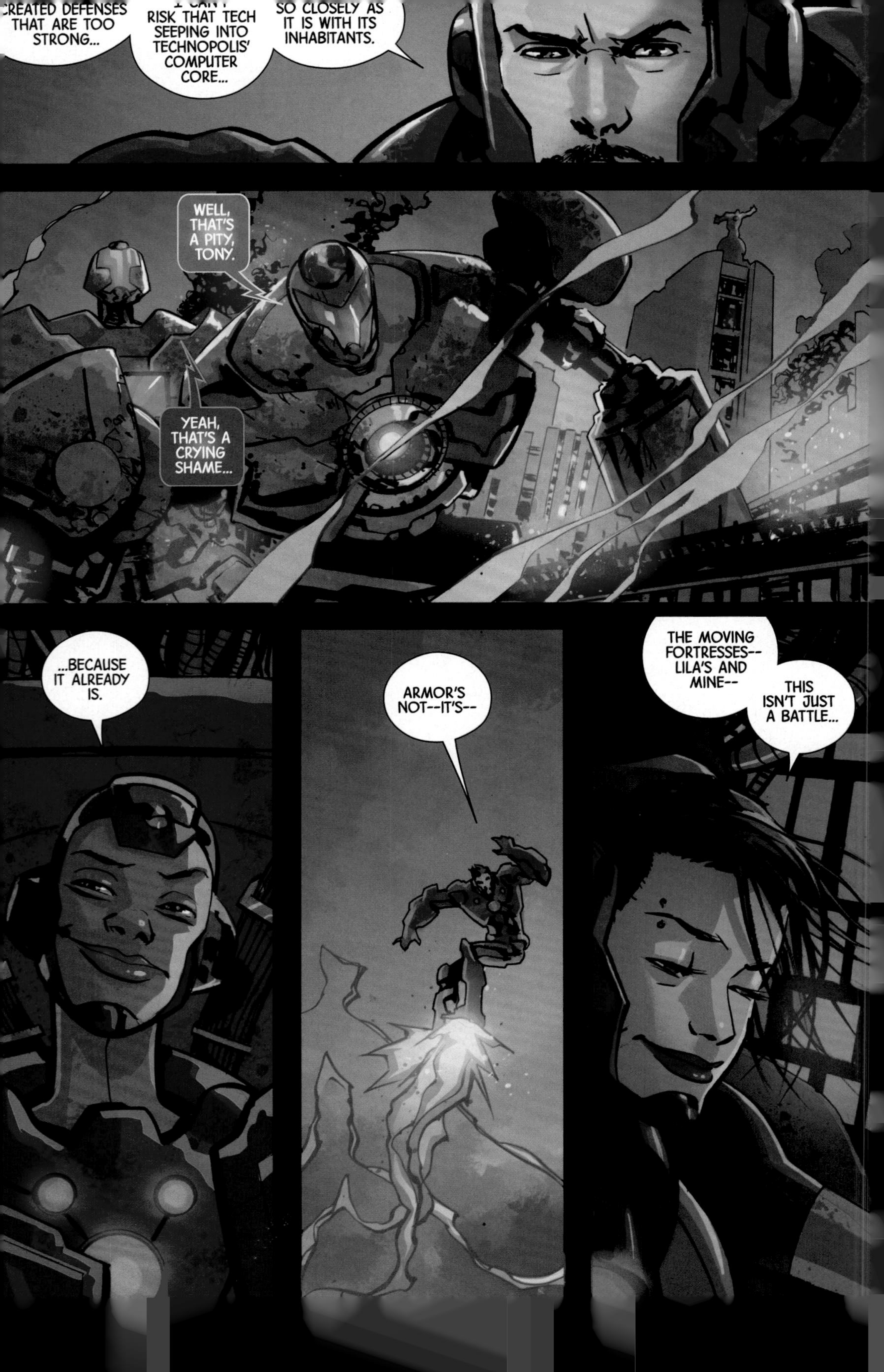
CREATED DEFENSES THAT ARE TOO STRONG...
RISK THAT TECH SEEPING INTO TECHNOPOLIS' COMPUTER CORE...
SO CLOSELY AS IT IS WITH ITS INHABITANTS.
WELL, THAT'S A PITY, TONY.
YEAH, THAT'S A CRYING SHAME...
...BECAUSE IT ALREADY IS.
ARMOR'S NOT--IT'S--
THE MOVING FORTRESSES-- LILA'S AND MINE--
THIS ISN'T JUST A BATTLE...

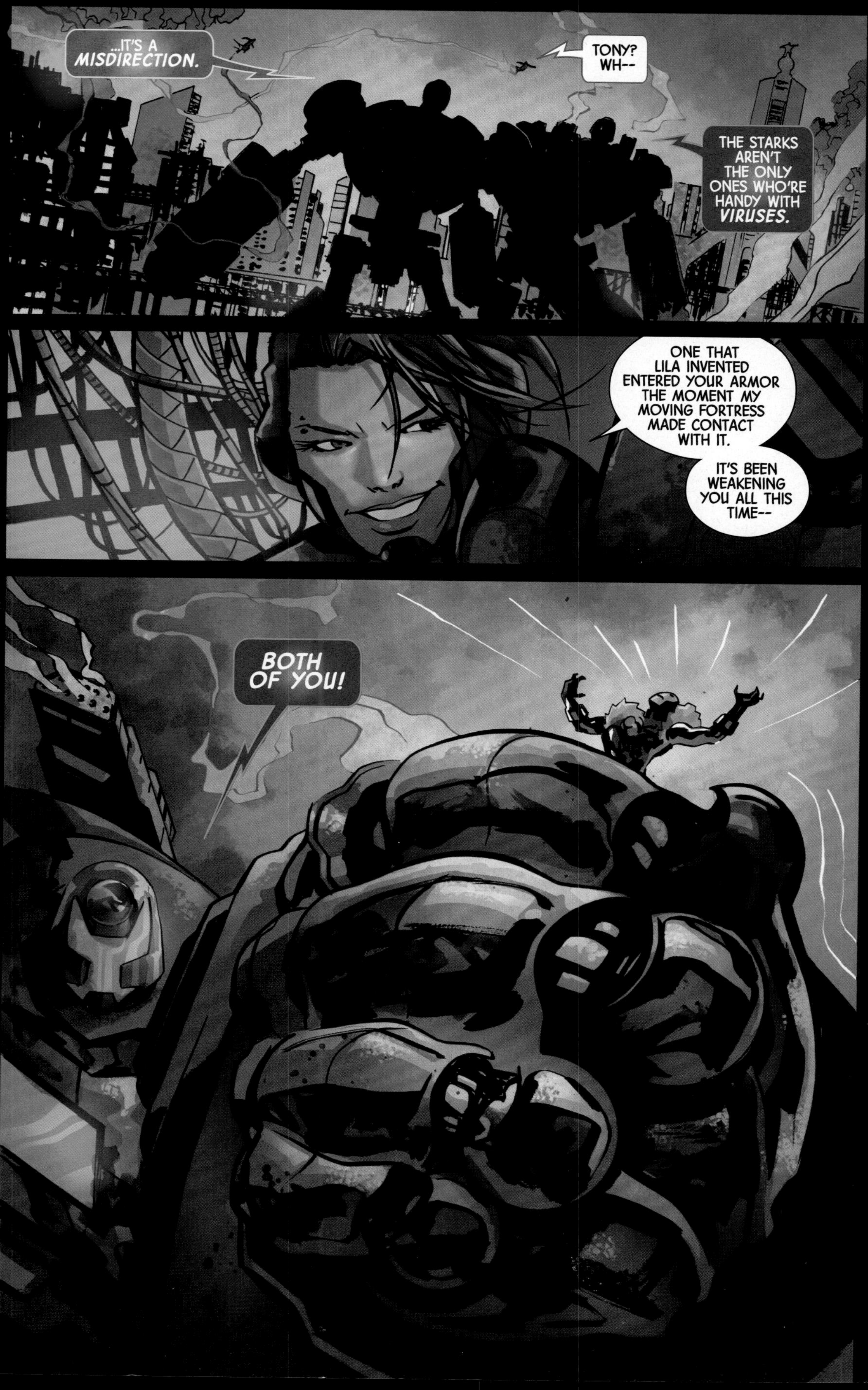
...IT'S A MISDIRECTION.
TONY? WH--
THE STARKS AREN'T THE ONLY ONES WHO'RE HANDY WITH VIRUSES.
ONE THAT LILA INVENTED ENTERED YOUR ARMOR THE MOMENT MY MOVING FORTRESS MADE CONTACT WITH IT.
IT'S BEEN WEAKENING YOU ALL THIS TIME--
BOTH OF YOU!

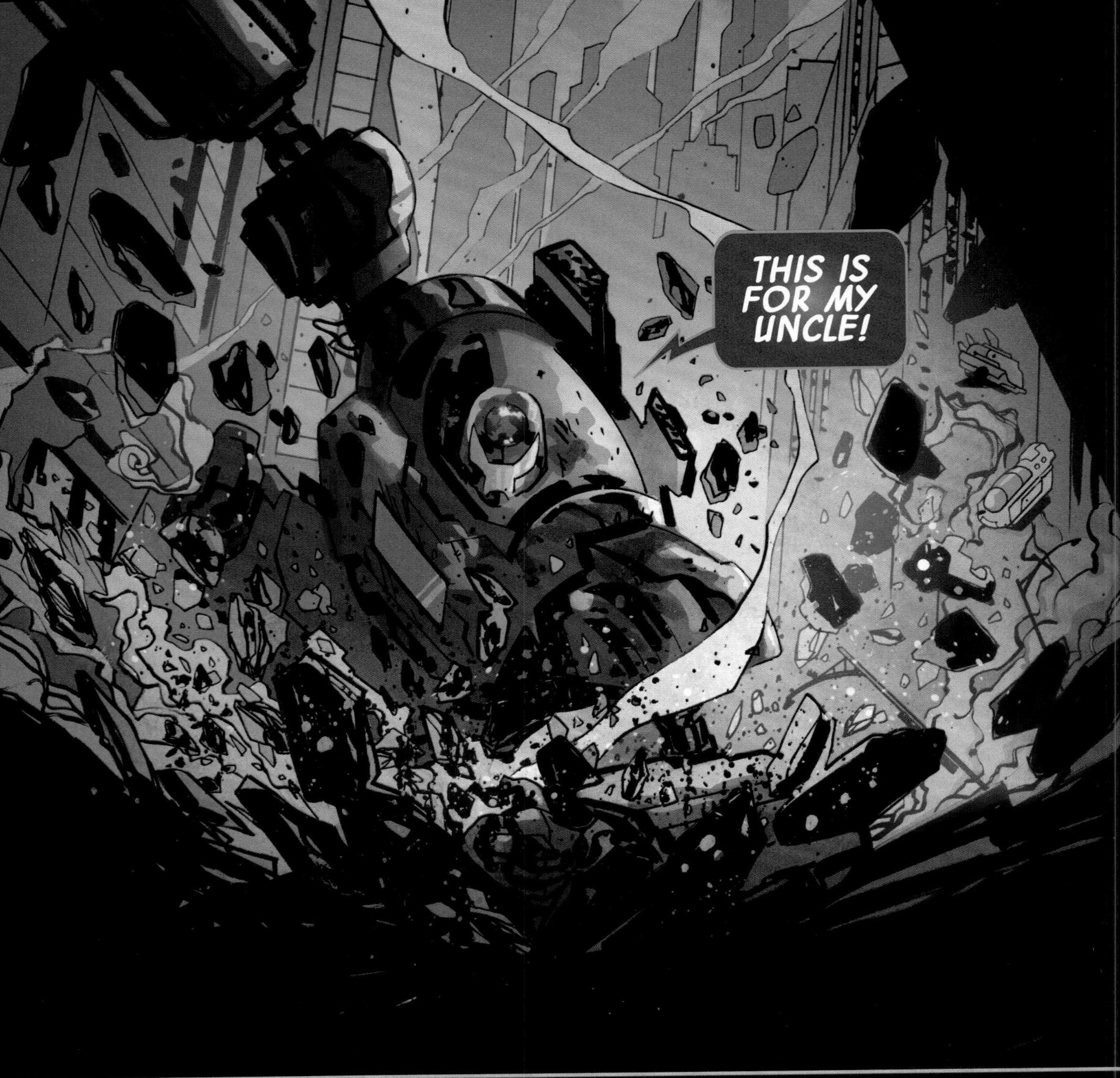
THIS IS FOR MY UNCLE!

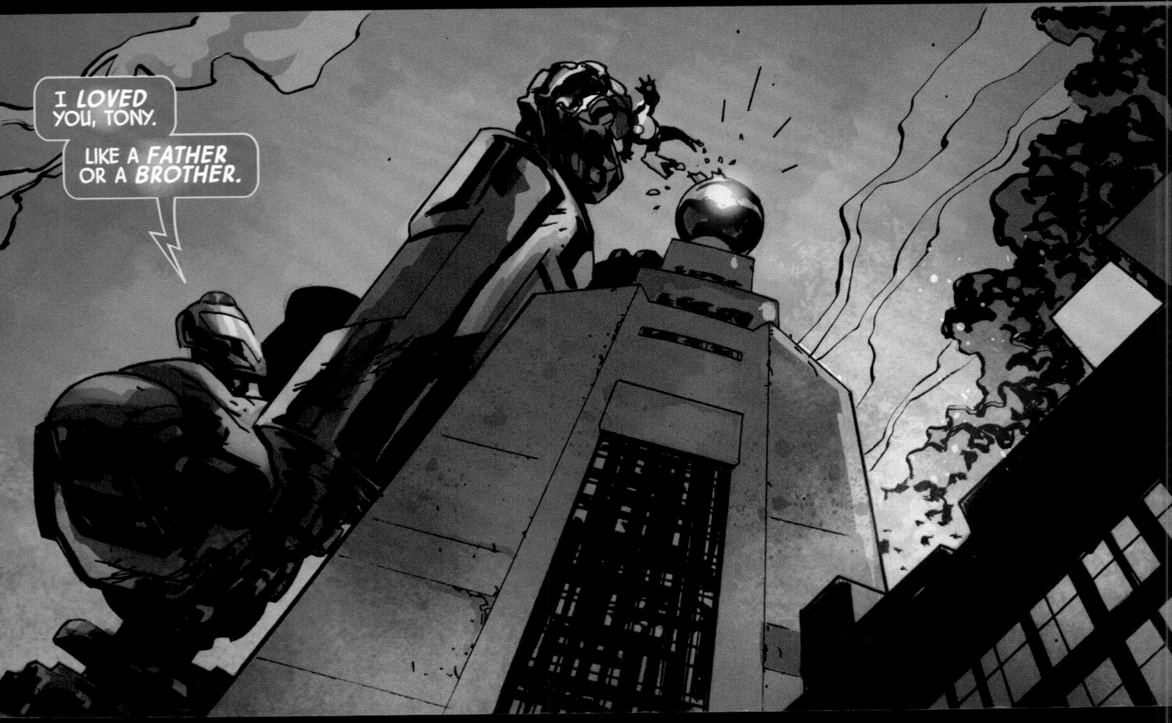
I LOVED YOU, TONY.
LIKE A FATHER OR A BROTHER.

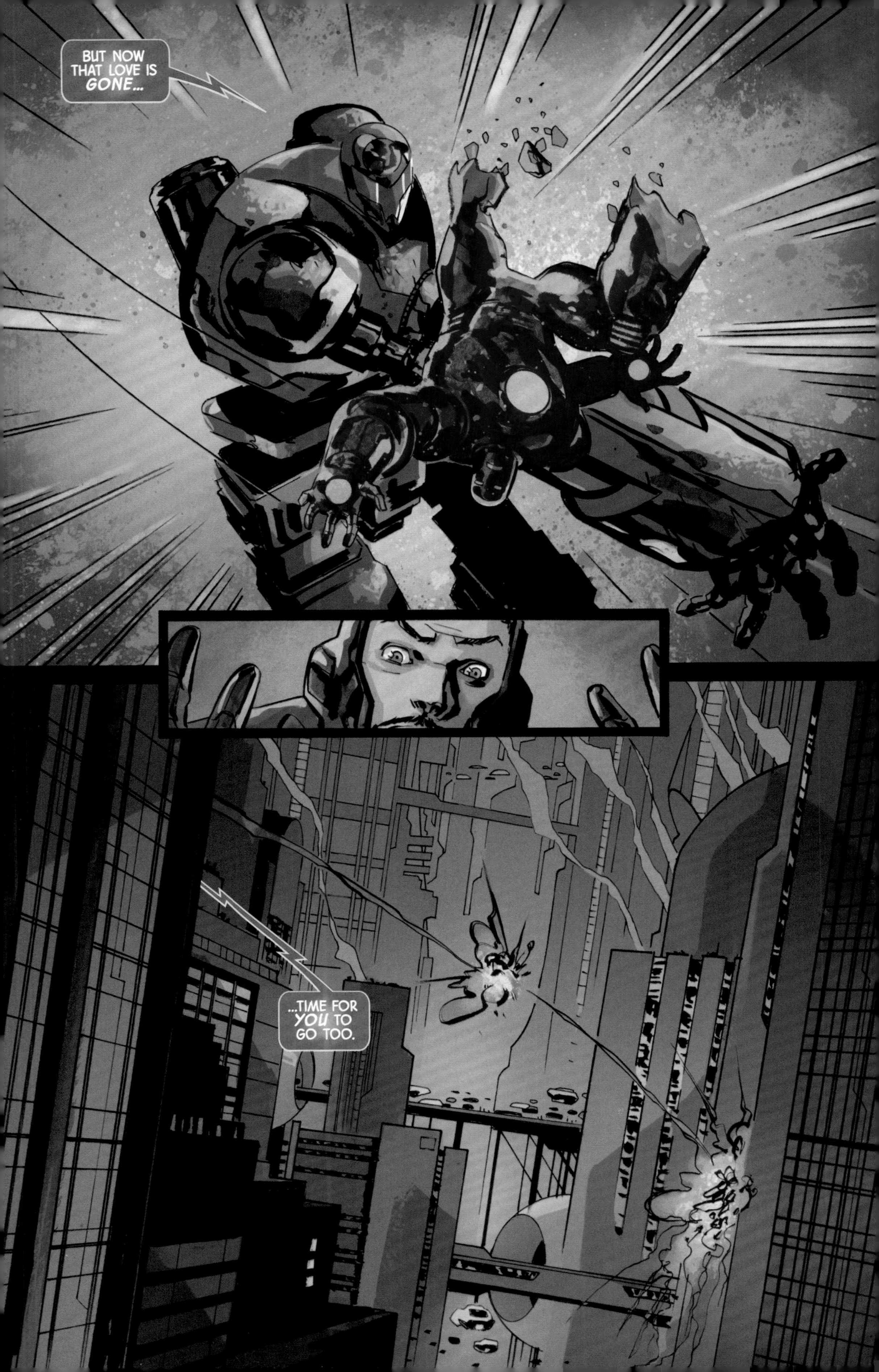
BUT NOW THAT LOVE IS GONE...
...TIME FOR YOU TO GO TOO.

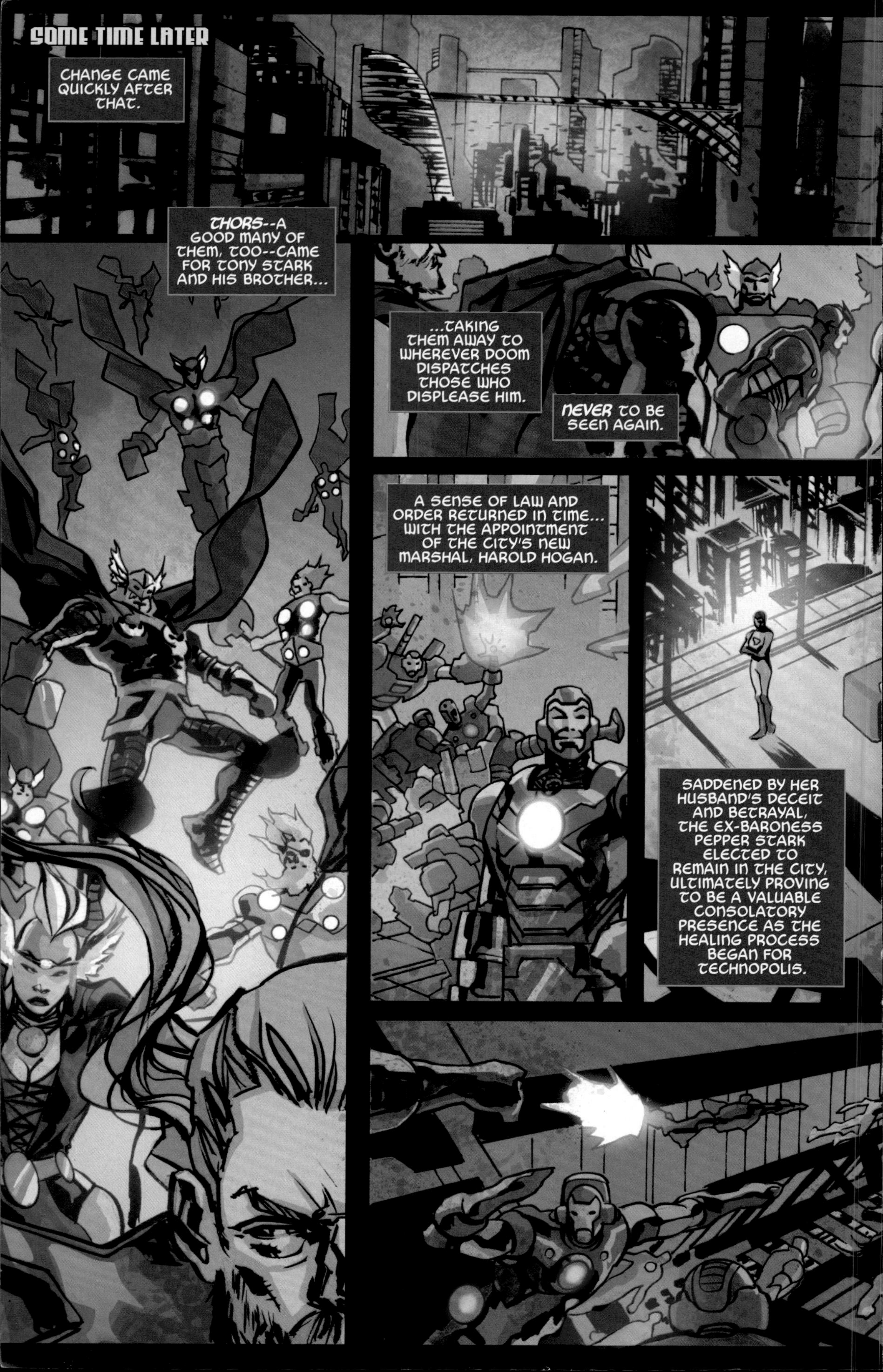
SOME TIME LATER
CHANGE CAME QUICKLY AFTER THAT.
THORS--A GOOD MANY OF THEM, TOO--CAME FOR TONY STARK AND HIS BROTHER...
...TAKING THEM AWAY TO WHEREVER DOOM DISPATCHES THOSE WHO DISPLEASE HIM.
NEVER TO BE SEEN AGAIN.
A SENSE OF LAW AND ORDER RETURNED IN TIME... WITH THE APPOINTMENT OF THE CITY'S NEW MARSHAL, HAROLD HOGAN.
SADDENED BY HER HUSBAND'S DECEIT AND BETRAYAL, THE EX-BARONESS PEPPER STARK ELECTED TO REMAIN IN THE CITY, ULTIMATELY PROVING TO BE A VALUABLE CONSOLATORY PRESENCE AS THE HEALING PROCESS BEGAN FOR TECHNOPOLIS.

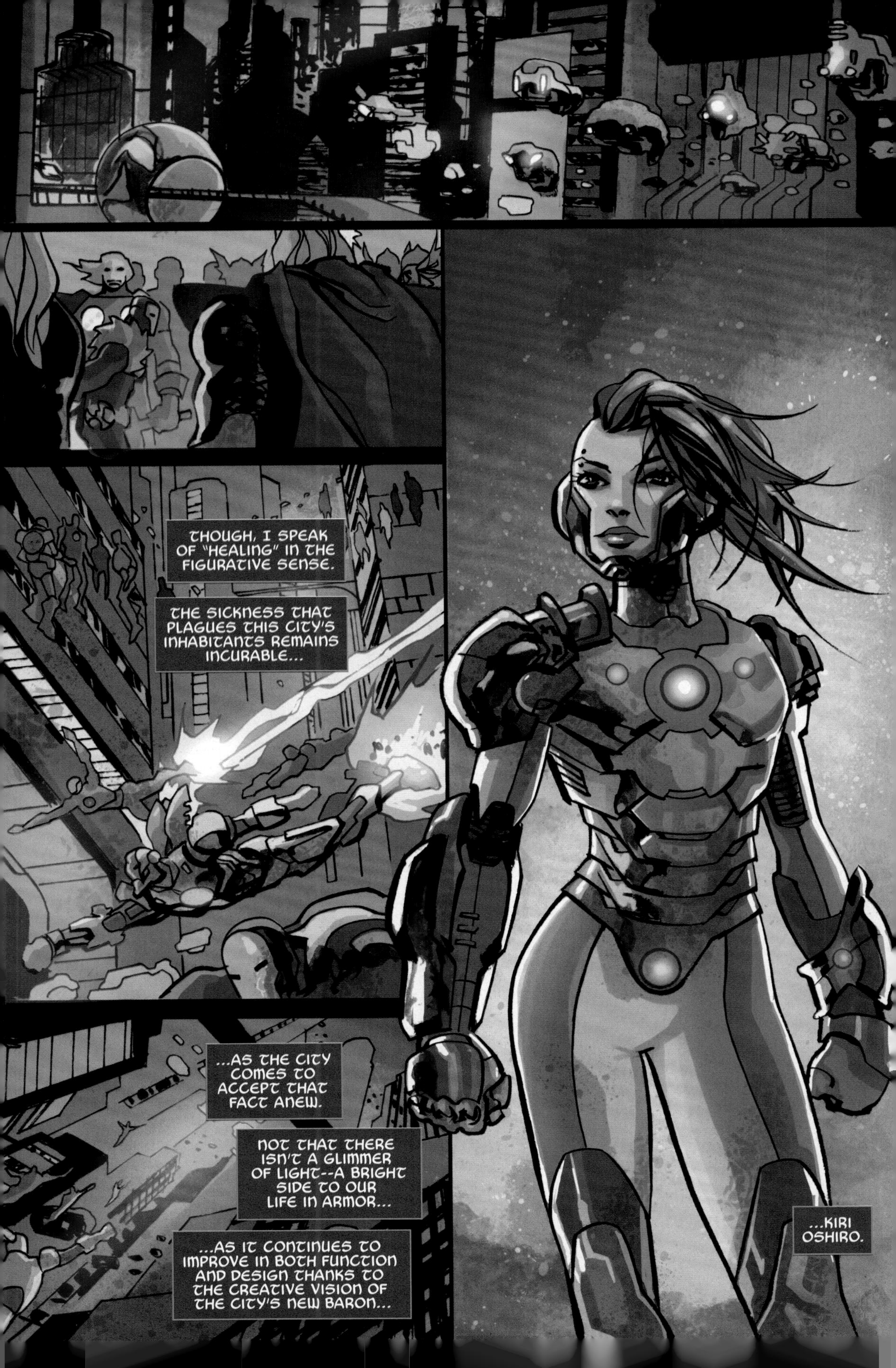

THOUGH, I SPEAK OF "HEALING" IN THE FIGURATIVE SENSE.
THE SICKNESS THAT PLAGUES THIS CITY'S INHABITANTS REMAINS INCURABLE...
...AS THE CITY COMES TO ACCEPT THAT FACT ANEW.
NOT THAT THERE ISN'T A GLIMMER OF LIGHT--A BRIGHT SIDE TO OUR LIFE IN ARMOR...
...AS IT CONTINUES TO IMPROVE IN BOTH FUNCTION AND DESIGN THANKS TO THE CREATIVE VISION OF THE CITY'S NEW BARON...
...KIRI OSHIRO.

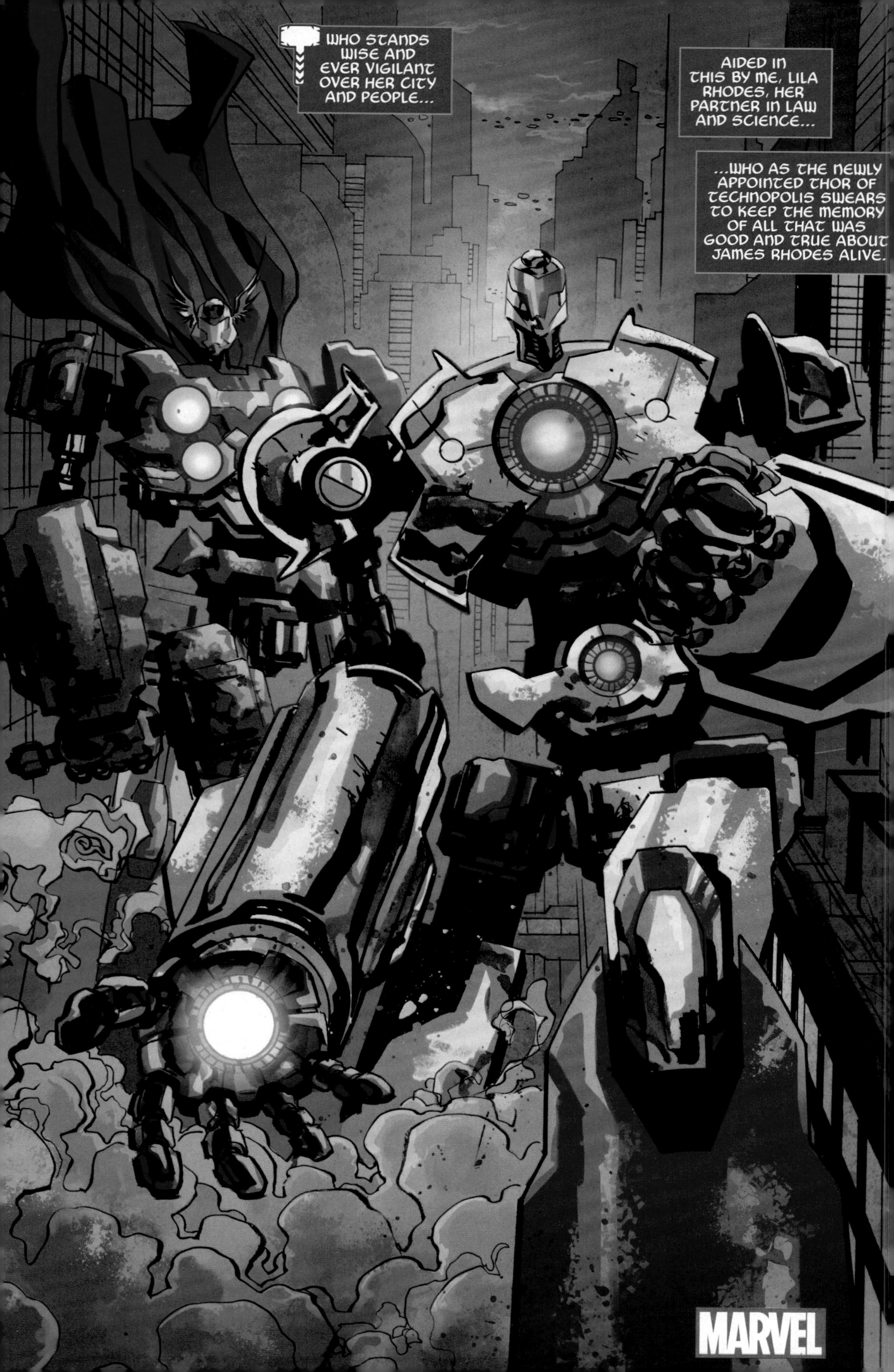
WHO STANDS WISE AND EVER VIGILANT OVER HER CITY AND PEOPLE...
AIDED IN THIS BY ME, LILA RHODES, HER PARTNER IN LAW AND SCIENCE...
...WHO AS THE NEWLY APPOINTED THOR OF TECHNOPOLIS SWEARS TO KEEP THE MEMORY OF ALL THAT WAS GOOD AND TRUE ABOUT JAMES RHODES ALIVE.
MARVEL

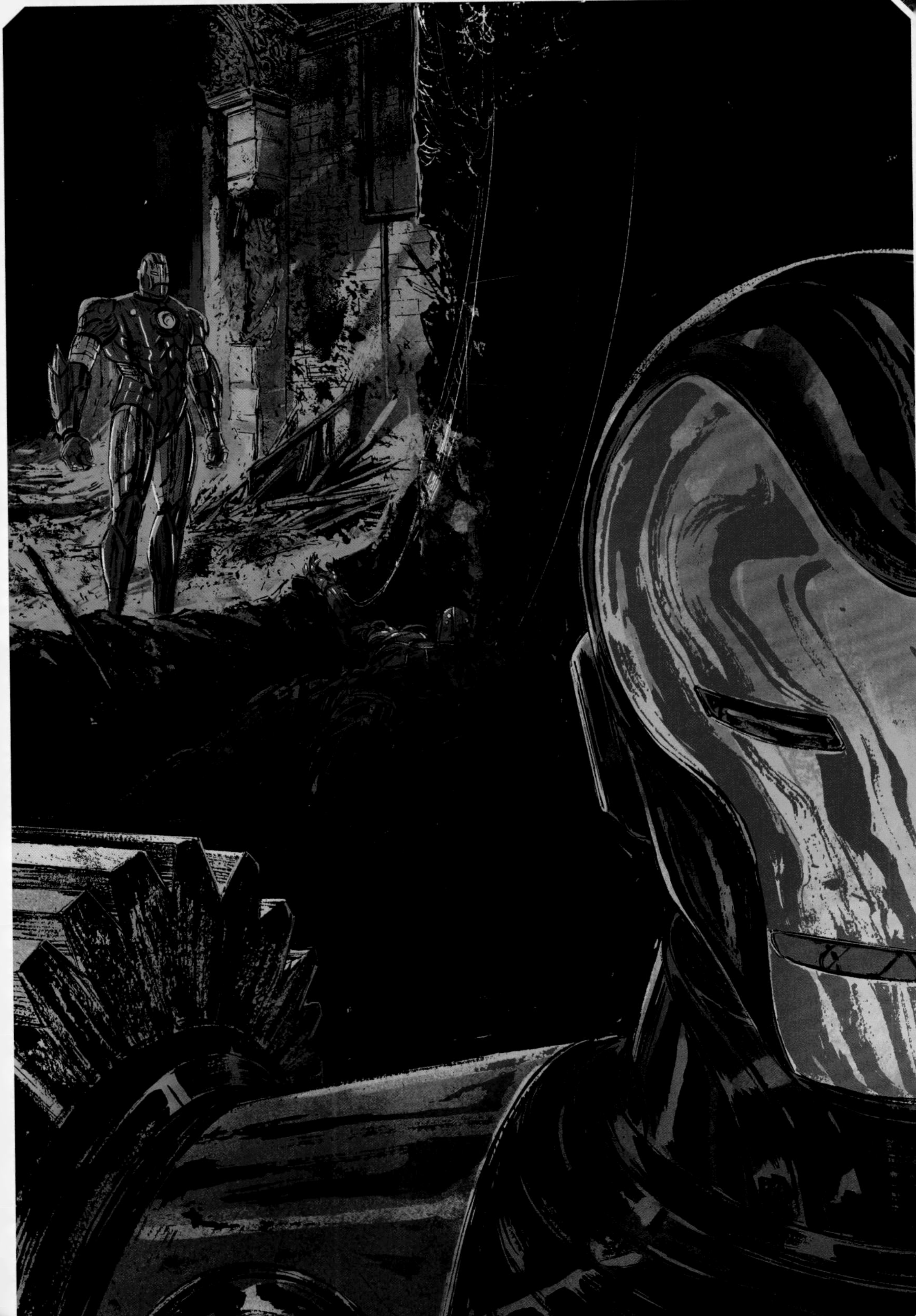

ARMOR WARS 1 VARIANT
BY VANESA DEL REY & ESTHER SANZ

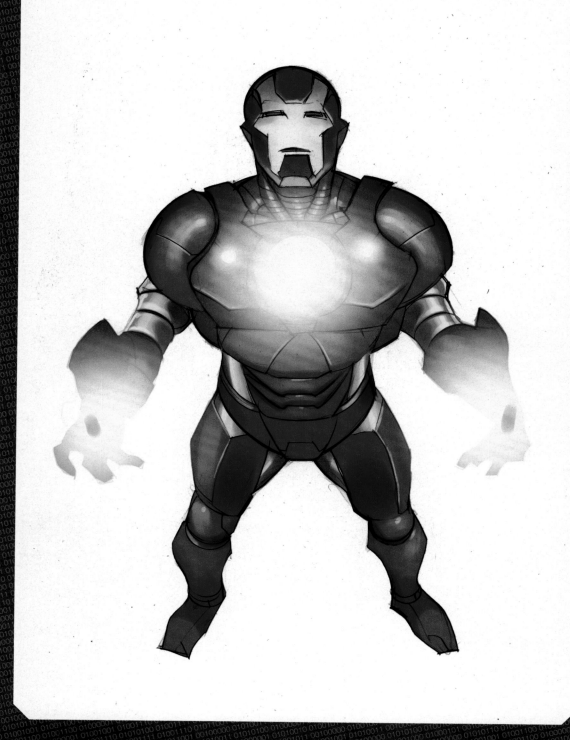

ARMOR WARS 1 ANT-SIZED VARIANT
BY PASQUAL FERRY & CHRIS SOTOMAYOR

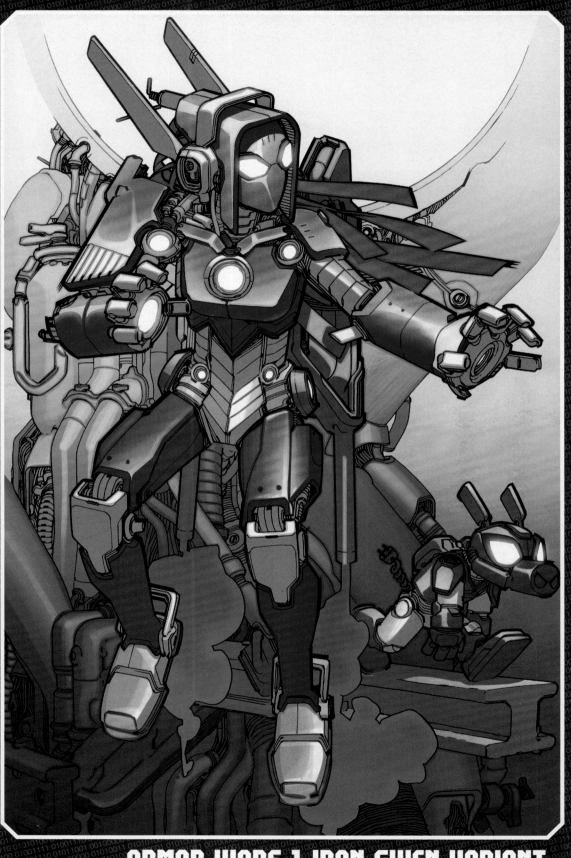

ARMOR WARS 1 IRON GWEN VARIANT
BY DAVID LAFUENTE & JOHN RAUCH

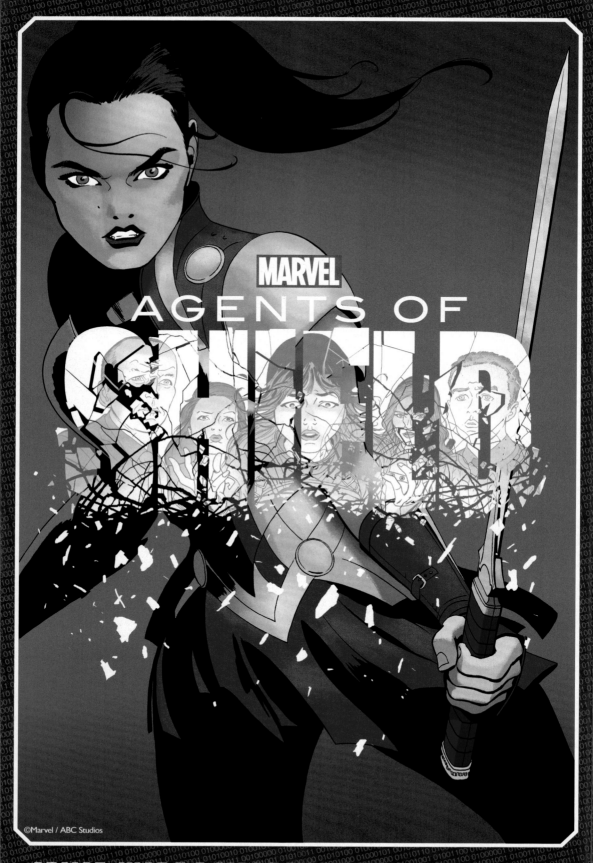

©Marvel / ABC Studios

**ARMOR WARS 1 MAOS VARIANT
BY MARCOS MARTIN**

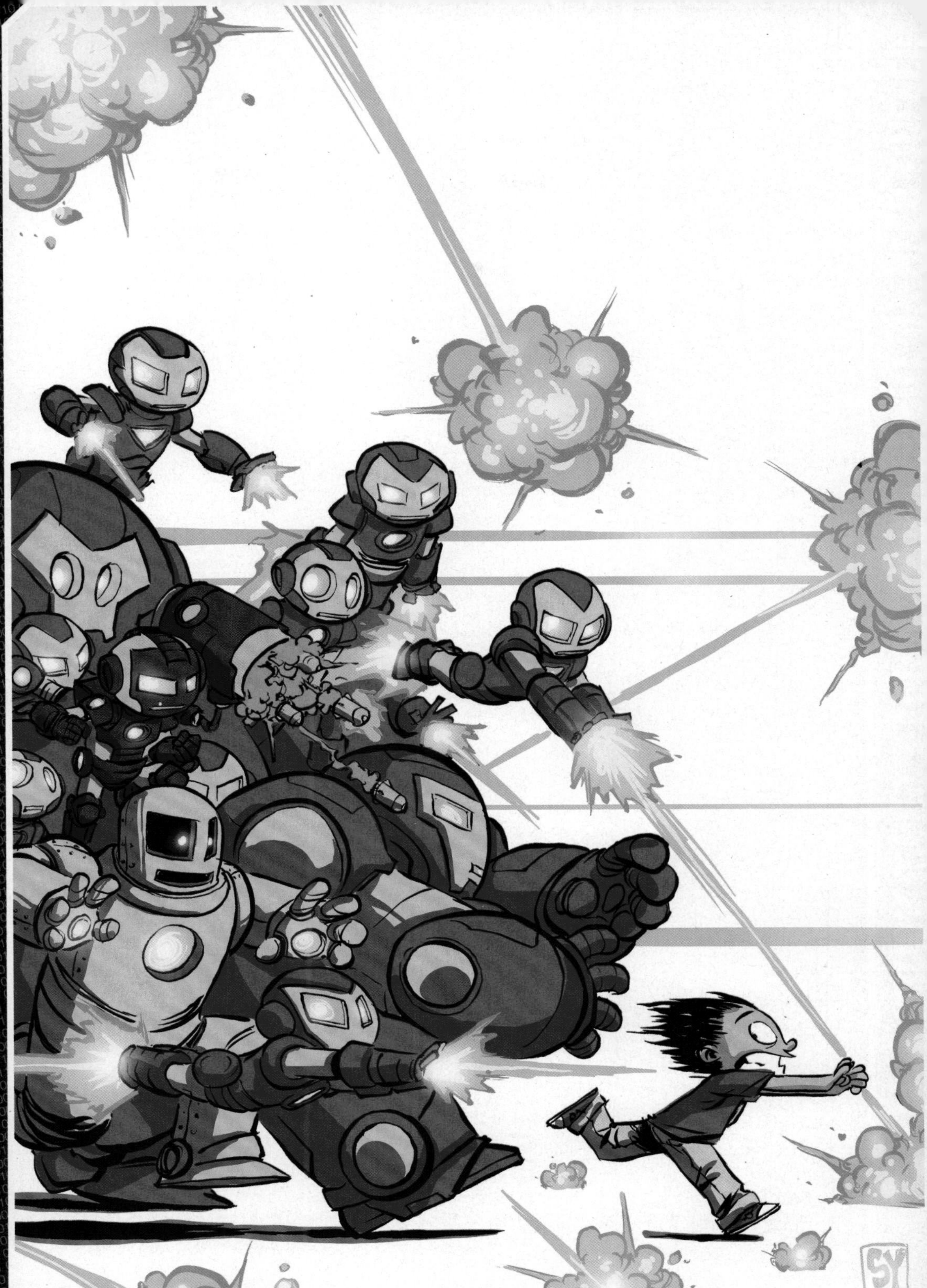
SY
15

ARMOR WARS 3 LANDSCAPE VARIANT BY ALEX MALEEV

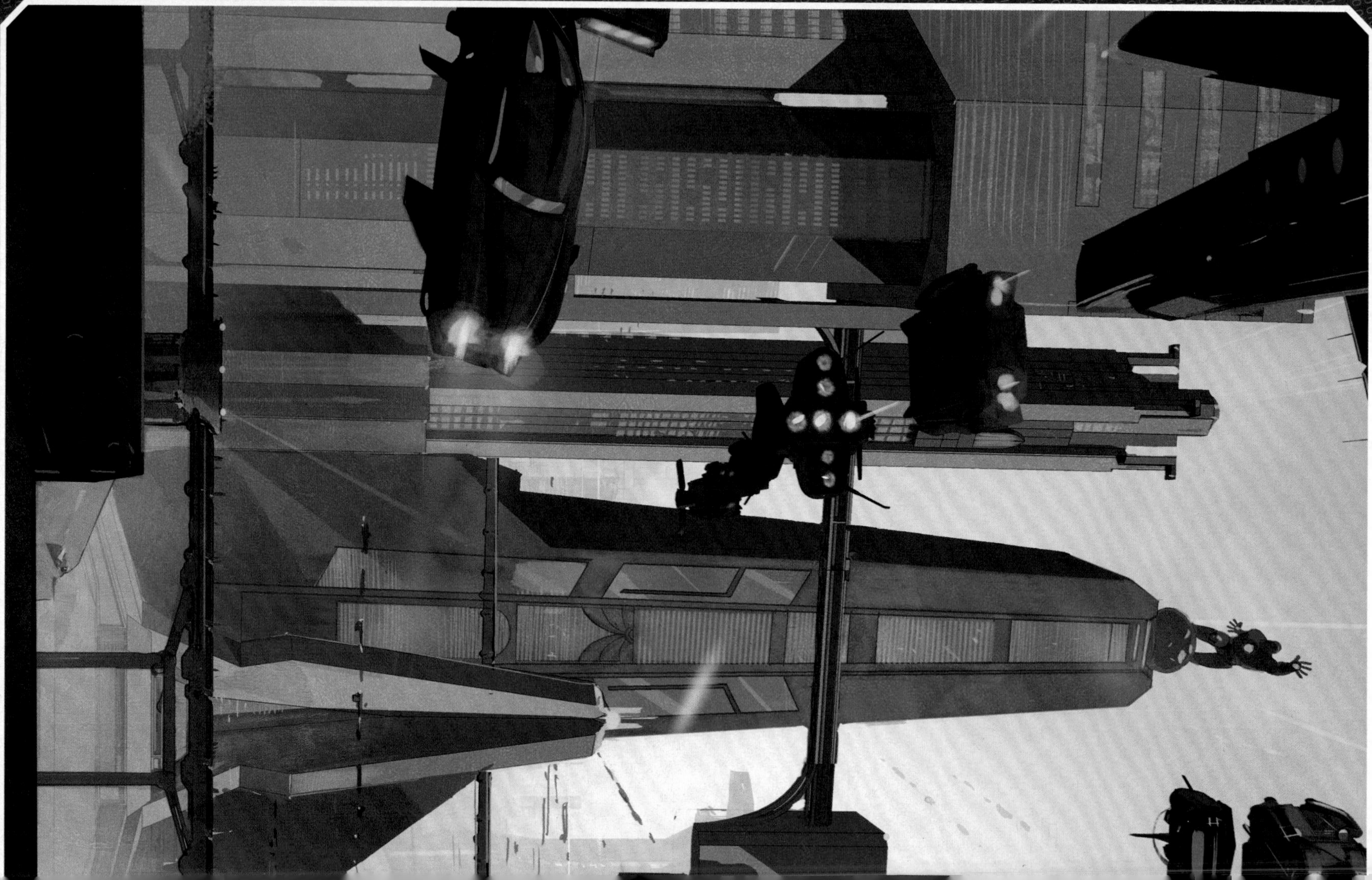

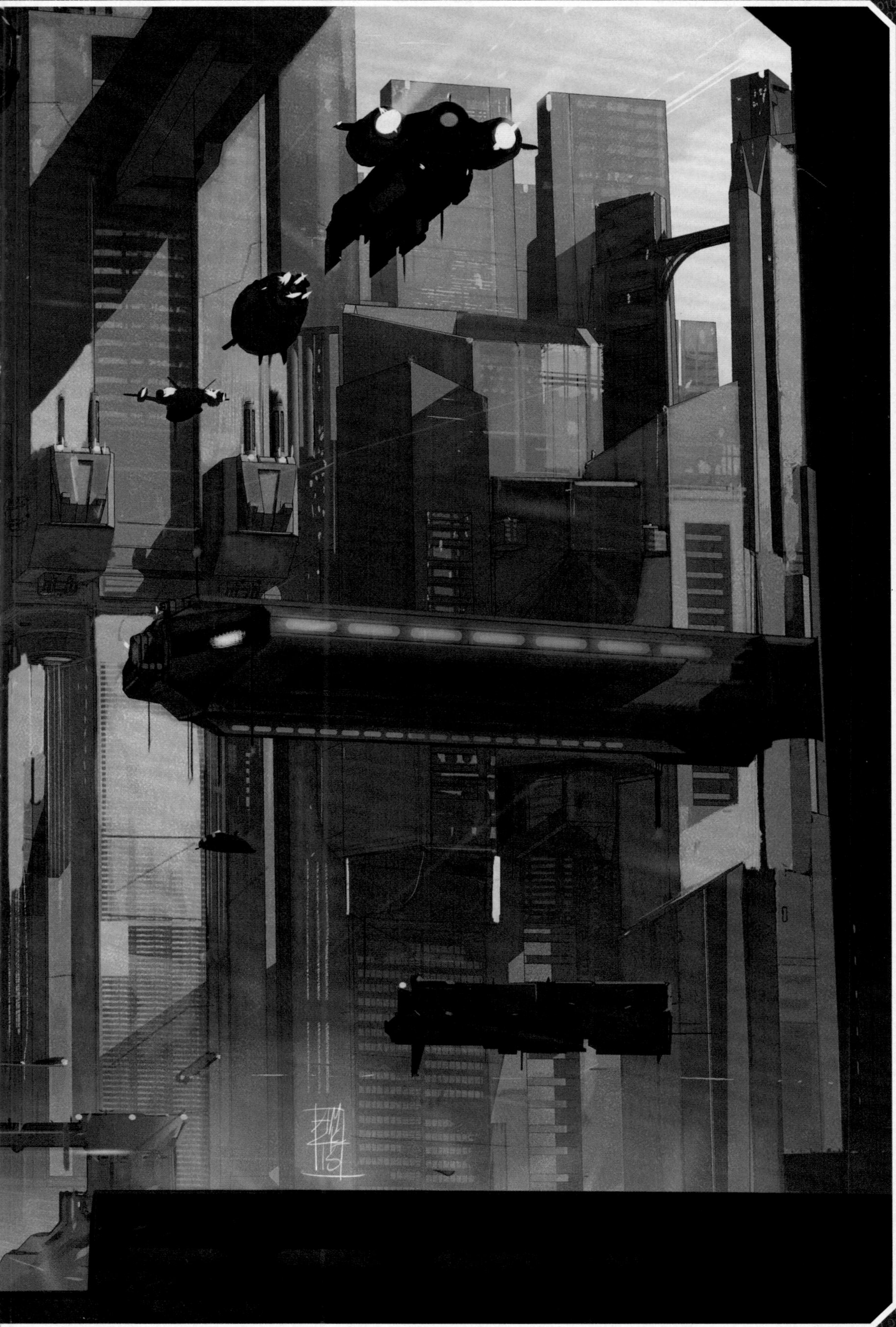

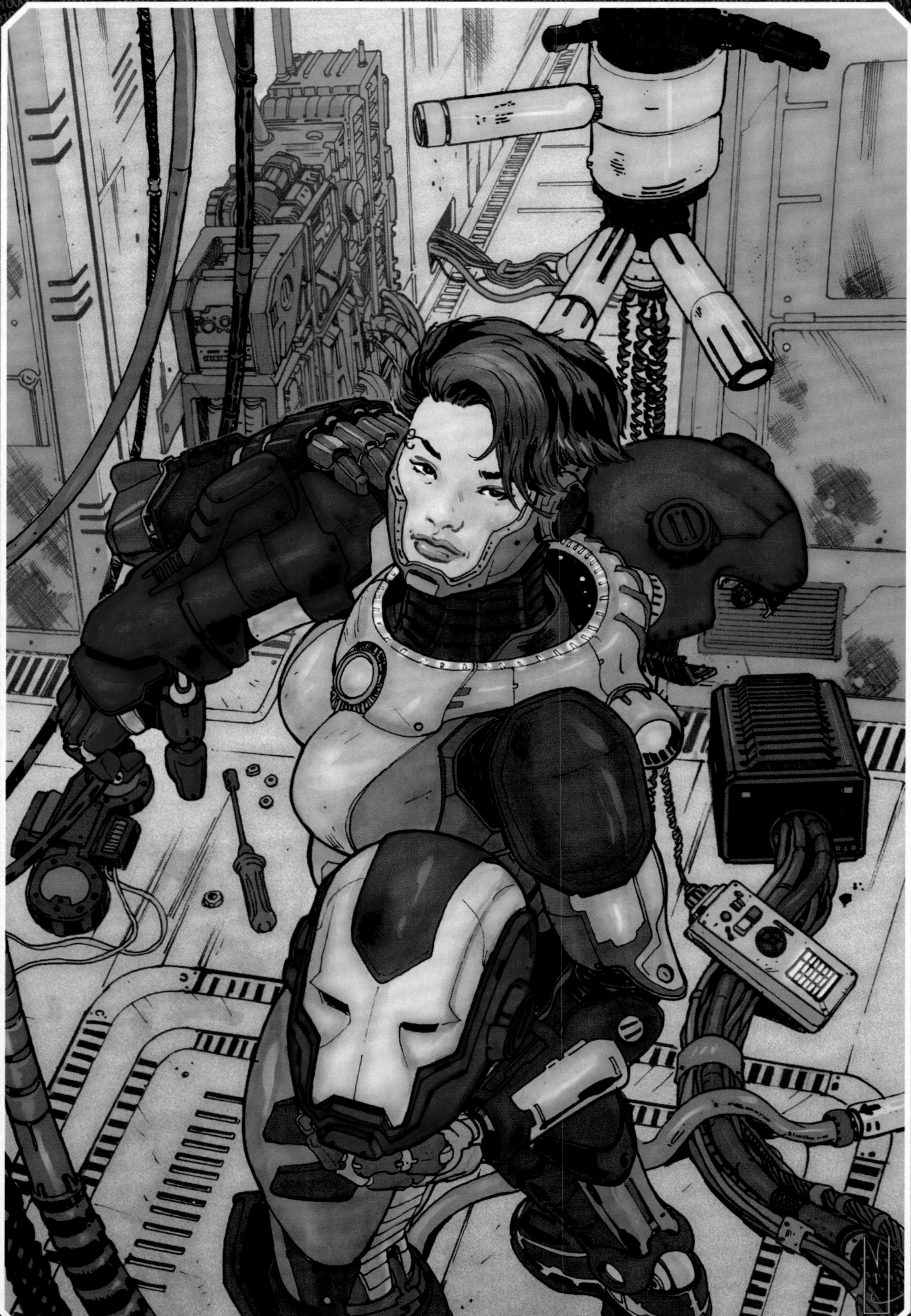

ARMOR WARS 2 VARIANT
BY VICTOR IBAÑEZ

ARMOR WARS SKETCHBOOK
BY MARCIO TAKARA

ARNO

I WAS ASKED TO USE THE CLASSIC IRON MAN 2020 DESIGN FOR ARNO. I THINK HIS COSTUME WORKS, BUT I WAS REALLY SCARED TO THINK THAT I'D HAVE TO DRAW THOSE COGS ALL THE TIME. COGS ARE TRICKY TO DRAW. I ENDED UP GETTING USED TO IT, THOUGH. ALSO, JAMES ASKED ME TO GIVE HIM THIS STEALTH MODE BLACK ALL OVER HIS BODY.

CITY

THE IDEA WAS FOR THE CITY TO HAVE THIS VERY SPECIFIC NOIR LOOK, MIXED WITH FUTURISTIC VISUALS. I SPENT A WHOLE DAY GRABBING REFERENCE FOR THE CITY ITSELF. THINGS LIKE ART DECO, DIESELPUNK AND CHICAGO FOR EXAMPLE. I WANTED TO MAKE THE CITY AS DISTINCTIVE AS POSSIBLE FROM A NORMAL FUTURISTIC CITY.

SPYDER-MAN

THOR MACHINE

AT FIRST I WANTED TO USE BLACK, RED AND GOLD. WE ENDED UP USING CLASSIC RED AND BLUE TO MAKE HIM MORE RECOGNIZABLE AS A SPIDER-MAN.

THE IDEA WAS TO COME UP WITH A SILHOUETTE THAT WOULD MAKE THIS GUY INSTANTLY RECOGNIZABLE, AND I GUESS THE ARM LIGHTS DO THE TRICK. I TRIED TO MAKE HIS ARMOR A LITTLE BIT MORE ORGANIC THAN THE OTHER CHARACTERS'.

RHODES WAS SUPPOSED TO BE A MIX OF WAR MACHINE AND THOR. I DIDN'T WANT HIM TO BE TOO SIMILAR TO AN EXISTING CHARACTER, SO MY MAIN FOCUS WAS THOSE FOUR THOR CIRCLES ON HIS CHEST. AND I WANTED HIM TO HAVE A SPECIFIC KIND OF HAMMER. I ALSO LOVE CHARACTERS WITH CAPES. CAPES MAKE MY LIFE A LOT EASIER COVERING TOUGH ANATOMY. THE ONLY THING THEY ASKED ME TO CHANGE WAS TO ADD THE BADGE ON HIS CHEST.

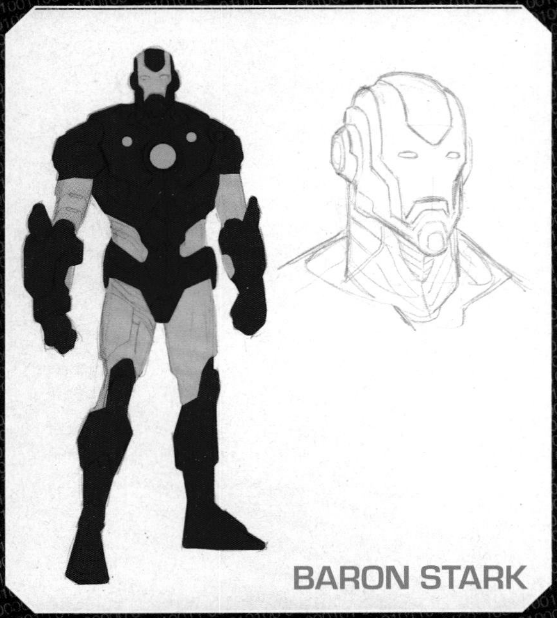
BARON STARK

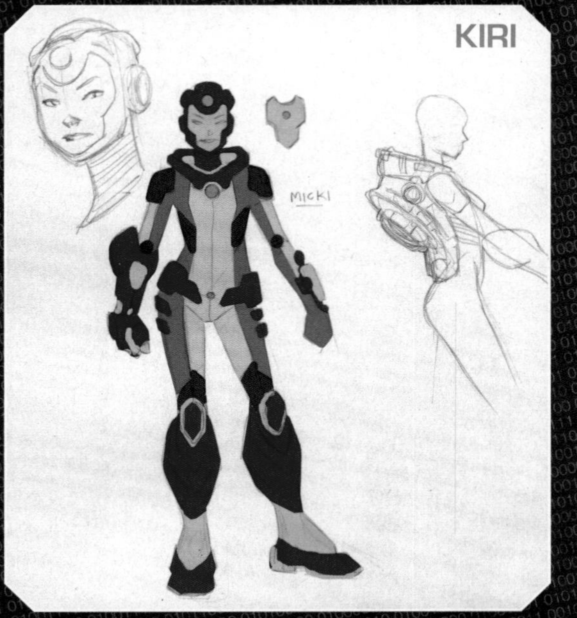
KIRI
MICKI

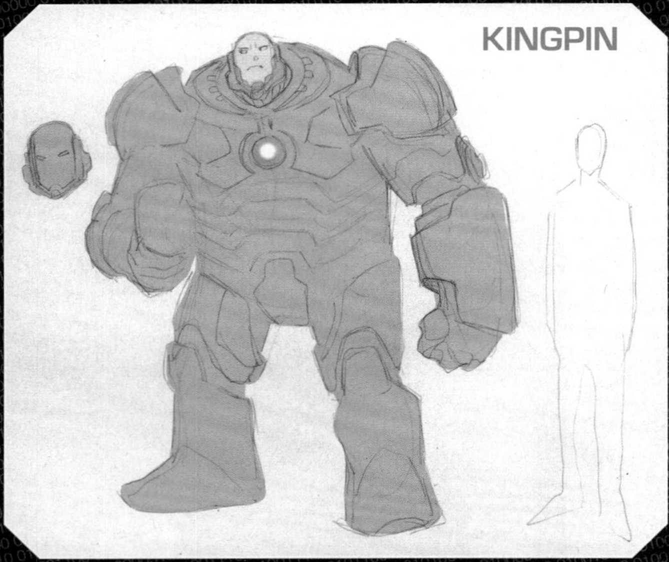
KINGPIN

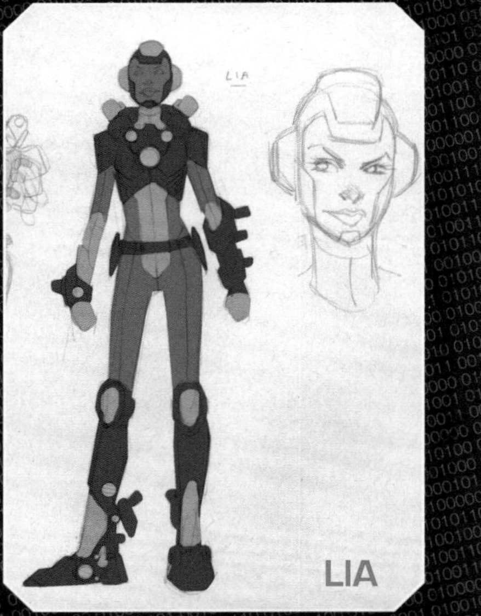
LIA
LIA

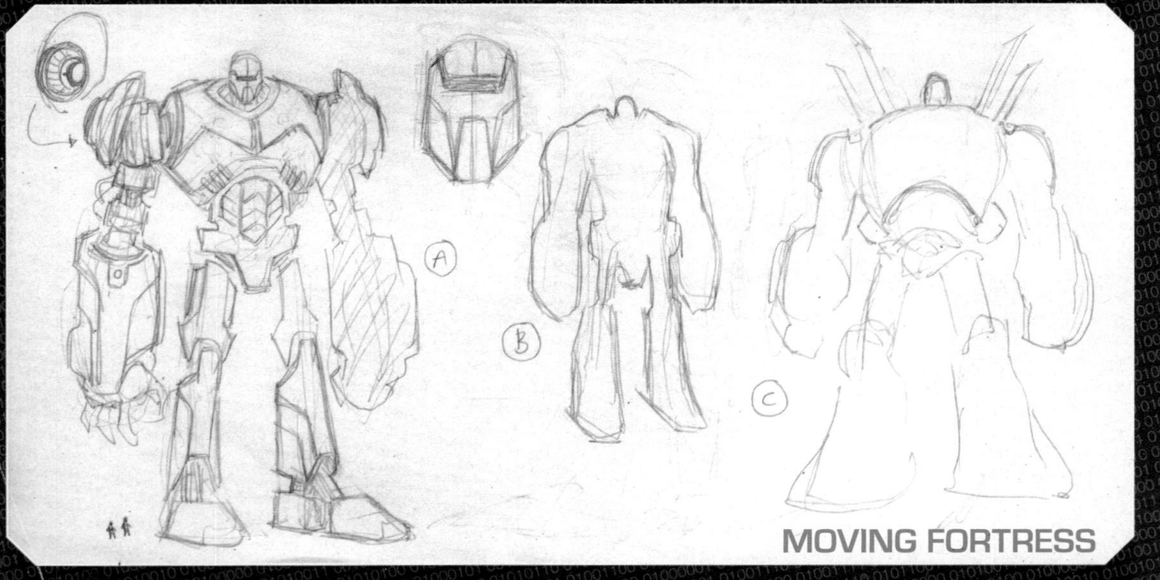
A
B
C
MOVING FORTRESS